POWER

versus

Liberty

Madison, Hamilton, Wilson, and Jefferson

POWER

versus

Madison, Hamilton, Wilson, and Jefferson

James H. Read

University Press of Virginia
Charlottesville and London

THE UNIVERSITY PRESS OF VIRGINIA
© 2000 by the Rector and Visitors of the University of Virginia
Printed in the United States of America

First published in 2000

♾ The paper used in this publication meets the minimum
requirements of the American National Standard for Information
Sciences—Permanence of Paper for Printed Library Materials,
ANSI Z39.48-1984.

Library of Congress Cataloging-in-Publication Data

Read, James H., 1958–
        Power versus liberty : Madison, Hamilton, Wilson, and Jefferson /
James H. Read
            p.   cm.
        Includes bibliographical references and index.
        ISBN 0-8139-1911-8 (cloth : alk. paper). — ISBN 0-8139-1912-6 (pbk.)
        1. Political science—United States—History—18th century.
2. Power (Social sciences) 3. Authority. 4. Liberty. 5. Madison, James,
1751–1836—Contributions in political science. 6. Hamilton,
Alexander, 1757–1804—Contributions in political science. 7. Wilson,
James, 1742–1798—Contributions in political science. 8. Jefferson,
Thomas, 1743–1826—Contributions in political science. I. Title.
JA84.U5R37   2000
320'.0973'09033—dc21   99-34633
                                                        CIP

To Pia

Contents

Illustrations

James Madison. Portrait by Charles Willson Peale.
From the collection of Gilcrease Museum,
Tulsa, Oklahoma.

24

Alexander Hamilton. Portrait by John Trumbull.
Courtesy, Museum of Fine Arts, Boston. Bequest of
Robert C. Winthrop.

54

James Wilson. Portrait by Jean Pierre Henri Elouis.
National Museum of American Art, Smithsonian
Institution, Museum purchase through the
Catherine Walden Myer Fund.

88

Thomas Jefferson. Portrait by Rembrandt Peale.
White House Collection, courtesy White House
Historical Association.

118

Preface

ABOUT FIFTEEN YEARS AGO, as I was writing a doctoral dissertation on the concept of power, I stumbled across Bernard Bailyn's chapter on "Power and Liberty" in *The Ideological Origins of the American Revolution*. I was fascinated by the interplay of these two ideas in American political discourse and the range of possible variations on this apparently simple theme.

I also was struck by the way late eighteenth-century debates over power and liberty echoed my own attempts to understand the concept of power. My investigation had focused on the so-called zero sum question: is one's gain of power necessarily another's loss? Americans of the Revolutionary and constitutional period wrestled with a somewhat different but related question: does every increase in the power of government entail a loss of liberty for the governed? Thomas Jefferson believed that it did. His friend James Madison and his rival Alexander Hamilton believed it did not. Their view was shared by James Wilson, a figure about whom I knew little at first but whose significance expanded as the project matured.

It seemed to me that the most important disagreements between late eighteenth-century American advocates and opponents of energetic government were not disagreements over the nature of liberty itself—over "positive" versus "negative" or "republican" versus "individualistic" liberty. They were disagreements over the nature of power and over the practical interconnection between power and liberty. Thus theorists and statesmen who understood liberty in broadly similar ways could draw very different conclusions about how much power to vest in government—especially national government.

A postdoctoral fellowship from the Program on Constitutional Government at Harvard University enabled me to begin the project in earnest. Since that time I have spent most of my available waking hours living in the eighteenth century. Yet because the question of how much power the federal government should exercise continues to be a politically live one, I had a kind of window to the present even as I buried myself in old books. I hope this work will be of interest not only to political theorists and historians but to anyone concerned with the inherently complicated and delicate problem of reconciling the power of government and the liberty of citizens.

I want to thank the Program on Constitutional Government and the Olin-Bradley Foundation for the 1991 fellowship that enabled me to begin the work. I especially wish to thank Harvey Mansfield and Delba Winthrop for their hospitality during that year and for providing a forum for presenting my ideas at an early stage.

Many scholars helped by providing feedback on work in progress at crucial stages. Some of them saw the central figures and arguments of the period very differently than I did, but this did not diminish their willingness to help me write a better book. They contributed to the book's strengths but are not responsible for its shortcomings.

Lance Banning, Charles Hobson, and Forrest McDonald were generous enough to read and offered detailed comments on writings sent to them, unsolicited, by someone they had never met. Samuel Beer read and commented on portions of the work twice, at early and late stages. These individuals demonstrate that the community of scholars really exists.

Michael Zuckert has helped in more ways than I can begin to describe here. He read the entire manuscript, a good portion of it more than once as it changed over time. He had a keen eye for what was best and weakest in my writing, and this might have been a better work if I had been willing to follow more of his recommendations. He also arranged for me to present a draft of the Hamilton chapter to the Political Philosophy Colloquium at Carleton College.

Peter Onuf read the manuscript for the University Press of Virginia. He immediately grasped what I was trying to accomplish in the work and showed me how to accomplish it better by paying closer attention to the work of scholars whose explorations intersected with my own.

I also want to thank Alan Gibson, Ruth Grant, Lauren Brubaker, Mark David Hall, and my colleagues Joe Farry and Eugene Garver for commenting on parts of the work.

My acquisitions editor at the University Press of Virginia, Richard Holway, took an immediate interest in this project and helped ease the anxieties of a first-time author.

The College of St. Benedict granted me a sabbatical during the 1995–96 academic year that enabled me to take the manuscript past the halfway point.

Suzanne Reinert provided indispensable help with the final stages of manuscript preparation. Deb Miller helped resolve several potentially disastrous software problems.

An early version of the Madison chapter was published as "'Our Complicated System': James Madison on Power and Liberty," *Political Theory* 23:2 (Aug. 1995): 452–75, copyright © 1995 by Sage Publications, Inc., reprinted by permission of Sage Publications, Inc.

Pia Lopez has read every word of the manuscript and has been my best and most critical reader from beginning to end. She helped convince me that I was onto something important, and I hope the finished product justifies her faith in me. To her I dedicate this book.

POWER
versus

Madison, Hamilton, Wilson, and Jefferson

1

Introduction

I own I am not a friend to a very energetic government.
It is always oppressive.
—Thomas Jefferson to James Madison, December 20, 1787

W HEN THE AMERICAN colonists fought for independence from Britain, they justified their action to themselves and to the world as a struggle to protect the liberty of the people from the power of an oppressive government. Later in the 1780s when they argued fiercely among themselves over what kind of national government to construct and in the 1790s when they contended over how to translate the sparse language of the Constitution into practice, the debate once again was phrased in terms of power and liberty. Opponents of a more powerful national government described it as a threat to liberty. Its advocates, whatever other good things they expected of energetic government, first had to reassure people it would not pose a threat to liberty. They had to challenge the widely shared assumption that was put into words by Thomas Jefferson when he wrote to James Madison that any "energetic" government posed a direct threat to liberty; they had to argue instead that it was sometimes possible to make government more powerful without making the governed less free.[1]

Their burden of proof was especially heavy in arguing for powerful national government. Compared to the state governments, the national government was more distant and represented a greater total accumulation of power; furthermore it was much newer than the state authorities and its effects on liberty more difficult to foresee. Anyone prone to be suspicious of power as such was likely to be particularly suspicious of national power. For this reason those hoping to establish an energetic national government had to address both the general suspicion of power and the special level of distrust directed against national power.

This book is a study of the way in which four theorists-statesmen of the age

1

wrestled with this problem. Three of them—James Madison, Alexander Hamilton, and James Wilson—challenged in different ways the widely held assumption that all governments tend to augment their power at the expense of liberty. Madison in a letter to Jefferson called this assumption "not well-founded."[2] But Madison, Hamilton, and Wilson challenged the assumption in very different ways, and the differences among them are as important as their shared opposition to the Jeffersonian view. This was not an argument that had only two sides.

Thomas Jefferson is included in this study for purposes of contrast, for he shared and reinforced the view that the others attempted to challenge. For Jefferson there was a permanent and irreducible antagonism between power and liberty: all governments tend to expand their power at the expense of the liberty of the governed, and for this reason their powers must be subjected at all times to close restraints.

Strategically, of course, as fellow architects and advocates of the Constitution, Madison, Hamilton, and Wilson had to argue against any simple opposition between power and liberty; for if a more powerful government meant a people less free, the Constitution was doomed from the start. But their theorizing about power and liberty neither began nor ended with the drafting and ratification of the federal Constitution. Therefore this study examines the trajectory of each man's action and thought from about the mid-1780s through the 1790s (and in some instances into the 1800s). The great divergence between Madison and Hamilton in the 1790s—which is almost routinely misrepresented by historians and biographers—is as central to this study of power and liberty as is their collaboration on *The Federalist*. James Wilson's opinions as a Supreme Court justice and his Law Lectures of the early 1790s are as important as his contributions at the Federal Convention. And Jefferson, too, must be studied over time; the Declaration of Independence may be the finest single expression of his thought, but the principles articulated in the Declaration do not explain Jefferson's initial reservations about the Constitution or why he was so suspicious of national power throughout the 1790s.

One of the purposes of this work is to underscore the wide range of political and theoretical possibilities available in republican thought in the 1780s and 1790s and to resist attempts to reduce that diversity to some single line of ideological division—such as democracy versus oligarchy, republicanism versus liberalism, agrarianism versus commercialism. Those divisions are there, of course, but they do not fully explain what these men supported and opposed and why. Wilson, for example, was as democratic as Jefferson and as nationalist as Hamilton; their respective commitments on questions of national power do not directly reflect their degree of commitment to democracy, or vice versa. Hamilton was probably the least democratic of the four men studied here, but to treat his commitment to national power as a function of his suspicion of democracy is to fundamentally misunderstand what he was trying to accomplish.

Another problem with the attempt to fit the theorists-statesmen of the age into prefabricated categories like "democracy," "oligarchy," "republican," and "liberal" is that this overlooks the degree to which the power of government itself was an independent problem that had to be addressed on its own terms. Jefferson advocated a thoroughgoing jealousy of governmental power, while Hamilton asked for a generous measure of trust; this is not a quarrel that can be obviously reduced to democracy versus oligarchy (even though Jefferson may have thought so). The preoccupation with the power of government characteristic of the age was not just a form in which other political, social, and economic conflicts were played out; it existed in addition to these other conflicts, shaped them, and sometimes took precedence over them.

This fixation on the power of government as such, in a way that crowds out other kinds of problems and de-emphasizes other kinds of power, may appear odd to modern readers. The preoccupation with governmental power was so strong that in the eighteenth century "power" was typically used as a shorthand expression for the power of government. In the twentieth century we have become much more sensitive to forms of social and economic power that do not fit easily into a narrowly governmental model. Works of social and economic history published in the last thirty years or so have made us much more aware of the kinds of social and economic power exercised in the past over women, paupers, debtors, indentured servants, slaves, and Native Americans (among others) by people who were not necessarily in government or directly involved in carrying out its policies.[3] For this reason the eighteenth-century preoccupation with governmental power might appear perverse, and a work of scholarship that takes that preoccupation on its own terms might appear old-fashioned.

The Founding era's fixation on the power of government may have been excessive; indeed it appeared so to those of the age who attempted to challenge the assumptions underlying it. But for better or worse it was there, in the political language and hopes and fears of the age. And those who believe that an excessive preoccupation with the power of government is a relic of eighteenth-century political discourse might take another look at present-day American politics.

I

This work takes the form of a four-way comparison structured by a set of interlocking themes and problems, all of which branch off from the basic question of how to reconcile the power of government with the liberty of citizens in a republican political order. Each of the four central chapters takes one of the four theorists-statesmen as its subject and can be read as a self-contained essay. But at the same time each individual portrait is an entry in a larger conversation about power and liberty.

In calling it a conversation, I mean this sometimes in a literal sense and sometimes in a figurative sense. Although there probably was no moment when Madison, Hamilton, Wilson, and Jefferson all sat down together and conversed about the power of government and the liberty of citizens, there were many particular exchanges among two or three of the men—sometimes in letters, sometimes at public or private gatherings, occasionally in shrill pamphlets of the kind Jefferson and Hamilton fired at each other in the 1790s. Perhaps it is stretching the term to call Jefferson's and Hamilton's battle a conversation; but when Hamilton said, "You must place confidence" and Jefferson wrote, "Free government is founded in jealousy, and not in confidence," there was an implicit exchange of ideas taking place even across an abyss.[4]

Madison's and Jefferson's long friendship and voluminous correspondence is well known.[5] The degree of intimacy and trust displayed in their letters to one another and their fundamental agreement on many issues (such as religious liberty) can easily cause us to overlook their very significant disagreements on other issues. Even when they took the same side politically (as they did in the 1790s in opposition to Hamilton), they often did so for different reasons. The present study concerns one of those matters upon which they disagreed, quite openly and respectfully.

Madison, Hamilton, and Wilson were three of the men most directly responsible for drafting the Constitution and arguing for its ratification, and this too was mediated by conversations. At the convention itself Madison was the single most influential figure in shaping the document, but Wilson was a close second and was clear and specific on a number of issues (such as the executive) about which Madison had no clear ideas coming into the convention. Early in the convention (May and June 1787) when fundamental questions of political principle were on the table, there was an impressive degree of cooperation among Madison, Wilson, and Hamilton, suggesting that each was responding to and building upon the thoughts of the others.[6]

Wilson, Hamilton, and Madison carried the ideological torch in the ratification struggle, Wilson doing so first in the key state of Pennsylvania. Wilson's crucial role in the ratification contest is overlooked in many histories of the period but was obvious to contemporaries. (Bernard Bailyn points out that Wilson's State House Yard speech of October 6, 1787, generated far more contemporary commentary and response than did *The Federalist Papers*.)[7] Wilson was the one most responsible for putting the idea of popular sovereignty at the center of the Federalist case for the Constitution. In *Federalist* No. 84 Hamilton borrowed Wilson's argument about the superfluity of a bill of rights under a constitution based on delegated powers. Jefferson, in complaining to Madison on December 20, 1787, about the lack of a bill of rights in the Constitution, explicitly mentioned Wilson's argument and criticized it; Madison, describing to Jefferson on October 17, 1788, his own change of position on a bill of rights, again mentioned Wilson by name and compared his own view with that of Wilson.

This work does not attempt to reconstruct every direct or indirect exchange among these four men. Instead their conversations function as a starting point, a way of identifying questions and problems that are then developed through the use of a wide range of sources. The advantage of a four-way comparison like the one presented here (as opposed to a full-length treatment of one of the figures that merely mentions the others in passing) is that certain kinds of problems can be fully understood only through comparison. One cannot, for example, adequately understand either Madison or Hamilton without comprehending how they could have worked together so closely in framing the Constitution and arguing for its ratification and then opposed one another so fundamentally on its application to practice in the 1790s.

Or to take another example, one cannot appreciate the significance of Jefferson's hostility to energetic national government and his endorsement of a strong version of state sovereignty unless one knows that James Wilson articulated an equally democratic but strongly national alternative. Whether Wilson's nationalist version of democracy could have taken hold then the way Jefferson's did is an open question; Wilson wholly lacked the capacity for Jefferson's style of political leadership. But the comparison demonstrates, at the very least, that Jefferson's suspicion of national power and his understanding of the Constitution as a compact among sovereign states did not directly follow from his belief in popular sovereignty, or his faith in the people, or from the alleged influence of Scottish moral philosophy on his political thought, for these faiths and beliefs likewise characterized James Wilson, whose political commitments were so different from Jefferson's.[8]

II

The conversations and arguments about power and liberty examined in this work take place against a background of Lockean political principles—best encapsulated in the Declaration of Independence. They also build upon, as well as transform, a tradition of oppositional Whig thought originating in eighteenth-century England. Both the shared Lockean principles and the oppositional Whig tradition shaped the way in which problems of power and liberty were raised, but they did so in very different ways. It is not that they conflicted, exactly, but rather that they addressed different kinds of problems.[9]

This is exemplified in the ambiguous relation between the Lockean principles of the Declaration of Independence and Jefferson's wider political thought. All four of the figures studied here—Hamilton no less than the rest—shared the principles articulated in the Declaration. None of them, however, shared Jefferson's view that energetic government is always oppressive.

The Declaration is Jefferson's most famous piece of writing, and no interpretation of his political thought can ignore it.[10] Yet for purposes of the present study, the Declaration poses some peculiar interpretive problems. It is, and was intended by Jefferson to be, not the statement of an individual but of the entire patriot cause: "Neither aiming at originality of principle or sentiment, nor yet copied from any particular and previous writing, it was intended to be an expression of the American mind, and to give to that expression the proper tone and spirit called for by the occasion."[11] Thus Jefferson would have deliberately suppressed any views and premises that did not command common consent (and Congress pared away at them even further when it edited Jefferson's draft). On the other hand, what remains in the document is certainly in accordance with Jefferson's own views and moreover—in Jefferson's own mental universe—is connected via certain well-oiled tracks with wider aspects of his thought that might not have enjoyed the common consent of the signers. The power of the document—and consequently Jefferson's fame—would have been significantly diminished if more of Jefferson's own views had been incorporated in it. It succeeds because it leaves so many questions open.

The Declaration dissolves a government without setting up another. It says nothing about how to set up another form of government, nothing about how to design and balance its powers so as to best preserve liberty, nothing about the appropriate distribution of power in a federated system. It merely declares the right of the people to establish a government based on consent while remaining silent about the form.

Nor does it say anything about how best to guard liberty during "normal" times. The Declaration is directed explicitly toward an extreme political case rather than the ordinary workings of government: a case in which there was a clear and radical choice between two fundamentally different sets of political principles. It thus provides no guidance about how to reconcile liberty and power during times when revolution is not the appropriate remedy.

One of the fundamental premises of Jefferson's political philosophy taken as a whole—testified to in scores of letters and especially in his draft of the 1798 Kentucky Resolutions—is the idea that there exists a permanent antagonism between the power of government and the liberty of citizens, an unequal contest in which the "natural progress of things is for liberty to yield, and government to gain ground."[12] But there is no statement to this effect, either direct or implicit, in the Declaration. It does not pretend to diagnose what flaws in the English constitution or what negligence on the part of the people set in process the chain of events culminating in the violation of the Americans' most fundamental rights. Instead it catalogs the violations themselves in order to assert the right of revolution. Jefferson certainly had his own views of what tendencies in English government had led to the crisis—he was well steeped in the thought of the oppositional Whigs—but there is nothing about this in the Declaration itself. The document does presuppose that a watchful people can distinguish between "light and transient causes" and "a long train of abuses and usurpations pursuing invariably the same object." Yet it does not explain the distinction; it lists the clear and present abuses but does not say anything about what early warning signs indicate a shift from "light and transient causes" to a "design" on liberty. If Jefferson had incorporated his own answer to this question in the draft, he might have encountered much disagreement with his fellow delegates.[13]

Jefferson's wider political philosophy makes a principle of "jealousy of power": every increment of power in government is dangerous. The Declaration, too, is implicitly about jealousy, but in a much more restricted and formal sense. To assert that "a people" has a right to alter or abolish an existing form of government when it becomes abusive of the rights it was designed to protect clearly implies that people practice a kind of watchfulness toward government; otherwise there would be no way of enforcing the principle. But to practice principled watchfulness is not necessarily to treat every increment of government power as a threat to liberty, nor does it necessitate the rejection of confidence in government officials under ordinary circumstances.

More generally, the Declaration of Independence is concerned not necessarily with powerful government but with abusive government. The practical relation between the amount of power vested in government and the possibility of its abuse is left entirely open.

It is also worth noting that the Declaration, although it asserts the right of "a people" to alter or abolish forms of government and establish new ones, leaves entirely open the question of whether there exists a single American people or thirteen separate peoples engaged in a strategic alliance against the British Empire. The opening of the document speaks of "one people" dissolving the political bands that have connected them with another, but the conclusion of the document asserts that the "united colonies are & of right ought to be free & independent states"—in the plural.[14] The people are sovereign, but whether the Declaration speaks in the name of a single sovereign American people or in the name of the various sovereign peoples of Virginia, Massachusetts, New York, etc., is a question upon which the Declaration is silent. How much power one is willing to vest in national government depends among other things upon whether one regards the United States as a single people or a coalition of peoples.

III

If the fundamental principles set forth in the Declaration offer little practical guidance for the conduct of government and protection of liberty in normal times, that gap was filled to a certain extent by the oppositional Whig tradition of thought in which Americans of the Revolutionary age had steeped themselves and whose importance has been underscored in a number of histories of the Revolutionary and constitutional period.[15] Political writers in this tradition whose influence was greatest in America would include Trenchard and Gordon (authors of *Cato's Letters*), James Burgh, and—though he was not really a Whig—Bolingbroke. Specific concerns addressed in these writings include the dangers of executive influence ("corruption"), the enormous English public debt, and the threat of standing armies. Above and beyond these specific concerns, they exhibit a general fear of governmental power. In a chapter from *Cato's Letters* entitled "The Encroaching Nature of Power, Ever to Be Watched and Checked," Trenchard and Gordon wrote: "Only the checks put upon magistrates make nations free; and only the want of such checks makes them slaves. . . . It is the nature of power to be ever encroaching, and converting every extraordinary power, granted at particular times, and upon particular occasions, into an ordinary power, to be used at all times, and when there is no occasion; nor does it ever part willingly with any advantage."[16] This political tradition provided Americans of the Revolutionary age with a distinct political language—including the characteristic use of the words *power* and *liberty*—as well as a checklist of signs warning of incipient corruption and tyranny.

However, these ideas had to be applied to a quite different American context and to the peculiar problems of establishing a new, wholly republican, federally structured nation. The England of *Cato's Letters* was not a republic but a limited monarchy with an aristocratic upper house. It was not immediately clear how the oppositional Whigs' suspicion of power, originally conceived in fear and resentment of a corrupt and overly powerful court, would apply to a political order wholly republican—where the people, not the government, were sovereign. Did the new republican context require greater or lesser suspicion of governmental power? A case could be made either way: Jefferson answered the question one way, James Wilson and Alexander Hamilton another.

Another challenge was to apply ideas of power and liberty that originated where there were only two basic entities, the government and the people, to a new context where there existed both state and national levels of government and where it was unclear whether "the people" referred to a national political community or something smaller. Although England had a self-conscious "country" gentry that defined itself in opposition to the "court," it had no counterpart to the states in the American political system. The oppositional Whigs never carried on their battle with entrenched power by claiming any kind of sovereignty for the counties of England. They never had to face the dilemma of two separate levels of government, each claiming a kind of supremacy; they never had to decide whether, in a federal system, the authority of state government in relation to national government represented liberty or merely a different form of power. Americans in the 1780s and 1790s had to face all of these questions, and their answers branched off in a number of different directions.

Another decision that had to be made in applying Whig ideas to a wholly republican American context was how to categorize the executive and judicial branches of government. In the English context it was clear that within the framework of government itself, liberty was peculiarly connected with the House of Commons, while the king and his ministers and court represented power. In a republican political order, founded on the principle that the people are sovereign, does it follow that executive and judicial power should be kept under even closer watch because of the seeds of monarchy and aristocracy they carry? Or can executives and judges be trusted with more power than under a hereditary order? Again, the Whig tradition could be made to speak with different voices on this question. When Jefferson observed to Edward Carrington on May 27, 1788, that "the natural progress of things is for liberty to yield, and government to gain ground," it was the perceived dangers of executive power that occasioned the remark.[17] James Wilson, on the contrary, insisted that extreme jealousy of executive power was natural and understandable in a hereditary order but inappropriate in a republic where all branches and levels of government equally express the will of the sovereign people.

The oppositional Whig tradition of thought could branch in a number of different directions in the American context. But not every branch was equally easy to follow. There was instead a grain, so to speak, which made movement along certain lines easier than others. Jefferson went with the grain. Madison, Hamilton, and Wilson all attempted to go against the grain in various ways and were conscious of doing so.

IV

One of the most crucial problems this work seeks to address is the convergence and divergence of James Madison and Alexander Hamilton. On that point this study differs from most of the historical and biographical literature.

There are dozens of book-length studies of *The Federalist* and probably hundreds of articles. A few preserve the fiction of a single author, "Publius,"[18] although most do not; some, reading Hamilton and Madison's later divergence back into the work, speak of a "split personality";[19] others, although admitting differences of emphasis and approach between Madison and Hamilton, stress their convergence of overall purpose.[20] But apart from a few references to later events, these remain studies of *The Federalist*, not comparisons of the political thought of Madison and Hamilton.

One would expect that biographies of Madison and Hamilton and studies of their political thought would remedy this problem by adding the necessary developmental perspective. But such works are at best a partial remedy. The degree to which a biography of Madison or Hamilton alone can introduce a comparative perspective is limited; studies of each man's political thought are similarly restricted. Both when they worked together on *The Federalist* and when they opposed one another in the 1790s, Madison and Hamilton reciprocally shaped one another's political thought. For this reason a comparison of Madison and Hamilton that includes both their collaboration in the 1780s and their opposition in the 1790s can explore aspects of their thought and its development over time that would otherwise be missed.

But there is a more fundamental obstacle to a serious comparative study of Madison and Hamilton, one that affects almost all biographies of them, studies of their political thought, and historical narratives of the period: the widespread belief that Madison reversed his constitutional principles between 1787 and 1792. Scholars offer different explanations of how and why he pulled this reversal, but that he did so is widely accepted.[21]

The explanation of Madison's conduct offered in Stanley Elkins and Eric McKitrick's *The Age of Federalism* is worth mentioning here for several reasons. It is the most comprehensive recent study of the 1790s and synthesizes an enormous range of scholarship both old and current. It devotes a great deal of space to both Madison and Hamilton and is especially insightful and subtle in its portrayal of Hamilton. It is arguably the definitive study of the historical period in which the great divergence between Madison and Hamilton took place. And yet in my view it is fundamentally askew in its portrayal of Madison.

The authors dismiss quickly, almost brutally, Madison's constitutional arguments against the Bank of the United States, claiming even that Madison himself "must have sensed" that he was "standing on very unsteady ground." The authors agree with Elias Boudinot of New Jersey (who during the 1791 congressional debate read out passages from *Federalist* No. 44, written by Madison, on the impossibility of a complete enumeration of powers) that there is no way of reconciling Madison's argument against the Bank with what he had held previously.[22] The authors argue instead that the key to understanding Madison was his visceral hatred of England—what they call Madison's "political economy of Anglophobia." He saw Hamilton attempting to reproduce the English system here and felt he had to be stopped. It was not just the economic system of England but what England on some less than rational level symbolized for Madison "that wrecked the personal and political relations between James Madison and Alexander Hamilton."[23]

However important Madison's and Hamilton's differences over political economy may have been,[24] however great their differences over what England symbolized and what United States policy toward it ought to be, there is no justification for a summary dismissal of Madison's arguments against the Bank or for the quick conclusion that he completely reversed his constitutional principles.

In his attack on the Bank, Madison at no point argued against the principle of implied powers as such; he never claimed that the mere text of a constitution could provide infallible answers to every question that arose under it (and therefore did not contradict what he said in *Federalist* No. 44). He did not claim, as Jefferson did in his brief against the Bank, that only absolutely indispensable means to a given end are constitutionally allowable. What Madison argued against—and believed he saw in Hamilton's rule of constitutional construction—was the use of implied powers in a way that allowed the indefinite expansion of governmental power. There is a difference between implied powers and complete powers, and Madison's argument against the Bank hinges on this difference. Neither those who drafted the Constitution nor the people when they ratified it had clear ideas of the extent of every power it granted. But they understood very clearly that the document was not designed to allow indefinite expansion of the powers of the national government.

For Madison the most authoritative guide in questions of constitutional interpretation was neither the text itself nor the intentions of the convention that drafted it; it was the sense in which it was understood by the people when they ratified it. It was not merely a matter of reading the text of the Constitution and finding in it no specified power to charter corporations. Much more important (in Madison's view, at any rate) was the fact that this specific power was considered at the convention and rejected; the supporters of the Constitution argued in the ratifying conventions that the national government would not enjoy such a power, and the people ratified the Constitution with the understanding that it would not include the power to charter corporations. It was not the power to charter corporations as such (Madison himself having originally supported such a power) but the willingness to disregard the clearly expressed sense of the people in their ratifying conventions that threatened liberty.

Whether there in fact existed so clear an understanding on this point as Madison believed is of course a debatable question. But Madison thought it existed, and his argument against the Bank—and his opposition to Hamilton's policies more generally—cannot be understood without taking this aspect of his argument into account.

Madison—like Hamilton and Wilson—rejected the common assumption that every augmentation of governmental power posed a direct threat to liberty; one could not assume that every time the government became more powerful, the people became less free. Sometimes greater power threatened liberty; sometimes it did not. It was not so much the total quantity of power vested in government that mattered (at least within a certain broad range); what mattered was that governmental powers stay within whatever limits have been clearly agreed upon. What frightened Madison about Hamilton's Bank proposal was not the power itself but the willingness to cross boundaries.

And far from marking a reversal from what Madison had said in *The Federalist,* this is in fact entirely consistent with it. In *Federalist* No. 38 Madison spoke with alarm about the Continental Congress's frequent practice of assuming powers "without the least color of constitutional authority." The fact that the Continental Congress was forced to exceed its constitutionally defined powers because of a defective system of government and that the assumption of power was done in the public interest did not change the fact that such a practice is dangerous to liberty. In this case, paradoxically, liberty would have been made more secure if national government had been authoritatively granted greater powers, for then it would not have to grasp for the needed powers in underhanded ways. Thus, surprisingly, Madison's critique of the too-weak government under the Articles of Confederation and his critique of the too-strong government that Hamilton tried to institute as treasury secretary have a common theoretical starting point: namely, that there should be a clear match between the powers publicly granted and the powers actually exercised. Liberty is threatened both by too much and by too little power.

A changed understanding of Madison requires a fresh look at Hamilton as well. If Madison's arguments against the Bank are taken seriously, and if they are consistent with what Madison had written in *The Federalist,* then this puts Hamilton's political and constitutional thought in a new light.

This does not necessarily mean accepting Madison's critical view of Hamilton or that it was Hamilton rather than Madison who pulled a reversal. (Hamilton's consistency has rarely been questioned, and I do not intend to do so here.) The political and constitutional thought of both men was broadly consistent over time, after making allowance for the usual problems of applying theory to the twists and turns of political life. Their collaboration on *The Federalist* represents not a common political theory from which Madison later diverged but the convergence, on a limited number of points, of two rather different ways of thinking.

According to the received view of Hamilton (to oversimplify somewhat), his broad-constructionist method of reading the Constitution (as exemplified in his "Opinion on the Constitutionality of a Bank")—which in time became the standard method of construction—seems so reasonable that it is hard to imagine how intelligent men like Madison and Jefferson could have disagreed.

On the other hand, it is equally assumed that Hamilton had little concern for liberty and that his political outlook, if not literally antirepublican, certainly contained more than a touch of authoritarianism.

The interpretation of Hamilton offered here turns the received view upside down. I argue that he was more concerned with liberty than is commonly assumed—and as a value in itself, not just as a means to his nationalist and economic ends. At the same time I attempt to show how problematic and daring his approach to the Constitution really was.

The starting point for understanding Hamilton is to realize that on at least one point, Madison's criticism is entirely accurate: not only did Hamilton attempt to create a more powerful government than the American people had expected when they ratified the Constitution, but he knew that he was doing so. In his "Opinion on the Constitutionality of a Bank," he in effect argued that a previous understanding of the kind Madison considered authoritative, even if it existed, was irrelevant; and in subsequent writings (the "Vindication" letters of 1792), Hamilton conceded that many well-intentioned men who ratified the Constitution did not possess "an accurate view of the necessary compass of the authorities which ought to constitute" the national government. People knew a more powerful national government was necessary, but they did not know how powerful it would need to be to accomplish what it was expected to do. Hamilton believed he had a better understanding of the necessary powers than the people did when they ratified the Constitution. The task was not to defer to their past understanding but to convince them to change their minds.

It is impossible to understand Hamilton's thought and action—at the Federal Convention, during the ratification contest, and as treasury secretary—without giving due weight to the problem of powerful states making claims to sovereignty. He had no illusions that the mere ratification of the Constitution would put an end to the sovereignty contest between national government and states, though it was bound to change the form in which that contest played itself out. If the national government did not establish itself—in practice, not just on parchment—as clearly superior to the states in authority and power, the Constitution eventually would fail. Unlike Madison, he had no faith that "the sovereign people" would be able to stand above this authority contest between national government and states and regulate it. The national government had to act first to establish itself; popular acceptance of its augmented power would come after the fact.

Perhaps the best way to dramatize what was at issue is to consider how

Hamilton's drive to strengthen national government must have appeared to someone steeped in the radical Whig tradition—in *Cato's Letters,* for instance—which presupposes a delicate balance between power and liberty that is always endangered by the encroachments of power. Viewed with this set of lenses, Hamilton's policies as treasury secretary would appear in the worst possible light: as a bold and undisguised attempt enormously to expand power at the expense of liberty.

But there is a peculiarity to this set of lenses when applied to the American context. In the English political system there was no counterpart to the federal problem that had to be solved in the United States. Trenchard and Gordon in *Cato's Letters* never had to worry about the counties of England advancing claims of sovereignty at the expense of king and Parliament. And this means that in Hamilton's drive to increase the powers of national government, the question—increase those powers at the expense of who or what?—does not have the kind of straightforward answer it would have had in England.

The key to understanding Hamilton's views on power and liberty and why he aroused such extraordinary fears among his contemporaries is the fact that Hamilton made a basic distinction between the liberty of citizens and the power of states, while most of his opponents did not. He believed it was possible greatly to expand the power of the national government with respect to the states without upsetting the ordinary balance between the power of government and the liberty of citizens. But in a sovereignty contest between national government and states, no such balance was possible.

However, even if a strong distinction is drawn between the liberty of the people, which Hamilton sought to uphold, and the sovereignty of states, which he sought to suppress, Hamilton's drive to augment the powers of the national government is open to another objection: that the people did not want and did not consent to such extensive powers. That was Madison's objection: he too realized that the liberty of the people and the power of states were different things, and he would have preferred a somewhat different distribution of power between national government and states; but whatever distribution of power had been clearly agreed to in the ratifying conventions should be honored. To disregard the understanding with which the people had ratified the Constitution posed a direct threat to liberty.

To answer this objection to Hamilton's thought and action requires more than showing that it is possible—in theory—to increase the power of the national government relative to the states without depriving the people of their public and personal liberties. It also requires a description of when and how the people—the people out-of-doors, not just the members of Congress—actually consent to these new national powers.

If such consent does not exist before the fact, then it would have to occur during the fact or after the fact. In the Hamilton chapter I argue that a two-part case for substantive consent can be made. First, Hamilton seems to have believed that the people—or at least the most influential and enlightened among them—could be persuaded by his arguments in his various reports as treasury secretary (which are masterpieces of clarity in explaining extremely complex issues). He did not merely act with the intention of bringing about a fait accompli too difficult or costly to reverse; he wanted truly to persuade the public that the actions were right.

Second, Hamilton seems to have believed that the public would come to accept the powers of the national government in a way comparable to how, in the sphere of economics, people accept the idea of credit. In the case of credit, the appearance of substance must come first; it becomes real only after it is believed in. The same could be said for the creation of new political power. Many of Hamilton's plans to strengthen national government can be understood as attempts to make the thing look real, and the best way to make it look real is immediately to give it powers that directly touch the lives of ordinary citizens. Once people came to regard the national government as real, they would cease to pose objections based upon extravagant fantasies about its powers. Thus making the government more powerful (in the right way) would itself help remove the objection that its powers were too extensive.

V

If Madison and Hamilton form a kind of natural pair for examination, so for different reasons do Wilson and Jefferson. Both Wilson and Jefferson had a gift (and a weakness) for powerful simplifications. Both had an unlimited faith in the people. Both were preoccupied with the grand difference between popular and hereditary political orders and saw in every event and decision a battle between these opposed principles. Both believed literally in the principle that the people are sovereign and can alter their forms of government whenever they wish. But on two points, energetic government and federalism, the two men headed in opposite directions. For Wilson, the energy of government and the energy of a self-governing people reinforce one another; for Jefferson, an energetic government signifies lack of energy in the people, and vice versa.

Wilson's response to the complications of federalism was to assert the existence of a single, national sovereign people standing above all authority conflicts. Jefferson's version of federalism also relied on the sovereignty of the people—but the people of the individual states, not a national people, the very existence of which he sometimes doubted. Both feared that the seeds of monarchy and divine right could come back to life within a republic. But for Jefferson it was above all the power of the national government that kept alive these seeds. For Wilson the pernicious seeds of divine right made their appearance in the form of the doctrine of state sovereignty. What for Jefferson was the remedy was for Wilson the problem itself, and vice versa.

What is most important about Wilson is his appreciation of the symbolic dimension of politics and his understanding of the ways in which political symbolism can be translated into constitutional detail. Both as theorist and as statesman, James Wilson was a man of a single idea: the sovereignty of the people. He did not invent the idea, which went back at least to the English Civil War and was given new life by the American Revolution. Instead he took an idea that was already in the air and pursued it more relentlessly than anyone else, at the same time giving it a new cast and applying it to practice in new ways. During the American Revolution the idea of the sovereignty of the people had assumed a predominantly local form in which the idea of direct democracy was taken literally. The people were superior to their governments, even elected governments, which they held in check through written constitutions, annual elections, and local instructions to their representatives.

What Wilson did was to take this idea and give it a national form: there exists a single, national people that creates and remains superior to every branch and every level of government. Wilson was the man most responsible for making this idea an essential part of the Federalist argument for ratification of the Constitution: the sovereign American people were free to create whatever form of government they wished, even if it contravened the Articles of Confederation or the constitutions of the states. But for Wilson the idea of popular sovereignty was not merely a clever argument for use in the ratification contest. In his own way he believed as much in direct democracy as his localist opponents did, and he endeavored at the Federal Convention to make the relation between the people and every branch and level of government as direct as possible. He favored (among other things) annual elections, direct popular election of both president and Senate, and representation based on "one man–one vote" at all levels. He consistently opposed state sovereignty in any form, for in his view it elevated the "artificial beings" called states above the people who created them.

Wilson's version of the sovereignty of the people depended in turn on his faith that there truly exists a single American people. To say that national laws and a national constitution reflect the will of the sovereign people presupposes that there is indeed an American people, which many of his contemporaries denied and many others doubted. And the harmonization of power and liberty that Wilson believed possible—in which an energetic government is seen as the expression of, not the enemy of, an energetic and free people—also depends upon the assumption that a single nation exists. For otherwise—as the Antifederalists did not hesitate to point out—the acts of the national government will be seen as acts of an alien and foreign power, and there can be no freedom in obeying a foreign power.

Wilson's relation to Madison and Hamilton can be summarized in this way. All three believed it was possible to create a strong national government that did not threaten liberty; the three worked together (especially during the early weeks of the Federal Convention) to create such a government and to secure its ratification. All three accepted the idea of the sovereignty of the people in some form (Hamilton in a more attenuated form than Wilson and Madison) and used it to justify the decision to tear up the Articles of Confederation and start over, for if the people are sovereign, they can change their form of government any time they choose.

But how much theoretical work can the idea of popular sovereignty be expected to do? Wilson believed that the idea of the sovereignty of the people, if properly understood and developed, contained the answer to all the important political and constitutional questions. For Madison and Hamilton the idea of popular sovereignty was only one part of a wider analysis of problems of power and liberty. If one was to reject altogether the idea of popular sovereignty (as most modern-day theorists do), the descriptive value of Madison's and Hamilton's thought would remain; Wilson's thought would suffer heavy damage. Still, Wilson illuminates aspects of Madison and Hamilton that we might otherwise miss. And Wilson's unusual sensitivity to the symbolic dimension of politics deserves a close examination.

Thomas Jefferson's remark about energetic governments always being oppressive came in a letter to Madison expressing Jefferson's reservations about the proposed new Constitution. Unlike Madison, Hamilton, and Wilson, who were at the very center of events, Jefferson was in Paris when the Constitution was drafted and ratified. Jefferson was thus excluded not only from the for-

mation of the document itself but more importantly from the wider transformations of American political thought that were occasioned by the events
surrounding the Constitution. Madison, Hamilton, and Wilson (among others) used the drafting and ratification process to effect a fundamental rethinking of power and liberty. Jefferson's outlook in contrast remained
uncontaminated by these transformations of thought, so that when he turned
his attention to the Constitution, his oppositional Whig suspicion of power
remained undiminished.

Jefferson was in no sense a die-hard opponent. During the mid-1780s he
himself had supported additional powers for the national government with
respect to commerce (though these were quite limited and specific in comparison to what he saw in the Constitution). He expressed certain specific
objections to the Constitution, the most important of which were its lack of
a bill of rights and the perpetual reeligibility of the President. But he soon
enough made his peace with the document itself and went on to serve under
it as secretary of state, vice president, and president. He was able to reinter-
pret the document in a way that fit his own political principles but that also
conflicted in important respects with the views of many of those who had
drafted it.

Jefferson's original objections had less to do with the specific provisions
of the document than with his more general fear that the purpose behind it
was to elevate power at the expense of liberty. He feared that popular governments would overreact to disorders like Shays' Rebellion (Massachusetts, 1786)
and thus degenerate into despotism. In Jefferson's view energy in government
was practically synonymous with coercive force; the energetic governments of
Europe relied on bayonets. The notion that government can be energetic in
ways that are not coercive was alien to Jefferson's outlook. And in fairness to
Jefferson it must be admitted that at least some of the political momentum
behind the Constitution was of a repressive character.

Jefferson also opposed the shift of sovereign authority from states to
national government that was intended by at least some of those who drafted
the Constitution. He was able to nullify this shift without opposing the document itself by understanding the Constitution itself as a creation of, and compact between, sovereign states comparable to a treaty in international law.

One question that deserves to be considered is the degree to which the
novelty of the system of power established by the Constitution aroused Jefferson's suspicions. The governments of the states had roots going back more
than a hundred years; they were established powers. The national government

was a new power. Jefferson's principles entail suspicion of all political power but reserve a special degree of jealousy for new powers because in his view innovations in government almost always tend to be innovations at the expense of popular liberty.

This hostility to innovation may seem strange coming from a man famous for his maxim "The earth belongs to the living," so that every generation has the right to change or repeal any constitution or law.[25] This is indeed Jefferson's strongest and clearest formulation of the principle of popular sovereignty. How is it possible to reconcile the Jefferson who is especially suspicious of innovations in government with the Jefferson who leaves each generation free to rewrite all its constitutions and laws?

The answer is that for Jefferson the radical right of the people to innovate and the conservative opposition to innovations in government were two sides of the same coin. Both are founded in the fear of government power and on the premise of an essential dichotomy between government on one side and people on the other. People must be free to rewrite laws and constitutions every generation to protect themselves against what government will do in the meantime. An innovation either comes from the side of government (and is bad), or it comes from the people and expresses their sovereign will; there is nothing in between. Here again the contrast between Jefferson and Wilson is especially striking, because for Wilson the energy of government in a republic was the expression—not the enemy—of the people's sovereign will.

VI

A remark about the usage of the term *liberty* in this work is in order. Liberty as used here means both private liberties such as property rights and religious freedoms and public liberty as embodied in the practice of popular self-government. Madison, Hamilton, Wilson, and Jefferson certainly recognized that there were differences between private and public liberties and also recognized that these two kinds of liberties frequently came into collision with one another. But they would have been puzzled by the modern-day tendency to dichotomize them into two different and antagonistic "traditions" of liberty ("Lockean liberal" or "negative" libertarianism as opposed to "republican" or "civic humanist" or "positive" libertarianism). The dichotomy is no less misleading for Hamilton than for the more democratic Madison and Wilson. Hamilton was worried about the possible excesses of public liberty and probably would have drawn a different balance between private and public liberty than the other three would have. But popular self-government still was liberty for Hamilton; nowhere did he speak of "true" liberty as private liberty only, nor did he call for any clear subordination of public liberty to private liberties such as property rights. Neither Hamilton, Madison, or Wilson would ever have agreed with Hobbes's remark that the liberty of a man is no different in Constantinople than in Athens.[26]

In making the interplay between power and liberty the focus of this work, I deliberately return to what was a central theme of Bernard Bailyn's *The Ideological Origins of the American Revolution* (1967). *Ideological Origins* did not develop this theme past the conclusion of the Revolutionary War; Bailyn's *Faces of Revolution* (1990) included some suggestive essays that carried the power-liberty theme into the constitutional period but lacked the comprehensive examination he had accorded the Revolutionary period.

It was Gordon Wood in *The Creation of the American Republic* (1969) who took up the challenge of developing the power-liberty theme into the constitutional period and beyond, and in doing so Wood transformed the next generation of scholarship on the Founding era. But in Wood's narrative the interplay between power and liberty becomes a kind of subplot to a larger story, the supposed shift from "republican" to "liberal" political paradigms over the course of the Founding period.

There is growing recognition now among scholars that the republican versus liberal distinction, although useful in many respects, is highly overdrawn.[27] In this work I return to the power-liberty theme inspired by Bailyn and attempt to develop it twenty years into the future without presupposing any radical shift of political discourse from republican to liberal during that period. In my view the discursive shifts that occurred between the Revolution and the mid-1790s entailed creative modulations of key ideas rather than radical breaks.

Hamilton, Madison, and Wilson all sought to challenge the Whig idea that power and liberty are inherently antagonistic. This is an important innovation, but it is not as radical a break as claiming that they sought to replace republican with liberal politics. They used a traditional language to say new things; the continuities are as important as the transformations.

VII

The central problems with which this book is concerned are as alive now as in Madison, Hamilton, Wilson, and Jefferson's time, despite fundamental transformations of American political, social, and economic life that they could not have imagined. No matter how sensitive one is to historical context, no matter how frequently one reminds oneself of the differences between late eighteenth-century America and the present day, the fact remains that one always has some motive for posing the historical questions one hopes to answer. My primary purpose here is to offer a historically accurate reconstruction of the views of four key Founders on the problem of national power. In posing questions to them and speculating about how they would answer, I have tried to restrict myself to questions that were actually asked or could have been posed by one of their own contemporaries and that they themselves would have recognized as fair and relevant to what they were trying to accomplish. But it would be disingenuous to claim that present-day political concerns have not shaped the inquiry in any way. Whether every expansion of governmental power comes at the expense of freedom—and if not, when and why some do and some do not—is a question worth putting to the Founders because it is likewise a question for us.

The question has taken on an additional significance in recent years. Since the 1980 presidential election, and even more since the election of a Republican Congress in 1994, the issue of the power and scope of government has been at the center of the national political agenda. One federal responsibility after another is being eliminated or devolved to state and local governments. This attack on "big government" can be either fruitful or destructive. At its best it can lead to a fundamental rethinking of which governmental powers are truly necessary or useful and which ones are unnecessary, too costly, or too restrictive of liberty. At its worst it becomes a simple-minded attack on government as such that makes no distinction among essential and inessential government responsibilities and that is blind to the wide array of private forms of power that only governmental authority can restrain.

The Founders—whether individually or collectively—cannot provide us with any direct guidance in this respect. Any of the four I examine here could be cited in support of many sides of many contested questions. There is not and can never be a single, straightforward Madisonian, Hamiltonian, Wilsonian, or Jeffersonian position on a problem they never faced. It is entirely fair to use their ideas to make political and constitutional arguments, so long as one realizes such arguments are one's own, not theirs. There is nothing wrong with the phrase "If Jefferson were alive today" (or Madison, Hamilton, Wilson) if this caveat is kept in mind.

The true practical value of the discussion of power and liberty I reconstruct here lies not in any specific answers offered or positions taken but in the conversation itself: the multiple perspectives it brings into play, the way it confounds any easy dichotomies. Madison believed that questions of power and liberty were inherently complicated and wished to dissuade Americans from simple propositions of any kind. That can serve as the watchword for our present-day examinations of power and liberty as well.

James Madison

1751–1836

2
James Madison
ON POWER AND LIBERTY

It has been remarked that there is a tendency in all Governments
to an augmentation of power at the expence of liberty.
But the remark as usually understood does not appear to me
well founded. . . . It is a melancholy reflection that
liberty should be equally exposed to danger whether the
Government have too much or too little power, and that
the line which divides these extremes should be
so inaccurately defined by experience.
—James Madison to Thomas Jefferson, October 17, 1788

How is it possible to make government more powerful without making those subject to its authority less free? That was one of the challenges Madison faced as he prepared for the Federal Convention (and faced again in drafting the Bill of Rights and in opposing Hamilton's policies in the 1790s). "According to the views of every member, the Gen[era]l Gov[ernmen]t will have powers far beyond those exercised by the British Parliament when the States were part of the British Empire," Madison observed on June 29, 1787, at the Federal Convention.[1] How could any government, even one republican in form, avoid being oppressive if it was to exercise more power over the United States than the British Parliament had exercised over the colonies? Did not Parliament become oppressive precisely because it had become too powerful? To argue for a government more powerful than Parliament but more protective of liberty as well, Madison must be able to argue—against the grain of much political thought of the age—that more governmental power does not necessarily mean less liberty, that power and liberty are not simply opposites to be balanced.[2]

This chapter explores the complicated relation between liberty and power in Madison's writings, especially in the crucial period between 1787 and 1791.

Within a relatively short span of time, Madison seems to have changed from a strong advocate of centralized power (1787) to an outraged critic of centralized power in its Hamiltonian form (1791). Before and during the Federal Convention he called for a national government that could strike down any law passed by a state legislature (which goes even further than present-day judicial review). It is necessary, he wrote to Jefferson in March 1787, "to arm the federal head with a negative *in all cases whatsoever* on the local Legislatures. Without this defensive power experience and reflection have satisfied me that however ample the federal powers may be made, or however clearly their boundaries may be delineated, on paper, they will be easily and continually baffled by the Legislative sovereignties of the States."[3] He stuck to this position through most of the convention and worried about the lack of a veto over state legislation in the final document.[4]

Yet when Hamilton proposed in 1791 that the federal government charter a national bank—a power which Madison himself had supported at the Federal Convention, and which would seem to be a far more modest exercise of national power than Madison's proposed negative—Madison was shocked and honestly feared that it undermined the foundations of constitutional government. His Virginia Resolutions of 1798 (protesting, among other things, the Alien and Sedition Acts) call upon the states to resist the unjust actions of the federal government. These resolutions would appear (though Madison denied it) to support the doctrine of nullification—a doctrine he strove with all his might to oppose in the last years of his life.[5]

Is there any theoretical consistency here? Or is this merely a pragmatist's response to shifting political alignments and diverse problems of policy? Throughout his life Madison was dogged with the accusation of inconsistency (an accusation made by many historians and biographers as well). He insisted, on the contrary, that he was more consistent than anyone else of his age.[6]

Lance Banning has written that "nearly all authorities discern a radical discontinuity between the Madison of the 1780s and the Madison of the 1790s" (though Banning himself argues for Madison's fundamental consistency).[7] Opinions vary as to the cause of Madison's supposed reversal. His nineteenth-century biographer Sidney Howard Gay wrote that Madison was a Federalist until he was "swept away partly, perhaps, by the influence of personal friends, particularly of Jefferson, and partly by the influence of locality."[8] Others have portrayed him as at heart an advocate of states' rights and strictly limited national power who was led by the peculiar conditions of the 1780s to favor powers (such as the negative) that went contrary to his later and better judg-

ment.[9] Still others attribute his shift to a tragic conflict between his nationalism and his republicanism in which Madison felt he could preserve republican principle only by sacrificing his nationalism.[10]

It is above all Madison's opposition on constitutional grounds to Hamilton's proposed Bank that epitomizes his supposed reversal.[11] Not only had
Madison at the Federal Convention favored granting the national government
the power to charter corporations, he also had argued in *Federalist* No. 44 and
elsewhere that a complete enumeration of powers was impossible and that
some powers must be left to implication. How then could he reject the implied
power to charter a Bank? For this reason his specifically constitutional arguments against the Bank are often discounted in favor of some other explanation for Madison's opposition.[12]

There is nothing necessarily inconsistent about favoring an increase in
national power at one time and opposing it at another. One can shift course
politically while holding to consistent underlying principles. The problem in
Madison's case was that he did not adequately clarify the principles that guided
his shifting political course.

The standard view that Madison reversed his political and constitutional
principles is challenged in two significant works of recent scholarship: Lance
Banning's *The Sacred Fire of Liberty: James Madison and the Founding of the
American Republic* (1995) and Jack Rakove's *Original Meanings: Politics and
Ideas in the Making of the Constitution* (1996). Both works portray a Madison
whose concerns of the 1790s are clearly founded upon and continuous with his
purposes in 1787.

For Lance Banning the key to Madison's consistency was his fundamental
commitment to preserving the republican experiment against threats resulting from both excessive fragmentation and excessive concentration of power.
The weaknesses of the Confederation were "more responsible than any other
fact for popular abuses in the states and thus for growing doubts about the
benefits of the republican experiment itself." Thus saving the republican experiment required a national government capable of regulating commerce, paying public debts, and protecting private rights. But Madison also feared that
"too much power, placed in hands too distant from the people, might endanger revolutionary ends." Through a careful study of Madison's political and
intellectual development during the 1780s, Banning demonstrates that Madison was never a nationalist of the stamp of Alexander Hamilton, Robert Morris, or James Wilson. Moreover, Banning argues that Madison's "respect for
written limitations of authority and charter boundaries between the powers

of the nation and the states did not develop after 1789" but was already apparent during the mid-1780s.[13] Therefore it should not be surprising that Madison opposed Hamilton's policies in the 1790s.

Rakove's *Original Meanings* examines a difficult and politically charged problem: in what sense can the "original understanding" of the Constitution serve as authoritative guide for subsequent questions of constitutional interpretation? And how is that "original understanding" to be ascertained? Madison is central to the inquiry by virtue of his peculiar insistence that the "oracular guide" to constitutional interpretation is the way in which the document was understood by the people when they ratified it. For Madison in 1788 the character of the ratification process itself was essential, not just whether the document was voted up or down. Madison was therefore entirely consistent when during the 1790s he insisted, against Hamilton, that the understanding of the ratifiers was the final authority in questions of constitutional interpretation. Rakove claims, however, that Madison's method of ascertaining the intent of the ratifiers was "marred by unresolved problems." For Rakove, in short, Madison was fully consistent but not always fully convincing.[14]

I agree with Banning and Rakove that Madison was fundamentally consistent; but my guiding question is different, and thus my argument emphasizes different things. The guiding theme of this chapter is the idea articulated in Madison's statement that liberty is "equally exposed to danger whether the Government have too much or too little power" and, moreover, "the line which divides these extremes" is "so inaccurately defined by experience": in short, Madison's rejection of any simple antagonism between power and liberty.[15]

The argument is this. For Madison the possibility of reconciling the power of government and the liberty of citizens depends above all upon the existence of clear boundaries to governmental power publicly agreed upon by an enduring majority of the people. In some cases (as with religious liberty) these boundaries are marked by natural right, and in other cases (whether or not the federal government can charter a bank) they are artificial; but in either case once they have been agreed upon, liberty is threatened if they are trespassed. It is this, and not the quantity of power as such, that matters.

I do not wish to push this argument too far. Madison would never have favored the kind of centralized power Hamilton argued for in his June 18 speech at the Federal Convention. But the break between Madison and Hamilton became irrevocable over a power, chartering banks and other corporations, that was well within the range of what Madison could have accepted—if the people in ratifying the Constitution had clearly understood that the national government would enjoy such a power. Madison's principal objection to Hamilton's Bank was that the people in ratifying the Constitution clearly understood that the national government would not have such a power.

The question of how power and liberty are and should be interconnected goes to the heart of Madison's republicanism. In a 1792 *National Gazette* essay (published soon after his open break with Hamilton), Madison wrote: "In Europe, charters of liberty have been granted by power. America has set the example and France has followed it, of charters of power granted by liberty. This revolution in the practice of the world, may, with an honest praise, be pronounced the most triumphant epoch of its history, and the most consoling presage of its happiness." He described republican constitutions as "instruments, every word of which decides a question between power and liberty."[16] The liberty Madison referred to here is not just private but especially public liberty: the political activity of the people in their sovereign capacity.[17]

What was new about the American (and Republican French) constitutions compared to traditional forms was not simply that in some mechanical fashion they struck a different balance between the power of government and the liberty of citizens. Who draws the line had also changed. One might suppose that once liberty becomes the fountain of power, all tension between them, and thus all need for limitation on power, disappears. But that was not Madison's meaning. Instead he meant that liberty must restrain itself; majorities must learn to respect the lines that majorities themselves have drawn.

I

Madison's sponsorship of the Bill of Rights and his support for civil liberties more generally in national as well as state politics provide an appropriate starting point for our search for underlying consistencies in his thought and action over time. At the very least—however consistent or inconsistent Madison may have been with regard to other questions of national power—he was a consistent civil libertarian.

Madison's principled support for civil liberties is also an appropriate starting point because it raises a key question. Did Madison reverse his principles on national power in order to preserve liberty as he understood it? (That is the central thesis of Irving Brant's biography of Madison.) Or might his consistent defense of civil liberties provide clues to a wider consistency on questions of national power?

Madison's first significant political act (1776) was a successful effort to strengthen the clause concerning religious liberty in Virginia's Declaration of Rights (from mere "toleration" to an absolute right of "free exercise according to the dictates of conscience").[18] Madison's support for civil liberties is the most visible link between the periods in which he favored expanding national power and those in which he opposed it. His proposed negative on state legislation (the apogee of his so-called nationalist period) had as one of its principal objectives preventing violations of individual rights by factious majorities.[19] His original draft of a bill of rights would have prevented both the national government and the states from violating religious liberty, freedom of the press, and jury trial (unlike the version that finally passed, which restricted only the national government). His Virginia Resolutions of 1798, which call upon the states "to interpose for arresting the progress of the evil" of the policies of the national government (the high point of his supposed states' rights period), are especially directed against the violation of freedom of speech and press under the Sedition Act.

In the attempt to discover whether a consistent understanding of national power underlay Madison's consistent defense of civil liberties, let us turn to his October 17, 1788, letter to Jefferson. The letter was written just as Madison was beginning to shift from opposition to support for a national bill of rights. Jefferson had argued from the beginning that the Constitution needed a bill of rights, and he was firmly convinced that (as Madison put it, implicitly summarizing his friend's view) "there is a tendency in all Governments to an augmentation of power at the expence of liberty." One of Madison's aims in the letter is to argue for a bill of rights but to do so on the basis of a very different and more complex understanding of the relation between liberty and governmental power.

Madison's argument in the letter could be summarized as: (1) liberty can be "equally exposed to danger whether the Government have too much or too little power," and (2) the "line which divides these extremes" of too much and too little governmental power must be stamped on public opinion, not merely drawn on parchment.[20]

Liberty can be endangered both by too much and by too little governmental power because there are so many different threats to liberty, proceeding from many different directions. The Antifederalists were certain that the greatest threat to liberty proceeded from government, and that the more powerful (and physically distant) the government, the greater the threat would be. For this reason the whole point of the Antifederalists' demand for a bill of rights was to reduce the powers of the national government significantly.[21] Jefferson, too, regarded a bill of rights exclusively as a limit on the national government, though he did not favor significantly reducing the powers proposed by the Federal Convention.

Madison, without denying the danger to liberty posed by powerful government, believed that an equal or greater threat proceeded from society itself in the form of factious majorities taking control of government. In such cases governmental power is not the source but merely the instrument of the threat to liberty. In other circumstances governmental power is the only available defense against threats to liberty. Such considerations make any simple opposition between liberty and governmental power a mistake.

Because threats to liberty can proceed from either too much or too little power, it follows that protecting liberty can require either limiting power or increasing it—perhaps even both at the same time. Madison's original draft of a bill of rights would have prevented both the national government and the states from violating religious liberty, freedom of the press, and jury trial. Madison explained in a speech in Congress on June 8, 1789, in which he presented his draft: "I have stated in the 5th resolution, that no state shall violate the equal right of conscience, freedom of the press, or trial by jury in criminal cases. . . . It must be admitted, on all hands, that the state governments are as liable to attack these invaluable privileges as the general government is, and therefore ought to be as cautiously guarded against."[22] Madison claimed this resolution was the most important of all. It is especially significant given the commonplace assertion that the original purpose of the Bill of Rights was to place limits on the national government exclusively; this may be accurate as a characterization of the form in which it passed, but it greatly misrepresents the purposes of its principal sponsor.

Biographers of Madison and students of the Bill of Rights have never quite known what to do with Madison's proposal to use the Bill of Rights to place limitations on the states. Sometimes it is passed over in silence.[23] Sometimes it is presented as evidence that Madison had not yet completely given up on his original idea of a negative on state legislation (implying that Madison's thought had not yet changed in this respect).[24] Sometimes it is cited as evidence that Madison anticipated the Fourteenth Amendment of the Constitution—which is true enough but does not explain the place of this proposal within his own thought.[25]

Clearly Madison envisioned a bill of rights that would have limited the power of the national government in certain respects but strengthened its power in other respects, because some branch or combination of branches of the national government would have to be responsible for enforcing these limits on states. (Madison himself never clearly explained how the limits on states would be enforced.)

Madison wished to challenge any simple opposition between liberty and governmental power. But what prevented him from running to the opposite extreme—of too closely associating governmental power (especially the power of national government) with the protection of liberty? In 1792, during the height of his battle with Hamilton, Madison wrote an essay for the *National Gazette* entitled "Who Are the Best Keepers of the People's Liberties?" In it he imagined a dialogue between a Republican, who expresses his own view, and an Anti-republican who seems a caricature of Hamilton:

Republican: "What a perversion of the natural order of things! to make *power* the primary and central object of the social system, and *Liberty* but its satellite."

Anti-republican: "Wonderful as it may seem, the more you increase the attractive force of power, the more you enlarge the sphere of liberty; the more you make government independent and hostile towards the people, the better security you provide for their rights and interests."[26]

The fictional Anti-republican here takes to an absurd extreme a general premise upon which Hamilton and Madison would have agreed: that at least some increases of governmental power are to the benefit of liberty. But clearly Madison believed that making the government "independent and hostile towards the people" was not the right way to go about protecting liberty. How then should it be protected? Madison's remarks about public opinion at the time of his conversion to support for a bill of rights may give us some clues.

Madison's original opposition to the Antifederalist call for a bill of rights was grounded in his unwillingness to make ratification of the Constitution conditional upon any amendments, thereby "giving an opportunity to the secret enemies of the union to promote its dissolution";[27] the reason for this opposition had now passed. Both James Wilson and Alexander Hamilton had argued that a bill of rights was unnecessary because the powers of the national government were limited to those enumerated in the document. Madison said that he accepted this argument to a certain degree "though not in the extent argued by Mr. Wilson."[28]

He wrote to Jefferson that "my own opinion has always been in favor of a bill of rights; provided it be so framed as not to imply powers not meant to be included in the enumeration. At the same time I have never thought the omission a material defect, nor been anxious to supply it even by *subsequent* amendment, for any other reason than that it is anxiously desired by others." He pointed to the different purpose of a bill of rights in a monarchy, where the greatest threat to liberty comes from the government, and in a republic, where the threat comes from society itself; he doubted that the "parchment barriers" of a bill of rights would be effective against "overbearing majorities." What then is the use of a bill of rights in a popular government? Madison identified two:

> 1. The political truths declared in that solemn manner acquire by degrees the character of fundamental maxims of free Government, and as they become incorporated with the national sentiment, counteract the impulses of interest and passion. 2. Altho' it be generally true as above stated that the danger of oppression lies in the interested majorities of the people rather than in usurped acts of the Government, yet there may be occasions on which the evil may spring from the latter sources; and on such, a bill of rights will be a good ground for an appeal to the sense of the community.[29]

Notice that "the sense of the community" is central to both of these arguments: in the first case a bill of rights may help create such a sense; in the second case (in this letter which prefigures the Alien and Sedition Acts controversy) it is a rallying point. Madison did not claim that such a "sense of the community" is so effective as to make governmental enforcement of rights unnecessary. He presumably meant that a sense of the community in favor of fundamental rights is an indispensable support for governmental efforts to protect rights and a restraint upon attempts to use government to violate rights. Thus, even if in practice these rights are to be enforced by the judiciary (again, Madison is not entirely clear on this point), the judiciary cannot do so effectively without "national sentiment" on its side.

In his June 8, 1789, speech in Congress introducing a bill of rights, Madison made the point again: "It may be thought all paper barriers against the power of the community, are too weak to be worthy of attention. . . . Yet, as they have a tendency to impress some degree of respect for them, to establish the public opinion in their favor, and rouse the attention of the whole community, it may be one mean to controul the majority from those acts to which they might be otherwise inclined."

He also made the argument in a negative way: given that the sentiment in favor of a bill of rights—as expressed in the various ratifying conventions— was so overwhelming, what kind of message would it send not to make such amendments? "It will be a desirable thing to extinguish from the bosom of every member of the community any apprehensions, that there are those among his countrymen who wish to deprive them of the liberty for which they valiantly fought and honorably bled."[30] Though he had little faith in the efficacy of words, Madison was enormously impressed with the potential power of the public opinion behind the words.[31]

There were two additional considerations that make this particular expression of public opinion especially important. First, the sentiment in favor of protecting fundamental rights was a truly national sentiment. In drafting his Bill of Rights, Madison sorted through recommendations originating in the ratifying conventions of seven states. He did not treat these recommendations as separate expressions of the public opinion of the peoples of several states; he viewed them as the public opinion of a single national people. (And, to be sure, he edited and reworked the recommendations to give them a more national character than they possessed in raw form.) The precise character of Madison's nationalism is difficult to describe, but clearly he believed a national "sense of the community" existed, or could be brought into existence in crucial matters.

Even more important was the fact that these declarations in favor of a bill of rights were expressed by the people in their ratifying conventions, which Madison regarded as the single most legitimate expression of the will of the sovereign people. The popular declaration in favor of a bill of rights, in other words, was not merely an ordinary expression of public opinion but public opinion in the highest and most sacred form of which it is capable.

From Madison's perspective this must have been a revelation: a national majority committing itself to the principle of restrictions on the power of majorities. This may have had the effect of filling an important gap in Madison's own thinking about the problem of protecting individual liberties. In his original idea of a negative on state legislation vested somewhere in the national government, his reasoning was that the national government, like a monarch, would be sufficiently distant and neutral with regard to disputes within states to play the role of umpire.[32] But what moral force could a distant, merely neutral, quasi-monarchical power have in a republic? A national majority, deliberately and explicitly committed to limits on the power of majorities, would provide much-needed support to the national judiciary in efforts to prevent violations of rights in the states and at the same time would serve as a check upon any attempt on the part of the national government to violate those same rights.

Lance Banning has remarked upon Madison's capacity to learn and change at the Federal Convention.[33] But the additional learning and changing Madison underwent in the course of sponsoring the Bill of Rights also deserves notice. His decision to switch from opposition to support for a bill of rights has sometimes been portrayed as a merely tactical shift—important in defusing opposition to the Constitution but of no real importance to Madison himself.[34] A recent study which recognizes the principled character of Madison's sponsorship and rightly stresses the importance Madison placed upon educating public opinion does not distinguish between his analysis of public opinion in *The Federalist* and the analysis of public opinion that informed his sponsorship of the Bill of Rights—thereby overlooking the new insights on public opinion he gleaned from the ratifying conventions.[35]

Madison failed to get an amendment prohibiting states from violating freedom of religion, the press, and jury trial included in the Bill of Rights. Yet he accomplished at least part of his purpose, which was to respond to, and further encourage, a national sense of the value of the most important public and personal liberties. An enduring national majority explicitly committed to fundamental liberties—a majority committed to restraints on majorities—provides an anchor against the tendency of government to vacillate between the extremes of too much and too little power.

II

On the surface there seems to be little in common between Madison's sponsorship of the Bill of Rights in 1789 and his staunch opposition to Hamilton's proposed Bank in 1791. Vesting the national Congress with power to charter banks and other corporations does not of itself pose any threat to personal or public liberty; it is well within the range of what Madison had earlier considered acceptable national powers. Madison's Bill of Rights left the ordinary powers of the national government untouched; it only prohibited certain powers that its drafters had not expected the national government to possess in the first place, and if Madison had had his way, it would have placed new restrictions on the states. Madison as sponsor of the Bill of Rights, in short, would still seem to be Madison the nationalist.

If his support for civil liberties provides the clearest evidence for Madison's consistency over time, the story of his intense opposition to Hamilton's proposed national bank seems to be the clearest evidence of inconsistency. The Bank controversy (1791) marks the point at which Madison seems to have made

a permanent shift away from support for strong national powers broadly interpreted over to strict constructionist constitutional theory and defense of states'
rights. At the Federal Convention, Madison himself had proposed a power "to
grant charters of incorporation where the interest of the U.S. might require &
the legislative provisions of individual States may be incompetent"—and this
probably would have included banks as well as internal improvements like
roads and canals.[36]

Madison's opposition surprised Hamilton, who had shown the Bank plan
to him before making it public, hoping for his support. How, he must have won-
dered, could this be the same Madison "whose politics had formerly so much
the *same point of departure*" as his own?[37] Hamilton certainly knew that he and
Madison differed significantly on matters of political economy. If Madison had
confined his objections to the particular policies Hamilton hoped to implement
with the aid of a Bank, Hamilton would not have been surprised. But that Madison would object to the power itself on principle—that was a shock.

To further augment the impression of Madison's inconsistency, later in life
as president (1815) he vetoed a bill to recharter the National Bank, but on policy rather than constitutional grounds: he stated explicitly, on the contrary,
that the Bank was no longer unconstitutional because it had operated now for
twenty years with "a concurrence of the general will of the nation" even though
the relevant constitutional language had not changed since 1791! A year later
he signed into law a new Bank of the United States.[38]

The easiest explanation for these shifts is that Madison simply subordi-
nated his constitutional theory to his substantive policy goals. Thus when he
realized that Hamilton wanted to use the Bank to perpetuate the public debt,
enrich a privileged class, and encourage manufactures at the expense of agri-
culture, Madison—so the argument would go—contrived constitutional arguments against banks and corporations even though he had earlier supported
these powers when he thought they would be used for different purposes. Then
he changed his mind again twenty years later when presented with a Bank bill
that matched his policy goals.

Madison's fears in 1791 about the Bank as a dangerous and indefinite
national power appear even more peculiar when contrasted with his support
in 1787 for a power vested in the national government to strike down state legislation "in all cases whatsoever." It would seem that Madison had one set of
constitutional principles for times when he believed the national government
was too weak and an entirely different set of principles for times when he
believed it was too strong.[39]

That is the picture of Madison I intend to challenge here. Madison opposed increased national power in 1791 for the same fundamental reasons that he supported it in 1787. The fundamental problem in both 1787 and 1791 was a disjunction between the powers the people expected the national government to exercise and the powers it actually exercised. Under the Articles of Confederation the problem was that the national government's actual powers fell far below what was required to accomplish what the people had charged it to do. The problem with Hamilton's Bank was that it assumed a power above what the people expected and understood it would have—an understanding best expressed in the conventions that ratified the Constitution. For Madison, in short, too much and too little power were different forms of the same problem. Liberty can be threatened by a disjunction in either direction.

This explanation of Madison's guiding principles also enables us to trace some interesting affinities between Madison's argument in support of the Bill of Rights and his argument against the Bank. Both arguments depend upon the anchoring effect of a national "sense of the community" expressed in the act of ratifying the Constitution. Madison supported the Bill of Rights because it tended to secure this anchor; he opposed the Bank because it loosed the anchor.

Before turning to Madison's argument against the Bank, it would be helpful to take a fresh look at the period of his most intense commitment to national power: his criticism of the Articles of Confederation and advocacy of a new constitution with greatly increased powers.

A careful examination of Madison's criticism of the Articles of Confederation shows that the problem he diagnosed was not simply that the national government was not powerful enough relative to the states. The more specific problem was that there was a gulf between the powers the Continental Congress possessed in principle (which reflected what the American people expected it to accomplish) and the powers it actually exercised. The people expected it to conduct foreign policy, provide for the national defense, pay off the public debt, and many other things. But its defective political machinery made these expectations difficult or impossible to fulfill. Thus the Continental Congress was chronically weak, a "lifeless mass" (as Madison described it). But this gulf between expectation and actual powers can just as well lead to usurpation and even despotism as a government strives in underhanded ways to secure the powers it needs. In *Federalist* No. 38 Madison made an argument that appears very strange unless this point is understood when one is reading his catalog of the alarming abuses of power by the Continental Congress:

Out of this lifeless mass has already grown an excrescent power, which tends to realize all the dangers that can be apprehended from a defective construction of the supreme government of the Union. . . . [The Continental Congress] have proceeded to form new States, to erect temporary governments, to appoint officers for them, and to prescribe the conditions on which such States shall be admitted into the Confederacy. All this has been done; and done without the least color of constitutional authority. Yet no blame has been whispered; no alarm has been sounded. . . . The public interest, the necessity of the case, imposed upon them the task of overleaping their constitutional limits. But is not the fact an alarming proof of the danger resulting from a government which does not possess regular powers commensurate to its objects?

This is not the language of one who favors sweeping, loosely defined powers! (One could not mistake this for one of Hamilton's contributions to *The Federalist.*) This passage supports Lance Banning's argument that Madison's "respect for written limitations of authority and charter boundaries . . . did not develop after 1789" but was already present during the mid-1780s.[40] It also helps make sense of Madison's claim in *Federalist* No. 45 that the change proposed by the Constitution "consists much less in the addition of NEW POWERS to the Union than in the invigoration of its ORIGINAL POWERS."[41] In practice, this would mean vesting the national government with substantially greater powers than it possessed under the Articles of Confederation. But the degree of power as such was not the principal issue; what was crucial was the match between expected powers and actual powers.

A dangerous disjunction between expected powers and actual powers can occur either when actual powers fall below expected powers—which was the case under the Articles of Confederation—or when actual powers exceed those expected and agreed upon. That is what Madison believed was wrong with Hamilton's proposed Bank.

Madison's February 2, 1791, speech in Congress against the Bank bill opens with some brief criticisms of the Bank on policy grounds but then proceeds to what is for Madison the central issue: "Is the power of establishing an *incorporated bank* among the powers vested by the constitution in the legislature of the United States?"[42] In denying the constitutionality of such a power Madison employed three different lines of argument.

One line of argument could be labeled strict constructionism, strictly speaking. Madison asked what specific language in the Constitution could include a power to incorporate a Bank. It cannot, for instance, be subsumed under the power "to borrow money" or "to lay and collect taxes" because it does neither. It cannot be subsumed under the "general welfare" or "necessary and proper" clauses because these are not intended to establish general powers but are merely "*incident* to the *nature* of the specified powers."[43]

But this kind of strict textual construction is not by itself conclusive, and Madison knew it. Later in the speech he remarked, "It is not pretended that every insertion or omission in the constitution is the effect of systematic attention. This is not the character of any human work, particularly the work of a body of men."[44] To argue against the constitutionality of the Bank, Madison could not rely on the claim that the language of the Constitution clearly excludes such a power.

But there is a very great difference between ambiguous language and an indefinitely expansive rule of construction. There is a difference between conceding that some powers must be left to implication and setting into motion a process by which governmental power can be continually expanded. This was his second (and much more convincing) line of argument. The principal danger lies not in the power to charter a Bank per se but in the rule of constitutional construction employed by the Bank's supporters by which every means to an end becomes in turn another end, opening up new means, which become ends, and so on indefinitely:

> Mark the reasoning on which the validity of the bill depends. To borrow money is made the *end* and the accumulation of capitals, *implied* as the *means*. The accumulation of capitals is then the *end*, and a bank *implied* as the *means*. The bank is then the *end*, and a charter of incorporation, a monopoly, capital punishments, &c. *implied* as the *means*.
>
> If implications, thus remote and thus multiplied, can be linked together, a chain may be formed that will reach every object of legislation, every object within the whole compass of political economy.[45]

To reject such a rule of construction, one need not rely on the clarity of any particular enumerated power in the Constitution. The fact that any enumeration of powers was attempted—however imperfect—excludes a rule of interpretation that would render enumeration itself absurd.

Madison's final and perhaps most important argument against the Bank is that the power it assumes was clearly considered and rejected by the people of the United States when they framed and ratified the Constitution. However useful and justifiable the power to charter corporations may be in the abstract, it is illegitimate and dangerous to override a clear expression of the will of the people. "A power to grant charters of incorporation," Madison explained, "had been proposed in the general convention and rejected."[46] (It was Madison himself who had proposed such a power.)[47]

The fact that the Framers of the Constitution considered and rejected a power of incorporation is important. But of even greater importance is that the people in ratifying the Constitution clearly understood that the national government would not be vested with such a power, and that

> the terms necessary and proper gave no additional powers to those enumerated.
>
> (Here he read sundry passages from the debates of the Pennsylvania, Virginia and North-Carolina conventions, shewing the grounds on which the constitution had been vindicated by its principal advocates, against a dangerous latitude of its powers, charged on it by its opponents.) . . .
>
> With all this evidence of the sense in which the constitution was understood and adopted, will it not be said, if the bill should pass, that its adoption was brought about by one set of arguments, and that it is now administered under the influence of another set[?][48]

Madison added that no one present in the chamber had had the opportunity to consult their constituents on the issue, so Congress would be proceeding altogether without popular endorsement. If Congress was willing to cross clearly defined boundaries in one respect, what would prevent it from crossing other boundaries as well? Madison even feared that Congress might begin incorporating religious societies.[49]

Throughout his life Madison insisted that the most legitimate guide to constitutional interpretation lay not in the words considered in isolation, or in the deliberations of those who drafted the Constitution, but in how it was understood by the people when they gave it their approval in ratifying conventions.[50] One clear statement of this view comes in a speech Madison gave in Congress on April 6, 1796:

But, after all, whatever veneration might be entertained for the body of men who formed our constitution, the sense of that body could never be regarded as the oracular guide in the expounding the constitution. As the instrument itself came from them, it was nothing more than the draught of a plan, nothing but a dead letter, until life and validity were breathed into it, by the voice of the people, speaking through the several state conventions. If we were to look therefore, for the meaning of the instrument, beyond the face of the instrument, we must look for it not in the general convention, which proposed, but in the state conventions, which accepted and ratified the constitution.[51]

This same principle, in some form, was central to Madison's decision to sponsor a bill of rights (which shows that he did not invent it in 1791 to oppose the Bank). The people in their ratifying conventions had declared themselves in favor of a bill of rights. At those same conventions they had declared themselves opposed to a national government as powerful as the one Hamilton hoped to administer into existence.

Madison, in contrast to Hamilton, took very seriously what had been agreed upon; for that reason there was no inconsistency in Madison's proposing at one time to include a power to charter corporations and opposing it now. He originally had desired a national government somewhat more powerful than the one the Federal Convention designed and the people ratified; but the matter having been settled, it would be illegitimate to press for additional powers. From the perspective of the proper relation between power and liberty, it is a secondary question how much power in absolute terms the central government is entrusted with; what is important is that it stay within whatever limits have been agreed upon. Power and liberty are reconciled only if power—which in a republican government is the creation, not the creator, of liberty—remains within those limits.

Whether there in fact existed in 1791 a clear public understanding opposed to the power to charter a Bank is of course an open question. As Jack Rakove has shown, Madison's attempt to find clear answers to questions of constitutional construction in the "original meanings" of the people who ratified the Constitution is beset by a number of practical and theoretical difficulties. And even if one accepts the principle Madison articulated, one can still argue that he applied it to practice in inappropriate ways. His later acceptance of the Bank's constitutionality may have been a backhanded admission of mistaken judgment. But his belated acceptance of the Bank can also be defended on grounds of principle: the fact that the Bank was approved by ten successive Congresses, under widely varying political circumstances, and that its operations were accepted by state authorities over time, proves that it had the support of an enduring, not a transient, majority and thus provides a kind of functional equivalent for the ratifying conventions.[52]

Madison never claimed that there was a clear "sense of the people" on every constitutional question. Instead he claimed that such a sense existed on certain very important constitutional questions. Whatever difficulties his argument encounters at the level of detail, one should not overlook one crucial piece of evidence in Madison's favor: Hamilton himself knew that he was vesting the national government with much more power than the people had expected when they ratified the Constitution. Hamilton believed he had the capacity and duty to persuade the people to accept such a government; Madison felt honor bound to stick with the agreement.

III

Madison believed that the American people in the act of ratifying the Constitution had clearly expressed the desire for a bill of rights. He also believed that the American people in ratifying the Constitution had a reasonably clear understanding of the extent of the national government's powers—an understanding that did not include chartering banks and other corporations.

Neither proposition makes sense unless there exists a single American people, at least in certain politically crucial respects. Thirteen separate peoples, politically unified only through the machinery of their common Constitution, could not possess the kind of clear and enduring "sense" that was central to Madison's theory of constitutional interpretation.

During the ratification debate the Antifederalists grasped immediately that the preamble to the Constitution and the mode of its ratification (approval of nine states, not thirteen, was required) assumed precisely what they questioned: namely, that there existed a national political community. The language of the Declaration of Independence was ambiguous on the question of whether independence was the act of one people or thirteen, and the Articles of Confederation had used the language of a compact among sovereign states. But the opening words of the Constitution—"We the people"—implied the existence of a single political community rather than a confederation of states, and some Antifederalists criticized it on these grounds.[53]

Several supporters of the proposed Constitution—above all James Wilson—argued, on the contrary, that there existed a single united American people, forged through the crisis of independence; that this sovereign people created both the state and federal governments and can delegate to either level of government whatever powers it chooses. In his notes of the Federal Convention, Madison recorded that "Mr. Wilson could not admit the doctrine that when the Colonies became independent of G. Britain, they became independent also of each other.... They were independent, not *individually* but *Unitedly*."[54] In Wilson's view a single American people existed not only before ratification of the Constitution but even before the Declaration of Independence.

Madison's own views on the matter, however, are much less straightforward than Wilson's and certainly exhibit some surface contradictions, even within the pages of *The Federalist* itself. On the one hand he often enough treated the American people as a single sovereign entity. The clearest statement of this position comes in *Federalist* No. 46, where he wrote: "The federal and State governments are in fact but different agents and trustees of the people, constituted with different powers and designed for different purposes. The adversaries of the Constitution seem to have lost sight of the people altogether on this subject; and to have viewed these different establishments not only as mutual rivals and enemies, but as uncontrolled by any common superior in their efforts to usurp the authorities of each other." He used this argument, among other things, to justify any irregularities with regard to the existing rules under the Articles of Confederation that may have occurred in drafting a new constitution. (See also No. 40 and No. 45.) If a sovereign people wishes to alter their form of government, a sacred right they always retain, then they are not bound by any rules that prevent them from doing so. James Wilson himself could not have presented a stronger and clearer statement of the position that there exists a single sovereign people—a "common superior." (One should note that the premise of a single sovereign people does not necessarily entail a single consolidated government, which Madison as well as Wilson opposed. A single people could choose any degree of centralization or decentralization it wishes.)

But *Federalist* No. 39 presents a rather different picture. Where No. 46 assumes the existence of a single sovereign people, No. 39 describes the act of ratifying the Constitution as "the act of the people, as forming so many independent States, not as forming one aggregate nation"; ratification "will not be a *national* but a *federal* act." The act of ratification must be "unanimous," meaning that no state could be forced to join the newly constructed Union against its will. "Each State, in ratifying the Constitution, is considered as a sovereign body independent of all others, and only to be bound by its own voluntary act." It would seem to follow, then, that the United States was not a single nation before ratification (as implied by No. 46); there were sovereign peoples but no sovereign people.

The obvious next question is: does the act of ratification itself make a single sovereign people out of what were previously separate peoples? Here too Madison refused to provide a clear-cut answer. Certainly the Union is more national than it was before: the House of Representatives "will derive its powers from the people of America," i.e., the people considered as a single political community. But the Senate will continue to derive its powers "from the States as political and coequal societies." The procedure for amending the Constitution does not require the concurrence of each state in the Union and thus signifies a major step in the national direction compared to the act of ratification; in this respect the character of the Union has been fundamentally altered by the act of ratification itself. But the amending process is still not wholly national because if it were, a majority of the people, not a majority of the states, would be competent "to alter or abolish its established government."

It should be kept in mind that in distinguishing between "national" and "federal" elements of the Constitution, Madison was not only speaking of the distribution of governmental powers. He meant that the people themselves are partly national, partly federal—which is to say, in some respects one people, in other respects several peoples.

Given the difficulties of reconciling *Federalist* No. 46 with No. 39, one might conclude that Madison was simply confused, or that he was hiding his truly nationalist views, or both.[55] A somewhat more sympathetic interpretation would be that it was the American people who were confused, not Madison; he was simply making the best of a messy state of affairs. The Constitution, after all, was not everything he had wished for. For instance, he had bitterly opposed at the Federal Convention the provision for equal state representation in the Senate, but he was willing to recommend its "federal" logic in *Federalist* No. 39. If the people freely drafted and ratified a document that is fundamentally unclear on the locus of sovereignty, one that mixes the logic of one sovereign people with that of several semisovereign communities, then it was Madison's duty to respect and argue for it. To make the document more consistent than it really is (as James Wilson did, especially in his

Chisholm v. Georgia opinion) would do violence to the concretely expressed will of the people.

Certainly Madison would defer on principle to the concretely expressed will of the people even where it differed from his own views. And there is no question that he disagreed with some of the "federal" characteristics of the Constitution he defended in *The Federalist*. But with respect to the fundamental point of *Federalist* No. 39—that the American people is in certain respects single and in other respects plural—Madison was articulating his own conviction. Perhaps his clearest description of his complex view of American nationhood comes in a 1791 essay from the *National Gazette,* where he wrote:

> Here then is a proper object presented, both to those who are most jealously attached to the separate authority reserved to the states, and to those who may be more inclined to contemplate the people of America in the light of one nation. Let the former continue to watch against any encroachment, which might lead to a gradual consolidation of the states into one government. Let the latter empty their utmost zeal, by eradicating local prejudices and mistaken rivalships, to consolidate the affairs of the states into one harmonious interest; and let it be the patriotic study of all, to maintain the various authorities established by our complicated system, each in its respective constitutional sphere.[56]

It seems not to have mattered to Madison that some saw the United States as a union of many communities and others as a single community. Both perspectives had something useful to add to the working of "our complicated system." He seems to have believed that political cooperation was possible among those with quite different theoretical views as to the single or plural character of the American people—so long as both recognized the need to keep government within the limits that had been agreed to.

Where did Madison himself stand on this question? His view of the matter could perhaps be summarized this way: (1) Nationhood need not be all-or-nothing but can exist in varying degrees. (2) The degree to which the United States is, or is not, a single nation is not fixed once and for all but can and should evolve over time. As "local prejudices and mistaken rivalships" are eradicated and the interests of states become harmonized, the United

States becomes more of a nation than before. (3) The people themselves are capable of directing and guiding this evolutionary process. Even where there are inconsistencies, he had faith in the ability of a free people to make them workable. (4) Wherever the American people clearly and deliberately intend to act in the character of a single nation, the political machinery should make it possible—thus the justification for circumventing the restrictions imposed by the Articles of Confederation, which prevented the American people from acting as a nation even when it chose to do so. But the process by which the American people become more of a nation must not be forced from above by a "consolidating" government (as Hamilton sought to do). Even a single, united American people would not choose to vest all power in a single central government.

A proper understanding of Madison's conception of American nationhood will in turn shed new light on his Virginia Resolutions of 1798, protesting the Alien and Sedition Acts, and their relation to Jefferson's Kentucky Resolutions, which advance an extreme version of individual state sovereignty. (The phrase "Virginia and Kentucky Resolutions" is commonplace in narrative histories of the period, as though Madison and Jefferson said and meant the same thing.) A careful reading of Madison's Virginia Resolutions (together with his "Report of 1800" which explains his reasoning more fully) shows that Madison was not a convert to state sovereignty.

Jefferson's Kentucky Resolutions (which Madison sharply criticized)[57] maintain that the states "constituted a General Government for special purposes,—delegated to that government certain definite powers, reserving, each State to itself, the residuary mass of right to their own self-government. . . . That to this compact each state acceded as a State, and is an integral party, its co-States forming, as to itself, the other party. . . . Each party has an equal right to judge for itself, as well of infractions as of the mode and measure of redress."[58] This is the language of a treaty that can be dissolved by any one of the parties to it. Jefferson's declaration that each individual state has the right to declare the acts of the national government "unauthoritative, void, and of no force" was later used, without distortion, to support the doctrines of nullification and secession.

Madison's Virginia Resolutions call upon the states "to interpose for arresting the progress of the evil, and for maintaining within their respective limits, the authorities rights, and liberties appertaining to them." He did not say, as Jefferson did, that the federal government is the creation of the states; he viewed instead the "powers of the federal government, as resulting from the compact to which the states are parties," which is a rather different thing. A single, though complex, American people can draw up a "compact to which the states are parties" and in doing so decide authoritatively which powers shall be delegated to which level of government.[59]

Madison intended the Virginia Resolutions as Virginia's contribution to a national expression of protest, on the part of a national majority, against the unjust policies of a faction that had seized control of the national government. He nowhere claimed the right of a single state to oppose a clear majority of the American people on this matter; he was instead attempting to create a national majority against the Alien and Sedition Acts. He did not maintain, as Jefferson did, that a single state can void the acts of the national government. Madison's protest uses the vehicle of the states because no other institutional mechanism is available. That it may be necessary in the last resort to use the states against the national government in this way is admitted in *The Federalist*, not only in Madison's contributions but even in Hamilton's.[60]

IV

For Madison an enduring "sense of the people" is the key to reconciling the power of government with the liberty of citizens. The power of government can be significantly increased without damage to liberty if the added powers accord with the deliberate sense of the people, while even small additions of power are dangerous if they proceed in violation of the deliberate sense of the people. This "sense" is most authoritatively expressed in the act of ratifying the Constitution, though it can take other forms as well. But in every case it is the sense of an enduring majority, even—perhaps especially—where it has the effect of restraining a momentary majority.

Is this characterization of Madison consistent with the antimajoritarian thrust of what is by far the most cited, most analyzed, and most anthologized of his writings? *Federalist* No. 10 is justly famous for its reversal of the assumption common at the time that republican government could survive only in a small territory. Madison argued on the contrary that the larger the territory, the greater the variety of interests and factions, the more stable republican government will be, provided it is properly designed.[61] And yet, read in isolation, the essay can leave a distorted impression of Madison's thought.[62]

In *A Preface to Democratic Theory*, Robert Dahl characterizes Madisonian democracy as an incoherent mix of clashing principles, majority power and minority power. Dahl regards as central to Madison's fractured theory the premise that minority tyranny poses no danger whatsoever in a republican government (taking as definitive Madison's quick dismissal of minority faction in *Federalist* No. 10) and thus that the only important political task is to break the power of majorities. (Dahl can thus maintain that Calhoun "enlarged upon" Madison's thought.) He claims that Madison ruled out any possibility of a majority restraining itself through some ethical principle; hence everything depends upon constitutionally prescribed external checks. Dahl overlooks Madison's equal fear of minority obstruction (which is central to Madison's criticism of the Articles of Confederation) and the importance he placed upon educating the "sense of the community" to respect individual rights. Such are the consequences of reading *Federalist* No. 10 as though it were the definitive expression of Madison's thought.

The fundamental purpose of *Federalist* No. 10—which it shares with all of Madison's writings—is to preserve a system of government based on majority rule. Madison made clear from the beginning of No. 10 that his purpose was to seek a cure for the "instability, injustice, and confusion" that serve as ammunition for the "adversaries to liberty" who would put an end to the republican experiment. As Lance Banning writes, if Madison "was deeply moved by his alarm about majority abuses, this was not the least because he was ferociously determined to preserve majority control."[63] An appreciation of Madison's lifelong commitment to majority rule must form the background of any discussion of his remedy for unchecked majorities.

Federalist No. 10 dismisses the problem of minority faction in a single sentence. Everywhere else in Madison's writing, including his other contributions to *The Federalist,* he worried about both majority and minority faction: his criticism of the Articles of Confederation centers on the tremendous obstructive powers of a minority; and in "Vices of the Political System of the United States" (April 1787), which develops many of the ideas presented in *Federalist* No. 10, he observed that "according to fact and experience a minority may in an appeal to force, be an overmatch for the majority."[64] Madison did not experience a sudden conversion to majoritarianism in 1791 any more than he converted at that time to strict construction of the national government's powers.

For Madison what counted was the existence of an enduring and deliberate, as opposed to a transient and passionate, majority. But this brings us to the central difficulty with *Federalist* No. 10: its argument depends upon a difference between good and bad majorities but says little about how they are to be distinguished. A faction (majority or minority) is by definition opposed to "the rights of other citizens, or to the permanent and aggregate interests of the community." A good majority, it would follow, is respectful of rights and promotes the permanent and aggregate interests of the community. But Madison said much more about how to prevent a bad majority from forming than about what enables a good majority to form. This lends plausibility to the interpretation, advanced by Charles Beard and others, that the argument is a shrewd divide-and-conquer strategy on the part of a well-connected elite.

Some scholars have carefully assembled Madison's scattered remarks, in *The Federalist* and other writings of about the same time, with the aim of reconstructing his implicit theory of what allows the right kind of majority to form. David Epstein argues that for Madison "justice" (the protection of rights) can be achieved negatively—i.e., through prevention—where extensive territory makes it more difficult for factious majorities to form, but realizing the "permanent and aggregate interests of the community" (which goes beyond mere justice) requires the positive and active efforts of "enlightened statesmen" capable of building a majority in the common good.[65]

But could enlightened statesmen accomplish this in the absence of an enlightened people? Alan Gibson argues that *Federalist* No. 10 relies upon the existence of a "public or civic consciousness" that "allows citizens to openly communicate and form coalitions which have the principles of right, of reason and of the Constitution on their side" while at the same time acting as "a barrier to the open communication of factious schemes."[66] In short, bad majorities are discouraged and good majorities facilitated by the same civic consciousness.

Both of these explanations are plausible and consistent with the limited and fragmentary textual evidence. But perhaps the limited textual evidence indicates that Madison himself, when he wrote *Federalist* No. 10, did not yet have a satisfactory answer to the question of how the right kind of majorities would form and what their character would be. *Federalist* No. 10 was written before the Constitution was ratified. We should consider the possibility that what Madison experienced and observed during the ratification process itself—for example, the widespread public commitment to a bill of rights—enabled him to fill some of the gaps in his thinking when he wrote *Federalist*

No. 10. One thing is certain: the majority that ratified the Constitution, whose "sense" Madison henceforth called the "oracular guide" to constitutional interpretation, is the highest example of the right kind of majority. *The Federalist* had depended upon the possibility of the right kind of majority but did little to show what such a majority looked like in practice.

It is instructive to consider what Madison had to say about conventions of the people in *Federalist* No. 49 and No. 50, which like No. 10 were written before the Constitution was ratified and thus before the "sense" the people would express in that process could have been known. In No. 49 and No. 50 Madison criticized Jefferson's recommendation that conventions of the people be called on a regular basis to remedy usurpations of power. Madison acknowledged that "the decision of the people ought to be marked out and kept open, for certain great and extraordinary occasions." (And clearly ratification of the Constitution qualified as such an occasion.) But "frequent appeals" would stir up passions rather than reason: "The *passions,* therefore, not the *reason,* of the public would sit in judgment. But it is the reason, alone, of the public, that ought to control and regulate the government. The passions ought to be controlled and regulated by the government."

Thus Madison provided a very abstract description of the difference between the right (reasonable) and wrong (passionate) type of majority. He also held out hope that if limited to "great and extraordinary occasions," conventions of the people can exemplify the reasonable kind of majority.

But Madison provided a far more detailed description of what can go wrong in popular conventions than of what a properly functioning convention looks like. Here, as in No. 10, majority factions receive the attention while the right kind of majorities remain in the background. His description of what conventions of the people accomplished in the past does not hold out much hope for the future: "We are to recollect that all the existing constitutions were formed in the midst of a danger which repressed the passions most unfriendly to order and concord; of an enthusiastic confidence of the people in their patriotic leaders, which stifled the ordinary diversity of opinions on great national questions. . . . The future situations in which we must expect to be usually placed do not present any equivalent security against the danger which is apprehended."

Although it is natural enough that Madison should argue against frequent popular conventions, what is strange about this passage is how little optimism it displays even toward the ratifying conventions immediately ahead. There was no equivalent external danger to "repress the passions," and although confidence in "patriotic leaders" such as Washington remained, this had certainly not stifled "the ordinary diversity of opinions on great national questions." One would never guess that three years later Madison would be speaking of the "sense" of the ratifying conventions with great respect. This further indicates that when he observed the actual process by which the Constitution was debated and ratified, Madison saw something good which he did not expect to see and which allowed him to fill some of the gaps in his political thought.

If so, this would signify a modification and deepening of his political thought—not a reversal, not a switch from liberal individualism to republicanism or from nationalism to states' rights. As long as scholars continue to assume that Madison radically reversed his political principles in the early 1790s, it will be difficult adequately to assess the strengths and weaknesses of his contributions to *The Federalist.*

V

I have argued that Madison held to a consistent, though complicated, view of the relation between liberty and governmental power. This does not mean that his views never changed, or that his political thought was unaffected by the demands and distractions of practical politics. Madison was always mindful of the need to temper theory with considerations of what Neal Riemer calls "prudent guidance."[67] But Madison's apparently shifting position, over time, on the crucial question of how much power should be vested in government was in fact deeply anchored in his political theory; it cannot be explained merely as a response to political opportunities and threats.

For Madison governmental power and liberty were not simple opposites (as though so much of the one always entailed so much less of the other). Because threats to liberty are so numerous and proceed from so many different sources, preserving liberty sometimes will require more governmental power, sometimes less. The degree to which governmental power threatens liberty in a republic may depend less upon the quantity of power vested in government than upon the existence of clear boundaries to whatever level of power has been agreed upon. This in turn depends less upon crystal-clear constitutional language (which Madison knew was not always possible) than upon an enduring "sense of the community" (as distinguished from a passionate, transient majority).

The concern for harmonizing governmental power with personal and public liberty has not diminished since Madison's time, though the forms power and liberty have taken have changed over the years. Nor has the temptation to draw simple conclusions about power and liberty been overcome. Ronald Reagan's 1980 campaign maxim declaring "Government is not the solution—Government is the problem" expresses the kind of simple antagonism that Madison rejected. A resurrected Madison would surely advise us against reducing problems of power and liberty to a simple formula.

The range and scope of governmental activity in the United States today are greater than anything Madison could have imagined. Far more spheres of activity are subject to laws or regulations than in Madison's time (partly, of course, because many of the problems which they address did not exist in his time). Is there something about this accumulation of governmental power and activity that chokes off human freedom even if it still respects freedoms of speech, press, religion, and the like? In other words, does governmental size itself diminish liberty? Many people believe this and argue that governmental activity as such must be reduced.

What would Madison say? One might attempt to resurrect his strict constructionism and argue that most of these historically accumulated powers should be cut away. Such a line of argument would fail for reasons Madison himself would be the first to understand: if these added powers are in fact accepted, desired, and expected by an enduring majority over a long period of time, then they acquire a presumptive legitimacy (just as the Bank eventually did). We could not restore Madison's Constitution even if we wanted to.

Perhaps instead Madison would ask us whether or not this expansion of governmental power has occurred with the considered acceptance of an enduring majority. If it has, then it need not threaten our freedom.

On precisely this question Madison would observe great disagreements among us (which tend to follow party lines). If—as is sometimes charged—the growth of government results primarily from the success with which "special interests" have captured government and created a mass of programs neither desired by nor beneficial to the majority of Americans, then fears for our freedom are justified (just as Madison's fears of the "special interests" who stood to benefit from Hamilton's policies were probably justified). If on the other hand these expanded activities (such as social security, aid to education, environmental protection, employment policy, national defense) do in fact serve purposes accepted by an enduring majority of Americans, then the problem is not that our freedom is threatened but simply that we want to avoid paying the bill. Madison would have understood this too: the battle he fought in the 1780s was against those who refused to be taxed on grounds that it threatened their liberty.

Madison would not pretend to answer the question of whether solving our urgent problems requires more government or less. We have to decide that for ourselves. He would, however, advise us that in the long run our liberty requires that we establish some kind of equivalence—one we clearly lack at present—between the functions we demand of government and the powers we are willing to vest in it.

Alexander Hamilton

1757–1804

3

Alexander Hamilton

AS LIBERTARIAN AND NATIONALIST

*Yet, however weak our country may be, I hope we shall never
sacrifice our liberties. If, therefore, on a full and candid discussion,
the proposed system shall appear to have that tendency, for
God's sake, let us reject it! But, let us not mistake words for things,
nor accept doubtful surmises as the evidence of truth.*

—Alexander Hamilton, remarks in the New York Ratifying Convention, June 20, 1788

A LEXANDER HAMILTON sometimes gives the impression of a man
who never lost much sleep over liberty. Everyone agrees that he was a
wizard of finance, a brilliant and realistic analyst of foreign policy, a
thorough and energetic administrator, a forward-looking political economist,
and many other things as well.[1] But liberty? Except for property rights and
market liberties, someone might claim, he never worried much about it except
as a means to the end of national prosperity and power.[2] Or if he did value liberty for its own sake, it was only private liberty (what in twentieth-century terminology might be called "negative liberty"), rather than public liberty,
popular self-government, the kind of liberty only citizens of a republic can
enjoy.[3] Hamilton's special concern was power—energy and efficiency of
government—and this he understood; but it was fortunate that his efforts on
behalf of power and energy were challenged and balanced by the efforts of others such as Jefferson and Madison whose first concern was liberty. So at least
goes a very common view.[4]

On the other side we have Hamilton's own insistence that he was "as zealous an advocate for liberty as any man whatever" though he "differed as to the
form in which it was most eligible"[5] and his admission that even an energetic
and effective government must be rejected if it entails the sacrifice of liberty.[6]

One can if one likes treat such assertions as merely the rhetorical tribute demanded by the circumstances. If however they are taken at face value—and we have no a priori reason not to do so—then Hamilton's enthusiasm for powerful and energetic government is explicable only if he had a different understanding of the interrelation between liberty and governmental power than did his more cautious contemporaries.

Comparison between Hamilton and Madison on this point is especially instructive. Madison and Hamilton agreed that it was possible—at least sometimes—to increase the power of government without diminishing the liberty of those subject to its authority; both rejected the notion that power and liberty are simply antagonistic. Their joint efforts on behalf of the Constitution, which established a far more powerful government than had existed previously, testify to their agreement on this general proposition. But Hamilton was willing to take the idea that power and liberty can be harmonized much further by vesting the national government with far more extensive powers than Madison was willing to accept. The preceding chapter quoted Madison's caricature of Hamilton in the form of a fictional "Anti-republican" who asserts: "Wonderful as it may seem, the more you increase the attractive force of power, the more you enlarge the sphere of liberty."[7] Madison in effect was accusing Hamilton of replacing a simple antagonism between power and liberty with an equally simplistic harmony. There is enough truth to the caricature to require some kind of explanation.

The difference between Hamilton and Madison on this question of power and liberty was not just one of the quantity of power each was willing to entrust to the national government. The difference was one of quality as well as quantity: they understood in essentially different ways the nature of the interconnection between power and liberty and the potential threats that each poses to the other.

For Madison, republican government—which is to say, a government based on the premise that the people are sovereign—presupposes a fundamental inversion in the traditional relation between power and liberty: liberty creates and defines power rather than power creating and defining liberty.[8] Hamilton, though he too was republican (various claims to the contrary notwithstanding), never believed that republicanism fundamentally changes the nature of politics or the extent of powers inhering in government. Any government—republican or otherwise—must have certain powers; he made this point in many places including *Federalist* No. 31: "A government ought to contain in itself every power requisite to the full accomplishment of the objects committed to its care, and to the complete execution of the trusts for which it is responsible, free from every other control, but a regard to the public good and to the sense of the people."

The principle of the sovereignty of the people, while it accurately describes the source of legitimacy in the republican form of government, does not change the fact that in an operational sense sovereignty inheres in government. A republican government—like any government—must be assumed to have complete powers except those specifically denied to it and/or incompatible with basic rights and liberties. Moreover, there is no reason why a government vested with complete powers should exercise those powers at the expense of liberty. Full powers for the national government would indeed come at the expense of the powers of states, but that is a different matter. For Madison the total quantity of power vested in government did not matter, at least within a certain broad range; what mattered was the existence of clear boundaries between what is permitted and what is not. The power to charter corporations, for instance, may or may not be a threat to liberty depending on whether the people, in agreeing to the Constitution, clearly understood it to have that power.

For Hamilton, on the other hand, the total quantity of power vested in the national government mattered very much, and even under the most flexible construction that quantity is barely sufficient to keep at bay the wolves of state sovereignty. Although there may be in principle a point at which the national government can become so powerful as to threaten liberty, that point is so far from being reached, and the danger lies so much in the opposite direction, that for all practical purposes supposed threats to liberty from the national government are purely imaginary.

The problem of conflict between state and national authority (and this cannot be emphasized enough in any attempt to understand Hamilton's political thought) in turn can be related to the differences between Madison and Hamilton on sovereignty. Madison believed that a sovereign people, given an adequate constitution, can monitor the balance of power between national and state governments, both of which are creatures of the people themselves. From Hamilton's perspective this was a dangerous delusion. Whatever "the sovereignty of the people" means—and Hamilton did accept the principle in some form—this "popular sovereignty" is not something capable of actively guiding and regulating the power contest between state and national government, a contest which follows a logic of its own that pays little regard to well-intentioned republican convictions. One cannot make sense of this power contest—which is in fact a sovereignty contest—without taking as a starting point the premise that in an operative sense sovereignty inheres in government.

This difference over sovereignty is related to a difference over the nature of consent. For Madison the overriding question in all matters of national power was this: what did the people understand themselves to have agreed to? For example, what particular balance between national and state authority did the people agree to in ratifying the Constitution? This presupposes two things: first, that there is a clear intention, a "sense of the people," that can be ascertained in constitutional questions; and second, that this "sense of the people" can be practically effective in guarding those boundaries that have been agreed upon.

Hamilton would deny both of these premises: there is no clear "sense of the people" to be ascertained; and even if we could find one, it would be irrelevant to the task of constitutional construction, which follows rules and imperatives of its own. Consent did matter to Hamilton, but in his thought it had neither the clarity nor the orientation toward the past that one finds with Madison. Instead for Hamilton consenting to government—at least to a new and untried form of government—is somewhat like the creation of credit: one must place confidence in something that does not yet exist but which can come into existence only after confidence is placed. One consents after the fact to something one cannot have clearly discerned at the beginning. Obviously in any such undertaking there is an enormous element of risk.

I

One of the things most difficult to understand about Hamilton is his peculiar blend of conservatism and radicalism.[9] With respect to sovereignty, for example, he remained a Blackstonean traditionalist, locating sovereignty in government and accepting its partition among national and state government in the American system only with reluctance. He attempted no radical transformation of the concept of sovereignty of the kind envisioned, in different ways, by Madison and by James Wilson, both of whom believed that republican forms of government required an entirely different understanding of sovereignty. In this respect Hamilton was a traditionalist, a conservative. He also had a conservative's distrust of energetic out-of-doors political activity.

In other respects he was a true radical.[10] This is most obviously true of his plans single-handedly to transform the American economy from agrarian to industrial. But it is equally true of his efforts to build a national state. His June 18 speech at the Federal Convention, which looks at first glance like a Burkean reverence for traditional order (with a president serving under good behavior to stand in for a monarch, a Senate serving under good behavior to fill the place of a House of Lords), is, considered from another angle, a bold and radical attempt to subvert the only traditional political and social orders that exist in America—the states. It is an attempt to conjure a national government out of thin air, against tradition, and vest it with an apparent solidity that will acquire substance only over time.

There is no point in attempting to decide whether Hamilton was really a conservative or a radical. He was both and neither, which is merely to emphasize that labels are of very limited value in understanding someone as complex as Hamilton. In another respect, however, labels are extremely useful as clues to the predispositions and prejudices of the historian and biographer. And few figures in American history carry as much troublesome baggage as Hamilton.

There is, to begin with, the surprisingly tenacious view that Hamilton was not a republican at all, that he was a secret monarchist or perhaps even a militarist who would have dispensed with republican forms gladly had the conditions been ripe. John Roche, for instance, suggests that Hamilton was not averse to a coup d'état: "Had Washington agreed to play the De Gaulle . . . Hamilton would willingly have held his horse." Similar charges were circulated widely in Hamilton's lifetime by his political enemies and have been taken up by some historians.[11] The principal drawback of this interpretation of Hamilton is that there is little evidence for it. The fact that some of his contemporaries claimed, and may even have believed, that he intended to subvert republicanism does not prove it to be true any more than the frequently repeated charge that he was corrupt as treasury secretary makes it true, in the face of all evidence. The fact that Hamilton had greater doubts than most of his contemporaries about the future prospects of republican government does not mean he wanted it to fail. (Had he wanted it to fail, his efforts as treasury secretary to give a fledgling republican government secure fiscal foundations would have been counterproductive.) So far as Hamilton's intentions are concerned, there is no reason to doubt the truth of what he wrote in 1803 to Timothy Pickering. The plan of government he presented at the Federal Convention, he wrote, "was predicated upon these bases—1. That the political principles of the people of this country would endure nothing but republican government—2. That in the actual situation of the country, it was in itself right and proper that the republican theory should have a fair and full trial—3. That to such a trial it was essential that the Government should be so constructed as to give all the energy and stability reconcileable with the principles of that theory."[12] There is an enormous difference between doubting a republican effort one hopes will succeed and trying to subvert the experiment itself.[13] And yet this slander, like many slanders, has a resonance beyond the range of those who actually believe it; its presence in the background lends an overtone to other interpretations of Hamilton.

In describing the antirepublicanism charge as a slander, I do not however mean to dismiss the argument that the actual effects of his policies might have been subversive of republicanism. That was Madison's charge, and it must be taken seriously. But it should be distinguished from the claim that Hamilton was consciously and deliberately antirepublican.[14]

A view that does contain elements of truth but is misleading all the same is this: that Hamilton, though a republican, was first and foremost an aristocratic republican and an enemy of democracy. The key to understanding his political thought and action, so the argument goes, is that he wanted to put the best people in office and keep the mob at bay. Gordon Wood, for example, speaking of the Federalists generally but in a way that would certainly include Hamilton, asserts that the struggle over the Constitution was only secondarily over national versus state authority; it was really a battle between the self-proclaimed "worthy" men against the "licentious" rule of ignorant men.[15] Because these "licentious" men had control of the states, the best hope for the "worthy" was to create a national government that would draw in the best and exclude the worst. (It follows, at least by implication, that had the state governments been in the hands of the better sort of men, there would not have been a serious effort to create a national government.) And Hamilton's June 18 speech could be read as a plea on behalf of just such a natural aristocracy.

This interpretation of Hamilton is true and misleading at the same time. It is certainly the case that Hamilton was a believer in a natural aristocracy (not an aristocracy of birth, of course, which would have no place for a West Indian upstart bastard) and that he—like most of the "worthy" men of his time—was no advocate of democracy as the term was understood then. Clearly he hoped to draw the most eminent men to national government by offering them service during good behavior in the Senate, which he indeed envisioned as a kind of natural aristocracy.

But this interpretation becomes seriously misleading if it is made into the supposed key to understanding Hamilton to which all other considerations are subordinate. It is especially misleading in its failure to take seriously the problems posed by state sovereignty—problems that, as Hamilton recognized, would lose none of their force even if the best men were in power in the states. Consider, for example, Hamilton's catalog in *Federalist* No. 7 of territorial and commercial conflicts among the American states. He insisted that it was useless to place blame on anyone; he went out of his way to remark that he did not intend "to convey the slightest censure on the conduct" of Connecticut in its territorial dispute with New York. "We should be ready to denominate injuries those things which were in reality the justifiable acts of independent sovereignties consulting a distinct interest." The problem caused by state sovereignty would not be resolved in the slightest if the better sort of men were in control in the states.

In fact, state control by the better sort of men might even make the problem worse because such men, with their love of honor and fame at stake, would want to vest state governments with more dignity than they deserved. Hamilton's June 18 Federal Convention speech can be read as a warning against precisely this danger. In spite of his remarks about "the amazing violence & turbulence of the democratic spirit," Hamilton's greatest fear here is that the states will become well ordered—internally—in a way that will ensure anarchy and conflict between the states. A dissolution of the state governments, he said, would be fatal, while a dissolution of the national government "would still leave the purposes of Gov[ernmen]t attainable to a considerable degree" within the states themselves.[16] Indeed, Hamilton feared that under such conditions the better sort of men would find their way into state government—thereby making the problem worse, not only by depriving the national government of their talents but also by vesting that much more dignity in the states. Unless national government provides "inducements for gentlemen of fortune and abilities to leave their houses and business," the power in the national government will be "thrown into the hands of the demagogue or middling politician, who, for the sake of a small stipend and the hopes of advancement, will offer himself as a candidate, and the real men of weight and influence, by remaining at home, add strength to the state governments."[17] He designed a national government with checks on democratic excesses not only because he feared unchecked democracy, but also because he feared that if its design was too democratic, prudent men in the states would not entrust it with sufficient powers.

In short, although it is true that Hamilton feared democracy, this is of very limited value in explaining his thought and policies, which require at the very least an equal attention to his fear of state sovereignty. Moreover, because most of the respectable men of his time—including those to whom his June 18 speech was addressed—had similar fears of democracy, this tells us very little about what distinguished Hamilton from his contemporaries. Many other delegates to the convention, on all sides of the various divisions, made similar critical remarks about democracy. Hamilton's diagnosis of the respective advantages held by the states in a power struggle with the national government—interest, influence, opinion, force, habit—on the other hand, is very distinctive, as is his radically nationalist proposed solution.

One more common view deserves mention, this one more sympathetic to Hamilton than the preceding two: Hamilton the builder of the modern state. If one begins with a modern industrial economy, a modern administrative state, or for that matter the modern American practice of judicial review based upon a flexible construction of the Constitution and then looks to the past for forerunners and prophets of the future, Hamilton will look infinitely more modern than Madison or Jefferson or most of the other influential men of the time.

It is not that this perspective is untrue (for certainly Hamilton's efforts did make an important contribution to a modern American state, a modern American economy, and the modern method of constitutional interpretation). The problem with this kind of retrospective evaluation of Hamilton is that it necessarily puts him on the side of history and puts Madison and Jefferson into the role of men who fought, unsuccessfully, against its tide. (The problem is compounded, in Madison's case, by the persistent though false view that in the early 1790s he made an 180-degree turn from nationalism to states' rights—as though he was rushing into the future at one point, panicked, and decided to run backwards into the past.) In truth all these men made their decisions for or against a powerful national government based upon reasons that had little to do with predictions of who was on history's side.

An examination of how Hamilton believed it was possible to harmonize power and liberty—an old-fashioned question expressed in old-fashioned words—can help break the hold of some of the common interpretations and give us a fresh perspective on this complex man.

II

Let us begin by examining some passages in which Hamilton used the words *power* and *liberty* in ways that might provide some clues to his understanding of the practical connection between them. The use of the two words in some connected phrase was common in the political language of the period, but Hamilton gave his own individual stamp to this common coin.

In his first "Continentalist" essay (1781), Hamilton observed that "an extreme jealousy of power is the attendant on all popular revolutions, and has seldom been without its evils." His purpose in this series of essays was to convince readers that the principal evil endangering the Revolutionary cause was "A WANT OF POWER IN CONGRESS."

> History is full of examples, where in contests for liberty, a jealousy of power has either defeated the attempts to recover or preserve it in the first instance, or has afterwards subverted it by clogging government with too great precautions for its security, or by leaving too wide a door for sedition and popular licentiousness. In a government framed for durable liberty, not less regard must be paid to giving the magistrate a proper degree of authority, to make and execute the laws with vigour, than to guarding against encroachments upon the rights of the community. As too much power leads to despotism, too little leads to anarchy, and both eventually to the ruin of the people.[18]

Hamilton's principal point here is that power (by which he meant the power of government) and liberty (which in this passage is identified with "the rights of the community") ought to exist in some sort of balance, a balance easily upset in popular revolutions by an excessive "jealousy of power." Hamilton here called for a readjustment of the power-liberty balance in the direction of greater power—but for the purpose of better preserving the liberty that remains. Too much liberty leads to the destruction of liberty itself.

He said something very similar seven years later at the New York Ratifying Convention:

> In the commencement of a revolution, which received its birth from the usurpations of tyranny, nothing was more natural, than that the

public mind should be influenced by an extreme spirit of jealousy. To resist these encroachments, and to nourish this spirit, was the great object of all our public and private institutions. The zeal for liberty became predominant and excessive. In forming our confederation, this passion alone seemed to actuate us, and we appear to have had no other view than to secure ourselves from despotism. The object certainly was a valuable one, and deserved our utmost attention: But, Sir, there is another object, equally important, and which our enthusiasm rendered us little capable of regarding. I mean a principle of strength and stability in the organization of our government, and vigor in its operations.[19]

Later in the ratifying convention he specifically applied this idea of a power-liberty balance to the division of power between Senate and House of Representatives: "Good constitutions are formed upon a comparison of the liberty of the individual with the strength of government: If the tone of either be too high, the other will be weakened too much. It is the happiest possible mode of conciliating these objects, to institute one branch peculiarly endowed with sensibility, another with knowledge and firmness. Through the opposition and mutual controul of these bodies [House and Senate], the government will reach, in its regular operations, the perfect balance between liberty and power."[20] In speaking this way Hamilton was squarely within Whig tradition, for a central idea of that tradition, which preceded the Revolution and provided it with a political language, was that power and liberty exist in some kind of balanced tension.[21] Tyranny results from an imbalance in one direction; anarchy from an imbalance the other way.

It is entirely consistent with this conception of balancing liberty and power that Hamilton, late in the Federal Convention, insisted that the number of members of the House of Representatives be increased: "He avowed himself a friend to a vigorous Government, but would declare at the same time, that he held it essential that the popular branch of it should be on a broad foundation. He was seriously of opinion that the House of Representatives was on so narrow a scale as to be really dangerous, and to warrant a jealousy in the people for their liberties."[22] If power and liberty are to be balanced, it would follow that efforts to preserve that balance would include some interventions on the side of liberty and against power—and that is what Hamilton did in this case. He was not always on the side of power.

But there is no indication whatsoever in any of these passages that Hamilton looked to a transformation of the relation between power and liberty of the kind expressed in Madison's 1792 *National Gazette* essay: "In Europe, charters of liberty have been granted by power. America has set the example, and France has followed it, of charters of power granted by liberty," which Madison called a "revolution in the practice of the world."[23] To speak of liberty as the creative and unlimited being, power as the created and limited being, is fundamentally different than speaking of a balance between them. Though Hamilton was capable of employing the new language of popular sovereignty when necessary, his heart was not really in it. The traditional idea of a balance between power and liberty is a better expression of Hamilton's thought at all stages of his career.

In the passages just cited Hamilton did not indicate precisely what he meant by liberty: did he mean individual rights, "private" or "negative" liberty, or the community's right of self-government, "public" or "positive" liberty? From the context it would appear that he meant both kinds of liberty. The idea that under the Articles of Confederation, the power-liberty balance had swung too far in the liberty direction would make little sense if liberty meant only private freedoms like property rights and rights of religious conscience. And in insisting that the House of Representatives be broadly based lest it endanger liberty, he showed again that he did not understand liberty merely in terms of private rights but also as popular self-government. He wanted to keep a closer rein on "public" liberty than did many of his contemporaries, but it is liberty all the same and must be protected in its proper degree.

III

The previous section challenged the perception of Hamilton as a man unconcerned with "public" liberty. That he was committed to personal or "private" liberty is more readily conceded. Yet here too he has been misrepresented. He is often portrayed as someone whose commitment to personal liberty began and ended with the rights of property. There is no question that like almost all of the politically active men of his generation, he was concerned about protecting property rights and upholding the sanctity of contracts. But his libertarian commitments were broader. This is demonstrated by three instances in which Hamilton intervened on the side of individual freedom from governmental authority even though these interventions did not advance his goal of national power in any discernible way, nor did they involve defending the property rights of privileged classes. All three occurred during his service in the New York Assembly in early 1787.

During the session Hamilton moved successfully to strike a provision of an election law that would have required an "oath of abjuration of ecclesiastical obedience" which was clearly directed against Roman Catholics. "Why should we wound the tender consciences of any man? and why present oaths to those who are known to be good citizens? why alarm them? why set them upon enquiry which is useless and unnecessary?"[24]

He successfully opposed a proposed article of the New York election law that would have authorized election supervisors "to take aside ignorant persons and examine them privately touching the persons for whom they meant to ballot." To this Hamilton objected that such a provision "not only is dangerous but it is totally contrary to the very genius and intention of balloting; which means that a man's vote should be secret and known but to himself— yet you not only permit him but even oblige him to discover his vote. . . . [It] deprives the unlettered person of what his fellow citizen who has it in his power to read, has secured to him. . . . I hope these reasons will be deemed sufficient to induce the house to reject the clause as repugnant to the genius and liberty of our republic."[25]

During the same legislative session he moved successfully to strike a provision of a bill concerning murder that would have required "that women who clandestinely were delivered of children and the same die, or be born dead, that the mother within one month thereafter, should before a magistrate be obliged to produce one witness at least, to prove that the child was not murdered; and in default of concealing the same, to be deemed guilty of murder."

> Mr. Hamilton observed, that the clause was neither politic nor just, he wished it obliterated from the bill; to shew the propriety of this, he expatiated feelingly on the delicate situation it placed an unfortunate woman in, who might by accident be delivered stillborn; from the concealment of the loss of honor, her punishment might be mitigated; and the misfortune end here. She might reform and be again admitted into virtuous society. The operation of this law compelled her to publish her shame to the world. It was to be expected therefore that she would prefer the danger of punishment from concealment, to the avowal of her guilt. He thought it would

involve courts in a delicate dilemma; the law would have no good effect as it would generally be evaded; such circumstances would be viewed leniently.[26]

The first case shows that Hamilton could be as passionate and effective an opponent of religious discrimination as Madison and Jefferson were. The second, in which Hamilton defended illiterate voters against the coercion of the literate (and of whatever political power appoints election supervisors), may come as a surprise to those who assume that Hamilton was always on the side of the better-educated and more privileged classes. The third not only demonstrates that Hamilton's concern for personal liberty was not limited to men but also shows his understanding of the self-defeating character of laws that intrude too much into the daily lives of men and women.

In relating these lesser-known episodes, I do not claim they were central to Hamilton's political agenda; they were not. But the fact that Hamilton was willing to defend liberty even when he had nothing politically to gain by it should warn us against dismissing or undervaluing his concern for liberty in cases that did advance his political goals. His defense of former loyalists against discriminatory legislation contravening the terms of the peace treaty, for example, certainly served national goals (national honor was at stake, as well as the treaty-making authority of the Continental Congress); but his arguments against the law (both as counsel in the law cases and in his "Phocion" pamphlets) show a disgust with the illiberal and unjust character of the legislation itself above and beyond its abrogation of the treaty.[27] His radical proposal during the Revolutionary War—a proposal that was of course rejected—to offer freedom to slaves willing to fight against the British was motivated not only by realpolitick but also by opposition to the institution of slavery.[28] (It would also have been thoroughly subversive of the entire southern social order, a fact that could not have escaped him.)

IV

Freedom of the press raises different kinds of problems than the liberties discussed so far, and in this sphere Hamilton's commitments were of a much more mixed character. On one hand he made an important contribution to American press liberty as counsel for the defense in the 1803 seditious libel case *People of New York v. Croswell*. On the other hand he supported the Sedition

Act and had himself gone to court in 1799 to testify against David Frothingham for an allegedly seditious libel against himself. This combination of cases could be used to charge that Hamilton did not care about press liberty as such but like so many men of the age—including Jefferson—valued a free press only for his own side while seeking to suppress opponents.[29]

But from Hamilton's own point of view he was consistent: he adhered to the same principles in defending Croswell and in supporting prosecution of men like Callender and Frothingham. My purpose here is not to present Hamilton as a towering champion of press freedom, though whatever his motives he did make a real contribution. The interesting question is: what does his argument for press freedom (and the limits he would impose on that freedom) reveal more generally about his views of governmental power and popular liberty? His arguments in favor of press freedom further illustrate the kind of balance he sought between power and liberty and at the same time underscore the differences between his political thought and that of Madison.

Harry Croswell was the publisher of the anti-Jeffersonian weekly *The Wasp*. The indictment charged, among other things, that Croswell had accused Jefferson in print of having secretly paid James Thomson Callender (who had been convicted in 1800 under the Sedition Act) to call Washington "a traitor, a robber, and a perjurer" and Adams a "hoary headed incendiary." Under the common law of seditious libel that was still in force in most of the states at that time, the truth or falsity of an allegedly seditious utterance was considered irrelevant; thus the judge in the case prohibited Croswell from entering evidence to the effect that Jefferson in fact had paid Callender. The jury was instructed by the judge that it could not rule on whether the statements were of a criminally libelous character but only on the fact of whether Croswell had published them.[30]

With an impressive display of legal scholarship citing both English and American precedents, Hamilton argued that the truth should be allowed as a defense (though the truth of a statement does not necessarily absolve) and that juries must have the right to pass judgment on whether the statement itself is of a criminal character. Though he lost the case, his efforts in this highly publicized case persuaded the New York legislature in 1805 to pass a more liberal libel law allowing truth as a defense. In his arguments before the bench, Hamilton defined liberty of the press as the right to publish "the truth, from good motives and for justifiable ends, though it reflect on government, on magistrates, or individuals." He made explicit the central role of a free press under popular government: it is "essential to say, not only that the measure is bad and deleterious, but to hold up to the people who is the author, that, in this our free and elective government, he may be removed from the seat of power. If this be not to be done, then in vain will the voice of the people be raised against the inroads of tyranny." He also reminded the court of the centrality of juries to the principles of the American Revolution. "This ought to be considered as a landmark to our liberties, as a pillar which points out to us on what the principles of our liberty ought to rest."[31]

But during the same oral argument, Hamilton praised the Sedition Act and even cited it as the most valuable of precedents because it allowed truth as a defense: "Let us advert to the sedition law, branded indeed with epithets the most odious, but which will one day be pronounced a valuable feature in our national character. In this we find not only the intent, but the truth may be submitted to the jury, and that even in a justificatory manner."[32] Hamilton saw no inconsistency between his defense of Croswell, on one hand, and his support of the Sedition Act and his role in the prosecution of Frothingham, on the other, for Croswell told the truth while the others were liars and thus were justly punished. (Just as Jefferson, from his own very different point of view, was consistent in opposing the Sedition Act and supporting state prosecutions for seditious libel: it was the national character of the law, not the restrictions on press liberty as such, that Jefferson objected to.) At no point did Hamilton challenge the basic principle of the doctrine of seditious libel: that the authority of government and its officials deserve special protection against writings that have a tendency to subvert public order. The truth of an allegedly subversive statement should be allowed to be entered as evidence but does not necessarily excuse. His argument for press liberty amounted to a modest liberalization of current practice that did not challenge in any essential way the full sovereignty of government.

A comparison of Hamilton's views with Madison's much more sweeping argument for press liberty in the "Report of 1800" serves to underscore wider differences between the two. Whereas for Hamilton the proper liberty of the press must be balanced against the legitimate right of government to protect itself against assaults on its authority, Madison denied government any authority over the press, just as it has no authority over religion. "Both of these rights, the liberty of conscience and of the press, rest equally on the original ground of not being delegated by the constitution, and consequently withheld from the government." Hamilton would have liberalized libel law to allow truth as a defense but still would have allowed error and untruth to be punished. Madison claimed that the "baneful tendency" of the Sedition Law "is little diminished by the privilege of giving in evidence the truth of the matter contained in political writings"—partly because this places a difficult burden of proof on the defendant, partly because in prosecutions for seditious libel, "opinions, and inferences, and conjectural observations . . . may often be more the objects of the prosecution than the facts themselves," and it is impossible for the defendant to prove the truth of such opinions and inferences. While Hamilton sought a moderate revision of a doctrine rooted in centuries of English practice (he cited a number of English precedents in the *Croswell* case), Madison insisted that liberty of the press in a republic rests on an entirely different basis and must be guided by quite different principles than in England: "The nature of governments elective, limited and responsible, in all their branches, may well be supposed to require a greater freedom of animadversion, than might be tolerated by the genius of such a government as that of Great Britain."[33] For Hamilton press liberty, like all liberty, had to be placed in its proper balance with power. For Madison it was not a matter of balance at all but one of properly recognizing which—the people or the government—is the superior and which the subordinate power: "If we advert to the nature of Republican Government," Madison said in another context, "we shall find that the censorial power is in the people over the Government, and not in the Government over the people."[34]

One can legitimately criticize Hamilton for the confined character of his case for press liberty. But whatever its merits, it was well within—even somewhat in advance of—mainstream republican thought of the time, and it cannot be dismissed as unprincipled.[35] It is entirely consistent with the idea that power and liberty coexist in a cautious balance that, as in the *Croswell* case, requires occasional readjustments.

V

Hamilton as described thus far comes off as a cautiously conservative republican, concerned with striking a fair balance between governmental power and private and public liberty, a balance that sometimes needs to be corrected in the direction of greater power, sometimes in the direction of greater liberty.

But this is clearly not the full picture. For in other respects Hamilton was unquestionably radical in a way not easily reconciled with the image of a cautious conservative ever in search of just the right balance. His political economy looked to a fundamental transformation of American life. His views of relations between national and state authority were anything but balanced. He would have preferred to reduce the states to mere administrative districts; failing this, he reluctantly accepted the principle of divided sovereignty between national and state authority, but the balance he favored was always on the side of national as opposed to state power. Any shift of power toward the national government and away from the states was from his point of view an improvement. A balance in which the scales always tip in the same direction is not a balance at all.

He was radical not only in his views of how much power the national government should have but in his method of securing it. Speed was of the essence. His actions as treasury secretary were characterized by one bold and controversial policy after another: funding and assumption followed by the Bank followed by the "Report on Manufactures," with little time for his opponents to catch their breath. For a traditional conservative the narrowness of a victory and the existence of a bitterly unreconciled opposition would be reason to slow down and build consensus before proceeding to the next measure. For Hamilton they were reasons to move even faster.

The purpose in pointing to Hamilton's radical side is not that it is especially important to pin the proper label on him ("conservative," "radical," "conservative radical," "radical conservative," etc.). The reason is that his radical side poses new and fundamentally different kinds of problems with respect to liberty than does his conservative side. Recall the image of a balance between liberty and governmental power, a language Hamilton himself employed and one which would have been perfectly comprehensible to his contemporaries. Within that framework a proposed modest adjustment in the direction of power, although it may encounter opposition, would not be perceived as a basic threat to liberty. A major shift in the direction of power, on the other hand, would be quite another thing: by the same logic this would mark a major reduction of liberty and thus would pose a fundamental threat to republican principle. And this was precisely how Hamilton's actions as treasury secretary were perceived by his political opponents.

There is no question that Hamilton favored a major shift in the direction of greater power. It is equally certain that he did not believe this posed a threat to liberty. How can these things be reconciled? It is clear that something besides the traditional idea of a balance between power and liberty is required.

VI

One of the difficulties with applying the idea of a power-liberty balance to the problems Hamilton sought to address is that such a balance assumes that there are only two essential agents: the government on one side and the people (whether collectively or as individuals) on the other. That may have been an appropriate assumption in England where this way of posing the problem originated. But in America there were three types of agents: the national government; the state governments, which claimed to be sovereign; and the people, caught between the other two with various and uncertain loyalties in both directions. Instead of a balance between power and liberty, there is instead a sovereignty competition between levels of government. And this is not in Hamilton's view a competition that can be resolved through some kind of balance. "The general power whatever be its form if it preserves itself, must swallow up the State powers. otherwise it will be swallowed up by them. . . . Two Sovereignties can not co-exist within the same limits," he said at the Federal Convention.[36] He later modified his views to take into account the existence in fact of divided sovereignty, each level of government having (at least in principle) its own peculiar objects. But it was only with great reluctance that he accepted any division of sovereignty, and without altering his view of the severe problems it creates. In Federalist No. 34 he can be heard trying to talk himself into accepting the thing: "To argue upon abstract principles that this co-ordinate authority cannot exist would be to set up theory and supposition against fact and reality. However proper such reasonings might be to show that a thing ought not to exist, they are wholly to be rejected when they are made use of to prove that it does not exist contrary to the evidence of the fact itself."

In the Constitution as written, divided sovereignty does exist, even though it ought not to. As a result the kind of sovereignty competition Hamilton hoped to avoid would take place in covert if not in open form under the new Constitution. And moreover it is a competition in which (as Hamilton made clear in his June 18 speech at the Federal Convention) most of the advantages lie on the side of the states: interest, opinion, habit, force, and influence. The Constitution as written and ratified was a vast improvement over the Articles of Confederation, but it still left the national government with much less power than Hamilton considered necessary. Madison's charge that Hamilton tried to administer the government into having the powers he considered necessary is entirely true.[37]

It is the existence of sovereign states, not the threat of democratic excesses in the people themselves, that drives Hamilton's push for as much national power as he can get, however he can get it. It is not ever greater power over individuals or over the people collectively but greater power over the states that he considers essential. This distinction between national government's power over the people and its power over states is essential to understanding how Hamilton can reconcile his libertarian commitments with his push for powerful national government. For a state to lose power does not mean that the individuals in that state become less free. "As states are a collection of individual men," Hamilton asked at the Federal Convention, "which ought we to respect most, the rights of the people composing them, or of the artificial beings resulting from the composition[?] Nothing could be more preposterous or absurd than to sacrifice the former to the latter. It has been s[aid] that if the smaller States renounce their *equality,* they renounce at the same time their liberty. The truth is it is a contest for power, not for *liberty.* Will the men composing the small States be less free than those composing the larger[?]"[38] The issue he immediately addressed in this passage was differences of power among states. But the same logic would apply to the greater power of the national government relative to the states: the liberty of people is altogether separate from the power of the state of which they are members—assuming, of course, that people are adequately and effectively represented in the national government.

Yet Hamilton at the same time knew that many people did believe there existed some privileged connection between the liberty of individuals and the power of the states. He attempted to clear up this confusion. But so long as the confusion remained in men's minds, the jealousy of power natural in republics would take the form of an excessive attachment to the prerogatives of the states. This had the effect of further stacking the deck against national government in an already unequal contest.

In Hamilton's view, because the national government (even after ratification of the Constitution) was too weak, or only barely strong enough, to accomplish what it needed to, it necessarily followed that it was too weak to pose any threat to liberty.[39] (Madison, by the way, would reject this line of reasoning. Even a weak government like the Continental Congress could threaten liberty if it assumed powers not clearly assigned to it.)

Of course in *The Federalist* and in his speeches at the New York Ratifying Convention, Hamilton accepted for the sake of argument the possibility that the national government might become despotic and showed how, if this was to happen, the combined power of the states would be more than a match for the national government. (In other words, he presented as an advantage the same thing he described as the principal problem in his June 18 speech: the fact that the states held most of the cards.) But what is striking about Hamilton's descriptions of possible despotic moves by the national government is how implausible and devoid of content they are. He spoke of possible "invasions of the public liberty," "projects of usurpation," "enterprises of ambitious rulers" on the part of the national government; but he never gave the reader any idea of what these would look like in practice or what might motivate them.[40] One suspects he considered the likelihood of a threat to liberty so remote, given the national government's small powers, that there was no point in forming detailed scenarios. All the real threats to liberty at present came from the states and/or from the results of a possible authority contest between national government and states.

If the national government ultimately achieved unchallenged sovereignty, then there would be no need for ever-greater power, and instead government and people could settle into a normal power-liberty balance. For in Hamilton's view there is nothing whatever about sovereign power as such to threaten liberty, except in the sense that all law involves some restrictions on liberty. Supreme power on one side can coexist perfectly well with rights and liberties on the other. It is nonsense to pretend that one is doing something to protect liberty by placing arbitrary restrictions on the extent of governmental power (restrictions like limiting its power to tax or to make military appropriations in peacetime).[41] What threatens liberty is competition between claimants to sovereignty, of the kind described in *Federalist* No. 8 and No. 15. Once the national government has achieved clearly superior power relative to the states, the dynamic will change, and the normal power-liberty balance between government and people can begin.

VII

But someone could object that although sovereignty competitions might have been real dangers under the Confederation and even more under a dissolution into two or three confederacies, the ratification of the Constitution put an end to them by establishing an authority—the people—superior to both national and state government. That was Madison's view. A free people, so long as it possesses adequate institutional forms (which it lacked under the Confederation but enjoys under the Constitution), is capable of regulating and balancing the respective national and state authorities so as to prevent destructive competitions and head off threats to liberty from either quarter.

From Hamilton's perspective this is impossible. Whatever "the sovereignty of the people" means—and he did accept it in some sense—it cannot mean the kind of active sovereignty capable of regulating such a competition.[42] The people may legitimate government in normal times through participation in elections and in times of crisis by exercising their right of revolution; they may be the ultimate source of power in a republic in the sense that "all the Magistrates are appointed, and vacancies are filled, by the people, or a process of election originating with the people" rather than by hereditary right.[43] In that very nebulous sense the people are sovereign. But in an operative sense sovereignty must inhere in government; this is true no matter how the objects of this sovereignty are divided between national and state governments: "To deny that the Government of the United States has sovereign power as to its declared purposes & trusts . . . [would] furnish the singular spectacle of a *political society* without *sovereignty,* or of a people *governed* without *government.*"[44] For practical purposes sovereignty equals government. (This view contrasts not only with that of Madison but to an even greater degree with the view of James Wilson.)

The ability of the people to play the kind of regulating role Madison foresaw was rendered impossible for Hamilton, not merely because it went contrary to his understanding of sovereignty but also for reasons arising out of what might be called Hamilton's political sociology. In *Federalist* No. 27 he spoke of the causes that will determine whether the people give their principal allegiances to national or state government:

> The more the operations of the national authority are intermingled in the ordinary exercise of government, the more the citizens are accustomed to meet with it in the common occurrences of their political life, the more it is familiarized to their sight and to their feelings, the further it enters into those objects which touch the most sensible chords and put in motion the most active springs of the human heart, the greater will be the probability that it will conciliate the respect and attachment of the community. Man is very much a creature of habit. A thing that rarely strikes his senses will generally have but a transient

influence upon his mind. A government continually at a distance and out of sight can hardly be expected to interest the sensations of the people. The inference is that the authority of the Union and the affections of the citizens towards it will be strengthened, rather than weakened, by its extension to what are called matters of internal concern; and that it will have less occasion to recur to force, in proportion to the familiarity and comprehensiveness of its agency. The more it circulates through those channels and currents in which the passions of mankind naturally flow, the less will it require the aid of the violent and perilous expedients of compulsion.

What is striking here is the after-the-fact character of popular support for strong national government. The people do not first choose to establish a strong national government and then carry out their intentions—which is what they would have to do if one were to take seriously the principle of popular sovereignty in Madison's and Wilson's sense. Instead it is government that takes the initiative to which people consent (or refuse to consent) after the fact. This idea is basic to the difference between Madison and Hamilton—above all to their battle over the Bank—and needs to be developed further.

VIII

Hamilton's "Opinion on the Constitutionality of a Bank" is justly famous in making the case for broad rather than strict construction of the powers of the national government. Hamilton's interpretation, or something close to it, has become the standard one, and it is difficult even to imagine what course American nation building would have taken had Jefferson's and Madison's constitutional interpretations won out. But precisely because Hamilton's construction looks so reasonable and natural to us it is easy to downplay the seriousness of the objections to it and to miss what is most adventurous and questionable in Hamilton's way of reading the Constitution.

For example, we are quite familiar with arguments against employing the original intent of the Framers as the criterion of constitutional interpretation. After all, that was more than two hundred years ago, and American society has been transformed in fundamental ways and faces problems that the Founding generation could not even have imagined. For this reason we are apt to find Hamilton's argument against original intent to be eminently reasonable—

unless we remind ourselves that when Hamilton wrote the following words the Federal Convention was only four years in the past and ratification less than three:

> Whatever may have been the intention of the framers of a constitution, or of a law, that intention is to be sought for in the instrument itself, according to the usual & established rules of construction. Nothing is more common than for laws to *express* and *effect*, more or less than was intended. If then a power to erect a corporation, in any case, be deducible by fair inference from the whole or any part of the numerous provisions of the constitution of the United States, arguments drawn from extrinsic circumstances, regarding the intention of the convention, must be rejected.[45]

Hamilton was in effect saying that his reading of the Constitution, if it is a better reading, should be accepted even if it diverged from the intentions of the men who framed it four years earlier and those who ratified it three years earlier.

If nothing else, his willingness to put aside original intent so soon after the fact demonstrates Hamilton's daring. It should also lead us to ask: what does consent mean under constitutional government, if an understanding reached three years earlier can be put aside in favor of a superior textual construction? By Hamilton's light the act of interpreting a text, however brilliantly done, has no necessary connection with the principle of popular consent. An interpretation may be logical and textually grounded and yet remote from anything the people intended.

Some scholars present Hamilton's constitutional argument as though it was routine rather than daring. H. Jefferson Powell argues that the eighteenth-century common-law understanding of intent was almost entirely a textual construction and rejected external evidence of the legislator's intention. Therefore, by excluding evidence of the intent of framers and ratifiers and relying entirely on textual construction, Hamilton presented "a picture that fit easily into the traditional interpretive wisdom of the common law."[46] Although it may be true that Hamilton drew upon traditional common-law devices, he was doing so under circumstances that were anything but traditional: both the Revolutionary invention of written, popularly endorsed constitutions superior to ordinary law and the theory of popular sovereignty that justified those constitutions were unknown to the traditional common law.

As Charles A. Lofgren points out in his rebuttal to Powell, the Constitution was not a "conventional legal document" but "rather elaborated a new system of government which rested crucially on the sovereignty of the people."[47] Thus the central question that distinguishes Madison's and Hamilton's method of interpreting the Constitution—whether the understanding of the sovereign people as expressed in their ratifying conventions should govern constitutional interpretation—cannot even arise under the common law, much less be resolved by it.

Nor is the problem dispensed with by pointing out that a popularly elected Congress approved the Bank bill. Hamilton no less than Madison believed that the enduring will of the people as expressed in their Constitution takes precedence over any mere act of Congress (that is one of the points of *Federalist* No. 78). So in putting aside Madison's criterion for an enduring will—the understanding of those who wrote the Constitution, and especially of those who ratified it—what standard of substantive consent was Hamilton putting in its place?

It is important to keep in mind Madison's objections to the Bank, especially because they are much less easily dismissed than the flawed arguments of Secretary of State Jefferson and Attorney General Randolph to which Hamilton was immediately replying in his "Opinion on the Constitutionality of a Bank."

At the Federal Convention, Madison himself had favored granting the national government the power to charter corporations; he did not believe there was anything about such a power, considered in the abstract, to pose a threat to liberty or to the practice of self-government in the states. But such a power had been proposed, considered, and rejected; and the ratification of the Constitution had been accomplished with the understanding that such a power was not included. There was something fundamentally wrong with adopting the Constitution under one set of arguments and then administering it under the influence of entirely different arguments.

At stake for Madison was the basic republican principle that liberty creates power rather than the other way around; that all powers not granted to government remain with the people. In practice this rules out any government whose powers are indefinitely expansive.

In his defense of the Bank, Hamilton agreed that it is an unquestionable republican maxim that "all government is a delegation of power." He pointed out that the national government is limited by its delegated power to certain objects of legislation but insisted that its powers must be regarded as sovereign "in relation to the objects" entrusted to it. But if the question is asked: is there anything here to rule out a continual expansion of the range of national objects of legislation at the expense of state objects of legislation?—the answer would have to be no. Nowhere did Hamilton clarify the difference between national and state objects in a way that would rule out a progressive expansion of the range of national legislation. The only example he gave of a power clearly outside the range of national legislation was that "a corporation may not be erected by congress, for superintending the police of the city of Philadelphia"—and even here he failed to explain the example in a way that would clarify where the actual boundary lies.[48] In short, the distinction between national and state objects, to which Hamilton frequently referred in his justification of the Bank, is radically underdefended. One must conclude either that he had a naively essentialist view of the difference between national and state objects, or (much more likely) that he was entirely comfortable with continual expansion of the powers of the national government relative to the powers of the states.

Nor did Hamilton make any attempt to show that the people did intend so expansive a national government. Indeed, in his 1792 "Vindication" letters, whose purpose was to defend his policies as treasury secretary against his increasingly numerous and powerful critics, he in effect admitted that the people, or a substantial portion of them, did not foresee so powerful a government. Although many of his critics, he said, were motivated by bad faith or ambition, he admitted that there were some "well-meaning" men who,

> sensible from experience of the insufficiency of the former system gave their assent to the substitute offered to their choice rather from general impressions of the necessity of a change than from an accurate view of the necessary compass of the authorities which ought to constitute it. When they came to witness the exercise of those authorities upon a scale more comprehensive than they had contemplated and to hear the incendiary comments of those who will ever be on the watch for pretexts to brand the proceedings of the government with imputations of usurpation and tyranny . . . some such men might be carried away by transient anxieties and apprehensions.[49]

Well-meaning men were misled by demagogues because when these well-meaning men agreed to the Constitution, they lacked Hamilton's own "accurate" understanding of "the necessary compass of the authorities which ought to constitute it." And it was that present necessity, not the possibly "inaccurate" understanding of those who ratified the document, that must take precedence.

From here it is a short step to concluding that Hamilton, in practice, favored the rule of an elite which alone possesses this "accurate" understanding and which is responsible only in the most attenuated degree to the majority of people outside the doors of government. To challenge this conclusion one has to show that it is possible to anchor his reading of the Constitution and his policies as treasury secretary with some form of substantive consent by the majority of the people. At what point and in what way do the majority of the people give to this greatly increased national power their considered and enduring consent? Madison's faith in a reasonably clear act of understanding—which occurred in the past—is one way of anchoring government in substantive consent. Hamilton rejected that kind of anchor. What then could he put in its place?

IX

If the people—meaning the people out-of-doors, not just their representatives in Congress—did not consent ahead of time to the extensive powers Hamilton considered necessary, then if they were to consent at all, they had to do so after these powers had come into existence. But if this means simply that Hamilton intended to present the people with a fait accompli which they did not want but which was impossible or too costly to reverse, then this kind of "consent" has nothing at all republican about it.

Nor is it an answer to say that if the people did not like the extensive powers assumed by Congress and the treasury secretary, they could vote them all out of office at the next election. In his discussion of executive power (*Federalist* No. 70) and in his case for unlimited reeligibility for election (*Federalist* No. 72), Hamilton argued that clear responsibility, together with the prospect of subsequent electoral reward or punishment, is an effective safeguard of republican government. But the creation of a new, untested, powerful national government is not like the passage of an ordinary piece of legislation or a routine act of administration; what is at issue is not a particular law or set of laws (which could be repealed) but the form under which lawmaking itself takes place and the domain of its authority. Suppose the people had voted the members of the Second Congress out of office for assuming too extensive powers for the national government; what would have prevented the members of the Third Congress from assuming the same powers while merely passing different measures?

No clear and unequivocal past act of consent to the extensive powers Hamilton wanted to bring into being—the kind of consent Madison considered essential—had taken place, while consent purely after the fact fails to satisfy republican principle. But a case can be made for a kind of Hamiltonian consent taking place over a several-step cycle.

Recall the passage from Hamilton's first "Vindication" letter in which he spoke of well-meaning men who "gave their assent to the substitute offered to their choice rather from general impressions of the necessity of a change than from an accurate view of the necessary compass of the authorities which ought to constitute it." There existed, before the fact, a popular directive of some kind though it was based upon "general impressions" of the direction of the necessary changes (a government more energetic than the Confederation) rather than an "accurate view" of where that process really needed to go. Hamilton did not criticize these men for lacking an accurate view of the necessary powers before they had come into being (he may even have considered it impossible for anyone other than himself and a few others to know ahead of time where the process must go). He criticized them for their lack of faith in the process and the men entrusted to implement it, which made them susceptible to the spurious alarms of demagogues. If they kept faith, they would in the end "accurately" recognize in Hamilton's policies the necessary fulfillment of the "general impressions" they entertained at the outset.

Hamilton was asking for faith but not blind faith. His brilliant public expositions of his policies—among them his "Report on the Bank," his "Opinion on the Constitutionality of a Bank," his "Report on Manufactures"—are a crucial component of his policies, not a mere adjunct to them. It was essential that the people—not just members of Congress but literate and politically active citizens out-of-doors—acquired an accurate understanding of what he was doing and why. Few American statesmen have taken to the pen as frequently and effectively as Hamilton, and these public expositions must have a central place in any consideration of Hamilton's republicanism. (Did Colbert explain his policies to the French people?) Hamilton's description in his "Report on the Bank" of how credit expands the effective quantity of money in circulation is clearer and more concise than what one finds in most modern-day economics textbooks. The same is true of his explanation in the "Report on Manufactures" of the way in which wealth itself is created rather than merely redistributed from one economic class to another.[50]

His aim in the "Opinion on the Constitutionality of a Bank" was to persuade Americans to read the text of the Constitution in a particular way, regardless of whether they had intended it to be read that way when they ratified it. But he was trying to persuade them of something else: that the government they had created was real. One of the most frequent lines of argument in the "Opinion of a Bank" is that any government requires the powers contended for:

> Now it appears to the Secretary of the Treasury, that this *general* principle is *inherent* in the very *definition* of *Government*.
>
> ... This rule [that powers ought to be construed liberally] does not depend on the particular form of a government or on the particular demarkation of the boundaries of its powers, but on the nature and objects of government itself.
>
> ... Why may not the United States *constitutionally* employ the means *usual* in other countries for attaining the ends entrusted to them?[51]

Hamilton was in effect saying: the true source of people's objections to national power is that they do not yet believe this national government is real, and for that reason they entertain the most fantastic fears about the shapes it could take. If they could for once convince themselves of its reality, they would willingly grant it the necessary powers. After all, no one complained that it violated republican principles when states chartered banks, even though their constitutions contained no explicit power authorizing them to do so: "It is to be remembered, that there is no express power in any State constitution to erect corporations."[52] The only difference (Hamilton might have pointed out) was that the state governments were established powers; people were accustomed to them. The national power was new and its reality a question mark. (He also made this point in his June 18 Federal Convention speech.) And if the men who drafted the Constitution did not clearly assign the national government these powers, perhaps it was because they only half believed in its reality themselves. Hamilton himself often seemed to doubt its existence ("I am still labouring to prop the frail and worthless fabric").[53]

It would follow, then, that the very exercise of these powers—assuming they were exercised professionally and responsibly—would remove the principal objection to the powers themselves. For the exercise of the powers of the national government, by making people sensible of its reality, would at once remove objections whose real source was disbelief in the reality of the thing. (The long passage from *Federalist* No. 27 quoted above should be read from this perspective.) Substantive consent to these new powers by the majority of men would naturally follow once they became accustomed to its operations and gave up the fantastic fears they entertained before the fact.

But if this was the real source of the objections to the national government's power, this obviously left Hamilton with a chicken/egg problem. How would people come to believe in this new government in the first place? How could Hamilton ask Americans to place their trust in something that did not yet exist—or barely existed—but which could come into full existence only if they trusted it?

The answer is that for governmental power as with credit, the appearance of reality comes first and prepares the way for the substance.[54] The analogy between the creation of political power and the creation of credit is an interesting one and suggests interconnections Hamilton may have perceived without spelling them out. In his first "Report on Public Credit," he remarked: "In nothing are appearances of greater moment, than in whatever regards credit. Opinion is the soul of it, and this is affected by appearances, as well as realities."[55] The deeply rooted character of the idea is shown by a similar remark made in his first known extended discussion of political economy, in a letter to an unknown correspondent sometime in late 1779 or early 1780: "A degree of illusion mixes itself in all the affairs of society. The opinion of objects has more influence than their real nature. The quantity of money in circulation is certainly a chief cause of its decline; but we find it is depreciated more than five times as much as it ought to be by this rule. The excess is derived from opinion, a want of confidence."[56] Here, as in the passage from the "Report on Public Credit," he was speaking of political economy rather than political power as such. But in writing to James Duane (a member of the Continental Congress) shortly afterward, Hamilton applied the same idea directly to political power; here the issue was confidence not in currency but in Congress:

> And, in future, My Dear Sir, two things let me recommend, as funda-
> mental rules for the conduct of Congress—to attach the army to them

by every motive, to maintain an air of authority (not domineering) in all their measures with the states. The manner in which a thing is done has more influence than is commonly imagined. Men are governed by opinion; this opinion is as much influenced by appearances as by realities; if a Government appears to be confident of its own powers, it is the surest way to inspire the same confidence in others; if it is diffident, it may be certain, there will be a still greater diffidence in others, and that its authority will not only be distrusted, controverted, but contemned.[57]

This stress on confidence echoes in turn a much later remark from the New York Ratifying Convention; here however the accent is on the need for the people to show confidence in a government which is their own creation: "The great desiderata are a free representation, and mutual checks: When these are obtained, all our apprehension of the extent of powers are unjust and imaginary. . . . When, in short, you have rendered your system as perfect as human forms can be; you must place confidence; you must give power."[58] This last passage supports a quite well-known line of argument for Hamilton: the call for confidence means, at minimum, that we should not assume that every power that can be abused will be abused.[59] But when read together with passages quoted above, it also suggests parallels between confidence in government and the creation of credit.

With this idea in mind, let us take a final look at Hamilton's June 18 Federal Convention speech, where he proposed a Senate and president serving during good behavior. The speech is often read as evidence of Hamilton's deeply conservative and antidemocratic views, perhaps even of a badly hidden longing for aristocracy and hereditary privilege. I propose instead that it be read as an answer to the question: how is it possible to make the national government look real? The states had all the advantages of a real existence on their side; the national government as yet had nothing. But if the most eminent men in America could be drawn away from service to the states and persuaded instead to lend their own prestige to the national government, that government would in time acquire a weight of its own independent of these eminent men.[60] The presidency and Senate in Hamilton's plan were designed, among other things, to attract such men to national service. One could compare such men to deposits of specie in a bank that, by creating confidence in the solidity of the bank, allow it to extend credit and circulate currency several times the value of its specie. The national government needed eminent men (Washington of course at the top of the list) not only for their actual talents but equally if not more so for the sake of appearances. By the same logic a national bank was important not only for its role in expanding credit but equally for symbolic reasons—for establishing a visible national presence in American economic life.

All of this was predicated on the assumption that once men clearly understood these increased national powers and the reasons behind them, they would consent. Hamilton knew that in a republic something the body of the people fundamentally opposes cannot endure. But what if they did not accept these new powers? There was no guarantee that they would. What then? Might this make the sovereignty competition Hamilton feared far worse than it would have been if the issue had never been pressed? This is not a question Hamilton ever answered, though he must have known he was taking an enormous risk.

X

The purpose of this chapter has been to show how Hamilton's nationalism was consistent with his commitment to public and private liberty. The impetus behind Hamilton's persistent attempt to strengthen national government was not any desire dramatically to augment the power of government over individuals or over the people collectively. In matters that concerned the power of government on one side and either the private liberty of individuals or the right of popular self-government on the other, Hamilton always sought a careful balance that sometimes entailed correction in the direction of power, sometimes in the direction of liberty. Fear of the power of states was the primary driving force behind Hamilton's efforts to strengthen national government. He insisted that the liberty of a citizen is not a function of the relative power of the state of which he is a member.

In matters of power and liberty, an equilibrium is possible. In a competition for sovereignty between national government and states, however, the conflict tends toward all-or-nothing, and in such a contest Hamilton felt the states had the upper hand. It is this, not any desire to establish an authoritarian regime, that explains his radicalism and the speed with which he felt he had to move.

Unlike Madison and Wilson, Hamilton did not believe that this contest between national and state power could be resolved by the sovereign people, standing apart from both levels of government and keeping each within its proper bounds. Although Hamilton accepted the principle of popular sovereignty in some sense (as the ultimate source of legitimacy and as an expression of the right of revolution in extreme circumstances), he did not believe the people were capable of practical sovereignty on a day-to-day basis. In an operative sense sovereignty inheres in government. Government must take the initiative and await the people's approval or disapproval after the fact. He was certain, for example, that in the end the people would freely accept and support a much stronger national government than they had originally intended, once they were persuaded of its necessity and disabused of objections founded in fantasy.

It was not Hamilton's intention, then, to sacrifice liberty—private or public—to the power of government or to tip the scales radically in the direction of power at the expense of liberty. Whether his approach may have in fact put liberty at risk, regardless of his intentions, is another question. Even if in principle the liberty of citizens and the power of states are separable, could the widespread belief that the two were connected be so easily ignored? Madison like Hamilton recognized that the liberty of citizens and the power of states were different things and often operated at cross-purposes, but Madison believed that failure on the part of national government to respect agreed-upon limits in regard to the powers of states would lead to failure to respect limits in regard to the liberty of individuals as well. Hamilton seems not to have recognized any such problem. Nor does he seem to have considered what the consequences would be if the people, after the fact, clearly and deliberately rejected the increased powers Hamilton put into place. The result could have been the destruction of the Constitution he had helped to create.

On the other hand, in defense of Hamilton, one can ask whether any truly energetic and innovative policy is possible in a popular government without running great risks. The periods of greatest innovation in American political history—which would certainly include the Civil War, Reconstruction, and the New Deal—have been characterized by bold action running far ahead of any clear popular intention; the specific innovations in each case were popularly accepted, with greater or lesser degrees of enthusiasm, after the fact. (The first hundred days of the New Deal make Hamilton look like a slowpoke.) In a more democratic age we justify such risky and energetic ventures by making use of the fiction of a mandate—the myth that this bold and risky policy is simply carrying out the clearly expressed intention of the people. Hamilton was less democratic and more honest than purveyors of mandate justifications: he recognized from the beginning that he was trying to persuade the people to take a path different from the one they had originally intended.

Many of the bold initiatives—whether of the Left or of the Right—that have been attempted in the United States since Hamilton's time have pursued policy aims remote from, in some cases directly opposed to, anything Hamilton himself would have supported. (He probably would have regarded the Great Society and the Reagan Revolution with equal repugnance.) That is only natural: every radical naturally becomes conservative as soon as the policies he or she considers valuable have been put in place. But the specific policies he favored are in the end less important than the energy with which he believed government should act and his attempts to reconcile that energy with liberty. Hamilton's activism established a precedent that deserves careful study by advocates—as well as critics—of bold and risky political initiatives in a nation committed to individual liberty and popular self-government.

James Wilson
1742–1798

4

James Wilson

AND THE IDEA OF POPULAR SOVEREIGNTY

*The dread and redoubtable sovereign, when traced to his ultimate
and genuine source, has been found, as he ought to have been found,
in the free and independent man.
This truth, so simple and natural, and yet so neglected or despised,
may be appreciated as the first and fundamental principle in
the science of government.*
—James Wilson, *Lectures on Law*

THE IDEA OF THE sovereignty of the people was central to the political discourse of the American Founding.[1] And no thinker of the age took the idea more seriously and pressed its implications with greater energy than the Scottish-born Pennsylvanian James Wilson.

That idea was the driving force behind Wilson's every action and remark at the Federal Convention, the Pennsylvania Ratifying Convention, and the Pennsylvania Constitutional Convention of 1789–90; in his written opinions as associate justice of the Supreme Court from 1790 to 1798; and in the law lectures he delivered at the College of Philadelphia in 1790–91. Wilson endeavored to put his theory of popular sovereignty into practice through the design of the various branches and levels of government; through election rules, representational schemes, and suffrage requirements; and through his strong advocacy of each individual's participation in political life.

He never wavered from his faith that there existed in the United States a single, national, sovereign people capable of distributing power between national government and state governments while remaining superior to both. And he saw no conflict whatsoever between a powerful and energetic national government (including a powerful executive) and a free and politically active people. At the Federal Convention, "Mr. Wilson contended strenuously for drawing the most numerous branch of the Legislature immediately from the people. He was for raising the federal pyramid to a considerable altitude, and for that reason wished to give it as broad a basis as possible."[2] The broader the base of the pyramid of power, the greater the height it could safely reach. If the question is asked: how is it possible to reconcile powerful government with the liberty of those subject to its authority?—Wilson's answer was simple: by making the people sovereign. He called the principle of popular sovereignty the "panacea" of politics: "There can be no disorder in the community but may here receive a radical cure."[3]

Wilson's political thought offers instructive comparisons with the thought of his better-known contemporaries—above all with Thomas Jefferson. Both Wilson and Jefferson believed literally in the concept of popular sovereignty; both had an unshakable faith in democracy and encouraged widespread political participation. But for Jefferson energetic government always threatens the liberty of those subject to its authority, even—perhaps especially—in a popular government. "I own I am not a friend to a very energetic government," Jefferson wrote to Madison. "It is always oppressive."[4] For Wilson energetic government and popular liberty reinforce one another. Furthermore Jefferson was especially distrustful of the power of national government and understood the Constitution as a compact among sovereign states. In Jefferson's view it is at the local and state level that popular sovereignty is most perfectly realized. For Wilson in contrast there was nothing more antagonistic to the sovereignty of the people than the sovereignty claims of states, and popular sovereignty is most perfectly expressed in national politics. Jefferson was ambiguous on the question of whether a single, national, American "people" existed; Wilson was absolutely convinced of the existence of a single American political community.

Wilson also offers fruitful comparisons with the political thought of Alexander Hamilton. Wilson was as much a nationalist as Hamilton; like Hamilton he supported a strong, unitary executive; like Hamilton he believed in the national government's inherent power to charter banks and other corporations (Wilson believed such a power existed even under the Articles of Confederation).[5] But he was significantly more democratic than Hamilton (especially with regard to their views of the Senate and the president) and was convinced, as Hamilton was not, that the American people were already national in their allegiances. They also differed on sovereignty: although Hamilton may have accepted popular sovereignty as a legitimizing principle, for all ordinary purposes he insisted that sovereignty inheres in government, which is precisely what Wilson denied.

James Madison believed in the idea of the sovereignty of the people without making it a panacea as Wilson did. Furthermore, Madison's nationalism was of a more complex and ambiguous character than Wilson's.

There are inevitable drawbacks to giving a simple answer to a complex question. For Wilson the will of the sovereign people expresses itself in so many different ways—through upper and lower branches of Congress, the executive, the judiciary, both national and state governments, common law, decisions of juries,[6] not to mention constitutional conventions and revolutions—that one wonders whether the idea has been stretched so far as to lose all definite shape. Furthermore, Wilson probably exaggerated the extent to which the principle of popular sovereignty could remedy the actual power contest between national and state authorities. Both Madison and Hamilton attempted in their different ways to manage this contest. Wilson insisted instead that the "respectability and power" of the state governments would increase along with that of the national government; conflict would be replaced by harmony.[7]

Wilson's greatest strength, on the other hand, lay in his appreciation of the symbolic dimension of republican government and in his ability to translate that symbolic dimension into constitutional detail. What distressed him most about the received Blackstonean conception of law and sovereignty was its pernicious symbolism: it immediately divided the human race into superiors and inferiors, into those who command and those who obey, a principle that would undermine republican liberty from within if left unchallenged.

The principle of popular sovereignty was commonplace in American political discourse of the time. What Wilson did was to take this commonplace idea and push it with greater consistency than anyone else. Naturally in the process of elevating a nebulous idea to the status of high theory, all of its inherent problems come out. Thus the strengths and weaknesses of Wilson as theorist mirror in many respects the strengths and weaknesses of the idea of popular sovereignty itself.

I

A brief biographical sketch is in order, for despite his contributions both as statesman and theorist, James Wilson is still largely unfamiliar except to specialists of the age.[8] He was born in Scotland in 1742 and received an excellent education at the University of St. Andrew before emigrating to Pennsylvania in 1765, where he took up the practice of law. In 1768 he composed "Considerations on the Nature and Extent of the Legislative Authority of the British Parliament" (which he did not publish until 1774), one of the first pamphlets to deny altogether any parliamentary authority over the colonies.[9] Wilson signed the Declaration of Independence and served two extended periods in the Continental Congress, where he worked alongside Hamilton and Madison in the effort to secure adequate funding for the national government. He also was a key figure in the faction-ridden Pennsylvania politics of the 1780s.

Wilson's greatest contribution came at the Federal Convention, where his influence in shaping the final document was second only to Madison's; he was arguably the single most important influence at the convention in designing the office of the presidency.[10] Wilson came to the convention with purposes as definite as Madison's and which served to complement Madison's ideas in important respects. Wilson, for example, pushed from the beginning—and more single-mindedly than Madison—for a national government that would derive its authority directly from the people rather than requiring the mediation of the states. Unlike Madison, who confessed to having no clear ideas about the design of the executive to bring to the convention,[11] Wilson pressed from the beginning for a single, energetic, popularly elected executive, an office which Wilson envisioned in democratic terms (unlike Hamilton, who likewise favored a single, energetic executive but did not regard it as a democratic office). Although Wilson was unable to get agreement on popular election of the president, the creation of the Electoral College was due in large part to Wilson's insistence on a mode of election that would bypass the state governments and involve the people directly in the choice of the president.

Wilson also favored popular election of senators (which finally came to pass in 1913 with the Seventeenth Amendment) and strongly opposed the view, entertained by many members of the convention including Madison and Hamilton, that the upper house should be more aristocratic in character and represent property as well as population. He opposed Madison's suggestion that suffrage under the national constitution be restricted to freeholders; his views on the franchise fell at the more liberal end of the spectrum of the period. He contended throughout the convention for the principle of representation in proportion to population in both houses of Congress. Like Madison he opposed to the end the decision to give each state equal representation in the Senate regardless of population. In accordance with the same principle of one man–one vote, Wilson successfully opposed the efforts of his fellow Pennsylvanian Gouverneur Morris to design a representational scheme that would have ensured the political dominance of the eastern seaboard states regardless of the growing population of the West.[12]

Wilson's State House Yard speech of October 6, 1787, marked the beginning of serious debate on the Constitution and introduced several arguments later taken up by other Federalists. (For example, Hamilton's argument in *Federalist* No. 84 to the effect that a bill of rights was unnecessary because in a republican government the people reserve all powers not explicitly granted was borrowed directly from Wilson's speech.) At the Pennsylvania Ratifying Convention the responsibility for explaining and defending the Constitution fell almost entirely on Wilson. The frequency with which defenders of the Constitution in every state employed the rhetoric of the sovereignty of the people probably owes much to the clarity and centrality Wilson gave this principle during the ratification debate in Pennsylvania.

Wilson was also the principal architect of the Pennsylvania Constitution of 1790. The 1776 constitution with its unicameral legislature, executive council, and test oath (which effectively disenfranchised a large percentage of the electorate) had been a source of bitter political battles. To a large degree the divisions in Pennsylvania over the federal Constitution mirrored the divisions over the state constitution. In these divisions Wilson had been aligned with the so-called aristocratic party, and despite his democratic commitments his political opponents accused him of having antidemocratic designs. Wilson was determined to secure for Pennsylvania a bicameral legislature and a single executive modeled on the federal Constitution. But in the course of the Pennsylvania constitutional convention, Wilson dramatically broke ranks with his erstwhile aristocratic allies, who favored an indirectly elected upper house, and made common cause with his former enemies in the successful effort to keep the franchise broad and to secure direct popular election of the upper as well as lower house. In the words of one member of the convention, Wilson "hitherto deemed an aristocrat, a monarchist and a despot, as all the federalists were, found his adherents on this occasion, with a few exceptions, on the democratic or anti-federal side of the house."[13] Wilson's apparent political switch was in fact entirely consistent with everything he said and did at the Federal Convention and underscores the difficulty he had fitting into the standard political divisions of his age.

Wilson was appointed by Washington to be associate justice of the Supreme Court (he had hoped for chief justice) and served from 1790 until his death in 1798. His most important opinion came in *Chisholm v. Georgia* (1793).

In 1790 and 1791 Wilson delivered a series of *Lectures on Law* at the College of Philadelphia in which he attempted to set forth his political theory in detailed and systematic form. His immediate purpose in delivering the lectures was to establish a specifically American jurisprudence, one more appropriate to a democracy than the English jurisprudence that still dominated the study and practice of law in the United States. Yet the lectures are in no sense narrowly legal but are instead an amazingly ambitious attempt to construct a system covering (among other things) human nature, the nature of society, the character of natural law and natural rights,[14] the common law, the law of nations, municipal law, and the true essence and locus of sovereignty. Moreover there is complete consistency between the theory Wilson set forth in the lectures and his words and actions at the Federal Convention as well as his opinion in the *Chisholm* case.

Despite his achievements Wilson died in obscurity and disgrace; his unbelievably reckless land speculations landed him in debtor's prison near the end of his life and ruined his reputation. Another reason for his eclipse was that his greatest accomplishment, his role in framing the Constitution, was performed behind closed doors and could not have been generally known until Madison's notes were published in 1840, by which time Wilson had already been forgotten. There has, however, been a modest renaissance of Wilson scholarship in the last twenty years or so.[15]

II

Informing all of Wilson's political thought and action (as maker and defender of constitutions, as Supreme Court justice, as lecturer on the science of law) is the concept of the sovereignty of the people. Wilson did not invent the idea of popular sovereignty; it was already in the air during the American Revolution. What he did was to give a particular shape to an idea capable of many different shapes. In order to appreciate Wilson's specific contribution to the theory of popular sovereignty, it is necessary to review the history of the idea in Anglo-American political discourse and to consider the range of possible directions in which such an idea could be taken.

In Anglo-American political thought and practice, the idea of the sovereignty of the people goes back to the English Civil War. The Parliament justified the deposition and execution of a sovereign king in the name of the sovereign people. But the sovereignty of the people quickly turned into the sovereignty of Parliament, which claimed to "embody" the people in a way that made spontaneous political activity by the people themselves unnecessary and even punishable.[16]Although it was admitted that in some ultimate sense the people were supreme (for this was necessary to justify Parliament's seizure of power), the people's own role could be pushed into a conveniently distant if not mythical past. For all ordinary purposes of government, sovereignty lay in Parliament.

It was the claim of the sovereignty of the English Parliament against which the American colonists did battle in the crisis leading up to the American Revolution. Bernard Bailyn goes so far as to claim that it was over the issue of sovereignty that the American Revolution was fought.[17] According to the Declaratory Act, Parliament "had, hath, and of right ought to have, full power and authority to make laws and statutes of sufficient force and vitality to bind the colonies and the people of America . . . in all cases whatsoever." If sovereignty was limited or divided in any respect, then it ceased to exist; sovereignty was all-or-nothing. The classic expression of this view comes from Blackstone's *Commentaries:* "There is and must be in all [forms of government] a supreme, irresistible, absolute, uncontrolled authority, in which the *jura summi imperii,* or the rights of sovereignty, reside," which in England was lodged in the king, Lords, and Commons whose actions "no power on earth can undo."[18]

Coming from a body in which they were not represented and which for the most part had left them alone until recently, the Declaratory Act seemed to the colonists destructive of all their liberties. Moreover this conception of sovereignty held no place for the colonial assemblies in which the colonists were represented and which, together with the royal governors, had served for generations as the actual ruling bodies in the colonies.

In response to the Declaratory Act, colonial pamphleteers challenged this all-or-nothing logic by attempting to describe some limit to Parliament's power over the colonies while still remaining within the British Empire. Attempts were made to distinguish between external and internal taxation and between legislation to regulate trade and legislation to raise revenue. Wilson himself, in an argument similar to the one advanced by John Adams, denied to Parliament all power to legislate for the colonies but tried to preserve the imperial attachment through the person of the king.[19]

All of these colonial pamphleteers explicitly or implicitly denied that sovereignty was an all-or-nothing quality located in a single governing body. So simple and orthodox a description of sovereignty contradicted their own experience as colonists, in a system which despite its ambiguities worked reasonably well for a long time.[20]

In the end these attempts to challenge Parliament's all-or-nothing claim to sovereignty failed: faced with a choice between complete obedience and complete independence, the colonists chose independence. But this left unanswered an important theoretical question. Did the attempts to resolve the sovereignty contest fail because of the pigheadedness of Parliament—its unwillingness to realize that sovereignty can be divided sometimes? Or did the attempts fail because Parliament was right—sovereignty was indeed all-or-nothing? With respect to the concept of sovereignty, the lessons of the break with England were very ambiguous, even contradictory.

The Declaration of Independence is silent about whether sovereignty existed anywhere in the newly independent colonies. By the time the Articles of Confederation were drafted, it was the states that had appropriated the language of sovereignty: "Each state retains its sovereignty, freedom, and independence." But this appropriation of the language of sovereignty by the states was carried out without any public debate comparable to the one that had preceded the Revolution. It occurred more by default than anything else: if sovereignty in the Blackstonean sense had to be placed somewhere, then given the wartime chaos and the weakness of the Continental Congress, there was nowhere else to place it than in the state governments.

Thus it was that during the ratification debate the all-or-nothing claim to sovereignty originally advanced by Parliament against the colonies turned up in the writings of several Antifederalists. The Minority of the Convention of Pennsylvania (in a passage that recalls the failed attempt to draw lines between parliamentary and colonial authority) wrote: "We apprehend that two co-ordinate sovereignties would be a solecism in politics. That therefore as there is no line of distinction drawn between the general, and state governments; as the sphere of their jurisdiction is undefined, it would be contrary to the nature of things, that both should exist together, one or the other would necessarily triumph in the fullness of dominion."[21] Alexander Hamilton, in his June 18 speech at the Federal Convention, accepted the same logic when he insisted that either the states would swallow the national government or the national government would swallow the states.[22] It was against this kind of all-or-nothing understanding of sovereignty (whether in Antifederalist or Hamiltonian form) that Wilson formulated his conception of a sovereign people who create and remain superior to both national and state governments.

I have mentioned the states' successful appropriation of the traditional claim of sovereignty in their external relations with one another and with the Continental Congress. But at the same time, within each state, the concept of sovereignty underwent a radical transformation. It is here, on the local and state level, that the idea of the sovereignty of the people was first put into practice.

Gordon Wood describes the way in which this new idea was implemented within the states. In every state there was a tendency toward making the people's authority as direct as possible:

> Developments in America since 1776 had infused an extraordinary meaning into the idea of the sovereignty of the people. The Americans were not simply making the people a nebulous and unsubstantial source of all political authority. The new conception of a constitution, the development of extralegal conventions, the reliance on instructions, the participation of the people in politics out-of-doors, the clarification of the nature of representation, the never-ending appeals to the people by competing public officials—all gave coherence and reality, even a legal reality, to the hackneyed phrase, the sovereignty of the people.[23]

It was this transformation of sovereignty within the states that later made it possible for supporters of the proposed national constitution to use the principle of popular sovereignty against the authority of the state governments: "the people" can override the authority of state governments or state constitutions if it wishes. But in Wood's view the Federalists' version of popular sovereignty was a clever appropriation of an idea that really belonged to their opponents. Popular sovereignty in its original and radical form was local, direct, concrete, and in its essence a weapon of "democracy" against "aristocracy." Popular sovereignty in its Federalist version was a disembodied, nebulous abstraction that conveniently "obscured the real social antagonisms of American politics" and was intended to restore the "better sorts of people" to political power.[24]

Edmund Morgan provides a somewhat different description of the discourse of popular sovereignty, one potentially more sympathetic to the national aspirations of the Federalists. Central to Morgan's description of the idea of popular sovereignty is the tension, within the concept of representation, between a representative's duty to pursue the general good and his duty to serve the particular interests of his district. Morgan describes the latter duty as the "local, subject" aspect of representation because it originated during the time when the king was still sovereign. Under these circumstances it was the king's job to look out for the common good of the realm; the representatives had only to be concerned with granting or withholding consent to taxation. But "when the king's authority was removed, as it was in England during the Commonwealth period and in America after 1776, the conflict of local interests with the sovereignty of the people at large became much more acute."[25] Many of the developments in the states that Wood describes as radical—the reliance on instructions, the heavily local bias—Morgan characterizes as expressions of the traditional local and subject aspect of representation.

The men who made the Revolution were not so provincial as to believe that the agent of a town or county, closely tied to his constituents, was necessarily well qualified to make laws and policy for a larger society of which his town or county formed a part. But in the contest with Parliament they had not been obliged to confront this inescapable contradiction of representation. After 1776 it emerged as the central problem of a new nation committed both to the sovereignty of the people and to a predominantly local view of representation.[26] It was this problem that the Federalist conception of sovereignty was intended to remedy: by creating a national House of Representatives elected directly by the people, instead of indirectly by the state legislatures as the Continental Congress had been, the Framers were able to combine the commitment to local and direct representation with a national legislative body capable of pursuing the interests of the whole nation.

Morgan agrees with Wood that one of the purposes of the Federalists' conception of a national sovereign people was to "subdue the unthinking many to the thoughtful few."[27] Just as the divine right of kings could be used not only to exalt but also to limit the power of monarchs, popular sovereignty could be used both to extend and to limit the power of the governed. But Morgan's account makes the local and state-centered version of popular sovereignty admired by Wood appear more problematic and in that sense evens the playing field between the Federalists and the defenders of state sovereignty.

It is not my purpose here to take sides between Wood and Morgan but to provide the background necessary to understand the specific practical problems that James Wilson's theory of popular sovereignty was intended to solve. Wilson attempted to accomplish at least three things: (1) to reject completely the Blackstonean conception of sovereignty as inhering in Parliament (or any other governing body), (2) to institutionalize the ideal of direct and participatory democracy, and (3) to give this ideal of direct democracy a national rather than local form.

III

In his opening speech at the Pennsylvania Ratifying Convention on November 26, 1787, Wilson provided a concise summary of popular sovereignty correctly understood and contrasted it with some mistaken conceptions of sovereignty:

> There necessarily exists in every government a power, from which there is no appeal; and which, for that reason, may be termed supreme, absolute, and uncontrollable. Where does this power reside? To this question, writers on different governments will give different answers. Sir William Blackstone will tell you, that in Britain, the power is lodged in the British parliament; that the parliament may alter the form of the government; and that its power is absolute and without control. The idea of a constitution, limiting and superintending the operations of legislative authority, seems not to have been accurately understood in Britain. . . .
>
> To control the power and conduct of the legislature by an over-ruling constitution, was an improvement in the science and practice of government reserved to the American States.
>
> Perhaps some politician, who has not considered, with sufficient accuracy, our political systems, would answer, that, in our governments, the supreme power was vested in the constitutions. This opinion approaches a step nearer to the truth, but does not reach it. The truth is that, in our governments, the supreme, absolute, and uncontrollable power remains in the people. As our constitutions are superiour to our legislatures; so the people are superiour to our constitutions. . . .
>
> The consequence is, that the people may change the constitutions, whenever and however they please.[28]

Wilson's immediate practical purposes here will help us understand the theoretical claims. His practical aim was to legitimate the work of the Federal Convention, which instead of merely revising the Articles of Confederation wrote a wholly new constitution—one which, if accepted, would take precedence over the constitutions of the states. To the objection that the convention exceeded its authority, Wilson answered that the American people are free to make or unmake forms of government whenever they wish, regardless of what was written in the Articles of Confederation or the constitutions of the several states. To tell the American people they cannot change their form of government because it contravenes a written constitution is to confuse sovereignty itself with what are merely its instruments. (The argument had an additional edge in Pennsylvania, where the supporters of the 1776 constitution claimed it was eternal and unalterable.) Wilson was not claiming that the work of the Federal Convention was the will of the sovereign people—not yet. At this stage it was merely a proposal which the people were free to accept or reject. As he said at the Federal Convention itself, in response to the claim that the convention was exceeding its authority, "With regard to the *power of the Convention*, he conceived himself authorized to conclude nothing, but to be at liberty to *propose any thing*."[29]

At minimum, then, the idea of popular sovereignty served to justify the work of the Convention. If this was its only purpose—if it was merely a rhetorically effective way of justifying and packaging the proposed constitution—then there might be reason to agree with Gordon Wood's characterization of popular sovereignty in its Federalist form as a disingenuous appropriation of an idea properly belonging to the other side.[30] But whatever may have been the case for other Federalists who employed the rhetoric of popular sovereignty, for Wilson the idea of popular sovereignty underlay every argument he made and every position he took at the convention itself.

On May 31 members of the convention were debating the question of whether members of the lower house of the national Congress should be elected directly by the people or indirectly by the legislatures of the states (as was the case under the Articles of Confederation). Sherman of Connecticut and Gerry of Massachusetts had just spoken in favor of indirect election, the former because the people themselves "want information and are constantly liable to be misled," the latter because "the evils we experience flow from the excess of democracy."[31] In reply Wilson declared himself strongly in favor of direct election:

> Mr. Wilson contended strenuously for drawing the most numerous branch of the Legislature immediately from the people. He was for raising the federal pyramid to a considerable altitude, and for that reason wished to give it as broad a basis as possible. No government could long subsist without the confidence of the people. In a republican Government this confidence was peculiarly essential. He also thought it wrong to increase the weight of the State Legislatures by making them the electors of the national Legislature. All interference between

the general and local Governm[en]ts should be obviated as much as possible. On examination it would be found that the opposition of States to federal measures had proceeded much more from the Officers of the States, than from the people at large.[32]

In this tightly packed remark Wilson was making the following claims:

1. that there is a positive correlation between the height of the power vested in government and the breadth of participation in it; in a republican form of government, power and liberty are not antagonistic but mutually supportive;

2. that the views of the people are more national in character than the views of those they have elected to state legislatures; and

3. that there must be a direct rather than an indirect relation between the people and each level and branch of government; the state governments should not be allowed to interfere between the people and the national government. Wilson favored direct popular election of both houses of Congress as well as the president: "He wished to derive not only both branches of the Legislature from the people, without the intervention of the State Legislatures <but the Executive also;> in order to make them as independent as possible of each other, as well as of the States.[33]

These points are further reinforced by a remark Wilson made on June 6; once again the point at issue was whether the first branch of the national legislature should be directly or indirectly elected:

Mr. Wilson . . . wished for vigor in the Gov[ernmen]t but he wished that vigorous authority to flow immediately from the legitimate source of all authority. The Gov[ernmen]t ought to possess not only 1st. the *force* but 2ndly. the *mind or sense* of the people at large. The Legislature ought to be the most exact transcript of the whole Society. Representation is made necessary only because it is impossible for the people to act collectively. The opposition was to be expected he said from the *Governments,* not from the Citizens of the States. The latter had parted as was observed (by Mr King) with all the necessary powers; and it was immaterial to them, by whom they were exercised, if well exercised. The State officers were to be losers of power. The people he supposed would be rather more attached to the national Gov[ernmen]t than to the State Gov[ernmen]ts as being more important in itself, and more flattering to their pride.[34]

This passage conveys the same ideas as the "pyramid" passage (the positive relation between vigor and popular support, the distinction between the people and their state governments, the allegedly national orientation of the people themselves) plus another important idea usually associated more with the Antifederalists than the Federalists: that "the Legislature ought to be the most exact transcript of the whole Society."[35] Only a directly elected body can serve effectively as a transcript of the people. Moreover a transcript requires frequent elections; Wilson was one of the few members of the convention who favored annual elections ("Mr. Wilson being for making the 1st. branch an effectual representation of the people at large, preferred an annual election of it.")[36] It also requires a consistent application of the principle of one citizen–one vote for purposes of apportioning representation, in opposition to any scheme by which property as well as individuals was represented or that privileged the original coastal states over newly created western states with growing populations:

> Conceiving that all men wherever placed have equal rights and are equally entitled to confidence, he viewed without apprehension the period when a few States should contain the superior number of people. The majority of people wherever found ought in all questions to govern the minority.... Again he could not agree that property was the sole or the primary object of Govern[men]t & Society. The cultivation & improvement of the human mind was the most noble object. With respect to this object, as well as to other *personal* rights, numbers were surely the natural & precise measure of Representation.[37]

And on the basis of this same principle of proportionality Wilson fought bitterly and unsuccessfully against equal representation in the Senate for states of unequal population.[38] To endow states as states with rights of equal representation was to confuse the source of sovereignty—the people—with what was in fact only their instrument: "Can we forget for whom we are forming a Government? Is it for *men,* or for the imaginary beings called *States?* ... We talk of States, till we forget what they are composed of."[39] (This same tendency to confuse men with the "imaginary beings" called states is central to Wilson's opinion in the *Chisholm* case.)

The admonition not to confuse these artificial beings, states, with the people who were their creators also turns up in Wilson's arguments against election of senators by the legislatures of the states:

He was opposed to an election by the State Legislatures. In explaining his reasons it was necessary to observe the twofold relation in which the people would stand. 1. as Citizens of the Gen[era]l Gov[ernmen]t. 2. as Citizens of their particular State. The Gen[era]l Gov[ernmen]t was meant for them in the first capacity; the State Gov[ernmen]ts in the second. Both Gov[ernmen]ts were derived from the people—both meant for the people—both therefore ought to be regulated on the same principles. The same train of ideas which belonged to the relation of the Citizens to their State Gov[ernme]nts were applicable to their relations to the Gen[era]l Gov[ernmen]t and in forming the latter, we ought to proceed, by abstracting as much as possible from the idea of State Gov[ernmen]ts. With respect to the province & objects of the Gen[era]l Gov[ernmen]t, they should be considered as having no existence.[40]

The fact that state governments "should be considered as having no existence" did not mean, however, that Wilson believed they should be annihilated or reduced to mere administrative districts as Hamilton ideally favored. Where Hamilton expected enduring conflict between state and national government, Wilson saw the possibility of harmony. Hamilton foresaw a destructive sovereignty competition between national and state governments and moreover was convinced that in such a contest the initial allegiances of the people would lie with the states; only with time and effective government could those allegiances be turned toward the national government. Wilson, by contrast, was convinced that the people's allegiances were already national. After Hamilton's June 18 speech in which he remarked that the national government must either swallow up the state powers or be swallowed up by them, Wilson replied that "he thought, contrary to the opinion of (Col. Hamilton) that [the states] might <not> only subsist but subsist on friendly terms" with the national government—this despite the fact that Wilson was just as committed to stripping the states of any claim of sovereignty as Hamilton was. Because the national government would represent the interests of all of the people, there was every reason to be confident that the national government would "leave the State Gov[ernmen]ts in possession of what the people wish them to retain."[41] In short, there is no need for a destructive sovereignty competition between nation and states because the people are sovereign and can distribute powers between national government and states however they wish.

Wilson's faith in harmony between national and state power may have been excessive, but it was not a delusion. Peter Onuf shows in *Origins of the Federal Republic* that there was some substance to Wilson's contention that "the fate of the states and the fate of the union were indissolubly linked in a positive rather than adversarial relation."[42] The states needed the support of the national government to secure contested boundaries and to uphold their own authority against internal secession movements. In this respect at least, the authority of state governments was indeed increased by the presence of an effective national government.

Just as the sovereign people can distribute powers however they wish between national and state governments, they can also distribute it as they choose between executive and legislative branches and between upper and lower houses of the legislative branch. All of these equally, though differently, express the popular will. In his *Lectures on Law* Wilson observed that before the American Revolution "the executive and the judicial powers of government were placed neither in the people, nor in those, who professed to receive them under the authority of the people. . . . Need we be surprised, that every occasion was seized for lessening their influence, and weakening their energy? . . . [But under the United States Constitution] they who execute, and they who administer the laws, are as much the servants, and therefore as much the friends of the people, as they who make them."[43] Wilson and Hamilton both favored a unitary, energetic executive (in *Federalist* Nos. 68–70 Hamilton echoed many of the arguments advanced by Wilson at the convention);[44] but Hamilton never regarded the presidency as an office expressive of the popular will to the same degree as Congress is.

Nor would Hamilton have agreed with Wilson's democratic description of the upper house of Congress. From Hamilton's perspective the purpose of the upper chamber was to balance the principle of popular liberty represented in the lower house against the principle of authority and stability represented in the more aristocratic upper house. Wilson by contrast, although he strongly favored a bicameral system both in the national government and in Pennsylvania, was able to give it a justification which does not introduce an aristocratic principle of any kind. Instead the benefits result from having "a double source of information, precision, and sagacity in planning, digesting, composing, comparing, and finishing the laws, both in form and in substance. . . . These effects of mutual watchfulness and mutual control between the two houses, will redound to the honour of each, and to the security and advantage of the state."[45] When during the convention to revise Pennsylvania's constitution the proposal was made to "refine" the popular will by establishing an indirectly elected upper house, Wilson was absolutely opposed and in the course of his argument in favor of direct election invoked, as he did at the Federal Convention, the metaphor of the "pyramid of government" which "must form the basis of every government, that is, at once, efficient, respectable, and free. ... The authority, the interests, and the affections of the people at large are the only basis, on which a superstructure, proposed to be at once durable and magnificent, can be rationally erected."[46]

And the basis can be durable only if the people participate actively in government. Wilson spoke in favor of political participation by ordinary citizens in a way that was certainly unusual among Federalists of the time.[47] One of the reasons advanced in favor of indirect election of the upper house of the Pennsylvania legislature was the allegation that most citizens were indifferent to their political rights or exercised them irresponsibly and thus were incapable of wise choice. In reply Wilson claimed that to the extent this was the case, it was the result of "the narrow point of view, in which the right of election, before the revolution, was considered; and by the few objects, to which the exercise of it was directed."[48] The problem would itself be remedied by a more widespread exercise of the right. And in his introductory *Lecture on Law*, he observed: "The science of law should, in some measure, and in some degree, be the study of every free citizen, and of every free man. ... In a free country, every citizen forms a part of the sovereign power: he possesses a vote, or takes a still more active part in the business of the commonwealth. ... The right and the duty of taking that share, are necessarily attended with the duty of making that business the object of his study and inquiry."[49]

To summarize: for Wilson there existed a single, national, sovereign people that creates and remains superior to governments, states, and constitutions to which it can delegate any powers it wishes and which it can alter any time it pleases. It expresses itself equally through national and state governments, through upper and lower branches of the legislature, through executive and judicial as well as legislative branches. Wilson is sometimes characterized, imprecisely, as a theorist of the American practice of "divided sovereignty."[50] Strictly speaking, sovereignty remained undivided for Wilson, for it inheres in a united American people.

IV

Wilson's opinion as associate Supreme Court justice in *Chisholm v. Georgia* (1793)—an important and neglected chapter in the history of judicial review—

is his most complete statement on the theory of popular sovereignty. All of the elements of the theory scattered throughout his remarks at constitutional and ratifying conventions as well as his *Lectures on Law* are here brought together in concise form and applied to a concrete case. The symbolic dimension of sovereignty and the link between popular sovereignty and liberty are especially central to Wilson's reasoning in the opinion.

The case involved an action brought by two citizens of South Carolina, acting on behalf of a British creditor, to recover debts owed by the state of Georgia. Georgia claimed that as a "sovereign" state it could not be sued. Furthermore, it refused even to appear in court on the grounds that as a sovereign state it was not subject to the authority of the United States Supreme Court. The Court, with Wilson in the majority, judged against Georgia by default. The decision outraged many, especially because many defenders of the Constitution during the ratification debate (not Wilson, however) had assured the public that states could not be sued for debts under Article III. (The Court's decision was soon overturned by the Eleventh Amendment.)

For Wilson what was at issue was not merely the obligation to pay debts but a fundamental and pernicious misunderstanding of the nature of sovereignty. He could have made his opinion brief by simply pointing out, as he did at the end of the opinion, that the Constitution specifically states that "the judicial power of the United States shall extend to controversies, between a state and citizens of another state" and that "no state shall pass a law impairing the obligation of contracts." But to proceed immediately to a textual argument would be to overlook the more basic issue of sovereignty that Wilson believed must be addressed first.

He began by observing that the question of whether Georgia was subject to the jurisdiction of the Supreme Court "may, perhaps, be ultimately resolved into one, no less radical than this—'do the people of the United States form a nation?'" Then, after quoting the Scottish philosopher Thomas Reid to the effect that it is impossible to make any innovation in philosophy "without using new words and phrases, or giving a different meaning to those that are received," Wilson went on to observe that "sovereignty" was one of those old words that must be used in a new way.

He then turns to the Constitution "ordained and established" by the people of the United States. "To the Constitution of the United States the term sovereign, is totally unknown. There is but one place where it could have been used with propriety. . . . [The people] might have announced themselves 'sovereign' people of the United States: But serenely conscious of the fact, they avoided the ostentatious declaration." But for a state (or even, for that matter, the national government itself) to proclaim itself sovereign was to make a master of what was properly only an instrument: "As the state has claimed precedence of the people; so, in the same inverted course of things, the government has often claimed precedence of the state; and to this perversion in the second degree, many of the volumes of confusion concerning sovereignty owe their existence." He then directly opposed the sovereignty of the American people to the claim of sovereignty advanced by the state of Georgia: "As a judge of this court, I know, and can decide upon the knowledge, that the citizens of Georgia, when they acted upon the large scale of the union, as a part of the 'People of the United States,' did not surrender the supreme or sovereign power to that state; but, as to the purposes of the union, retained it to themselves. As to the purposes of the union, therefore, Georgia is not a sovereign state."

Connected, in turn, with the perverted notion that sovereignty inheres in states and governments is an equally perverted understanding of law, by which—in the words of Blackstone—law is defined as a command by a superior prescribed to an inferior. (This issue is treated briefly in the *Chisholm* opinion but is discussed at length in Wilson's *Lectures on Law*.) In contrast to this definition of law and the slavish symbolism underlying it, Wilson linked the principle of popular sovereignty with that of equality and consent: "Laws derived from the pure source of equality and justice must be founded on the consent of those, whose obedience they require. The sovereign, when traced to his source, must be found in the man."[51] Only after establishing the true source of the Constitution's authority—the sovereignty of the American people—did Wilson turn to its actual language and its clear provision that states were subject to the judicial power of the United States.

Wilson's principal reason for insisting that sovereignty inheres in the people, not in states or governments, is ultimately moral: to vest sovereignty in governments or states is to set up some human beings as superior to others and thereby destroy liberty at its source. In his *Lectures on Law* Wilson developed his own theory of sovereignty and of law in opposition to Blackstone's definition of both. Blackstone's definition of sovereignty ("supreme, irresistible, absolute, uncontrolled authority") was, in Wilson's view, entirely consistent with Blackstone's equally pernicious definition of law as "that rule of action, which is prescribed by some superiour, and which the inferiour is bound to obey." Wilson claimed that through such definitions of law and sovereignty, "a character of superiority is inseparably attached to him, who makes [the laws; and] a character of inferiority is, in the same manner, inseparably attached to him, for whom they are made. . . . If I mistake not, this notion of superiority, which is introduced as an *essential* part in the definition of a law . . . contains the germ of the divine right—a prerogative impiously attempted to be established—of princes, arbitrarily to rule; and of the corresponding obligation—a servitude tyrannically attempted to be imposed—on the people, implicitly to obey." He was not reassured by the fact that men claimed not to believe such doctrines any more: "If they are not, and ought not to be believed; why is their principle suffered to lie latent and lurking at the root of the science of law? Why is that principle continued a part of the very definition of law?"[52]

This concern about "lurking" principles suggests two things. First, Wilson showed here that he was at least as concerned about how citizens think about themselves and their relation to government as he was about its actual operations. The power of government can be harmonized with the liberty of citizens only if citizens consistently regard the government as their servant, not their master. A small crack in the foundation—in this case a textbook definition of law—may have serious consequences later on.

Second, it shows how important Wilson considered political symbolism. What most troubled him about Georgia's claim to be a sovereign state or Blackstone's definitions of sovereignty and law was the perverted symbolic universe they established in which the artificial beings called states take superiority over their real creators, the people. (Recall this theme in Wilson's remarks at the Federal Convention.) Symbolism does not merely reflect but actually shapes practice. Wilson made this point explicitly in the *Chisholm* opinion. Even in our "convivial" life we must guard against "inaccurate" sentiments and expressions: "Is a toast asked? 'The United States' instead of the 'People of the United States' is the toast given. This is not politically correct. The toast is meant to present to view the first great object in the union: It presents only the second: It presents only the artificial person, instead of the natural persons, who spoke it into existence."[53]

If we want to take this idea further, we might perceive kinships between Wilson's belief in the power of symbolism and his call for active and widespread political participation. For political participation by ordinary citizens is to a high degree symbolically motivated. Because the actual impact of an individual participant on political outcomes is quite small, one is unlikely to participate unless participation is invested with meanings above and beyond one's probability of casting the deciding vote. And these meanings are condensed—but also sometimes perverted—by the political symbols we employ.[54]

V

The most difficult challenge to Wilson's conception of the sovereignty of the people is the one Wilson himself anticipated in his *Chisholm* opinion: the "radical" question, "Do the people of the United States form a nation?" In other words, do they form a community coherent enough to formulate a sovereign will? Can we speak of "the American people" as an active agent in any sense? Wilson's opinion in the case presupposed an affirmative answer to the question without giving grounds for it. What arguments, explicit or implicit, underlay his assertion that in 1793 a single American people existed?[55]

It is not enough for Wilson to establish that the people, not the government, are the locus of sovereignty, for an opponent might reply that sovereignty does indeed inhere in the people, but in the people of Georgia, not in the nonexistent "people of the United States." This would ruin Wilson's argument, for which it is essential to maintain that "the citizens of Georgia, when they acted upon the large scale of the union" did so "as a part of the 'People of the United States.'"

Many Antifederalist writings denied that any single American people existed. The dissent of the Pennsylvania Minority—in Wilson's own state, and written in large part in response to his own arguments at the ratifying convention—took issue with the very first words of the Constitution, "We the people of the United States," as did Patrick Henry in Virginia: "Who authorised them to speak the language of, *We, the People,* instead of *We, the States?*" "Brutus" of New York argued that the interests of the various states are too diverse to allow them to be regarded as a single people under a single government: "The laws and customs of the several states are, in many respects, very diverse, and in some opposite; each would be in favor of its own interests and customs, and, of consequence, a legislature, formed of representatives from the respective parts, would not only be too numerous to act with any care or decision, but would be composed of such heterogeneous and discordant principles, as would constantly be contending with each other."[56]

Thomas Jefferson's view of American nationalism was similar in spirit, though different in detail, from that of Brutus. In Jefferson's view the United States was one nation with respect to "everything external"—which would include national defense and foreign trade—and separate nations with respect to "interior government." A decade later, long after the Constitution had been ratified and put into operation, Jefferson's view had not fundamentally changed. His understanding of the federal Constitution in the Kentucky Resolutions

(1798) is that the states, through a compact similar in character to a treaty, created the national government and retain the right—even individually—to judge
and if necessary nullify its acts. The presupposition behind such a theory is that
the states, at least in certain crucially important respects, remain separate "peoples." Jefferson believed in popular sovereignty, just as Wilson did, but he was
much more certain that Virginia constituted a "people" than he was of the existence of any national American people.[57]

A different and more complex view—but still quite distinct from Wilson's—
was that of Madison, who spoke of an emergent American people, a nation in
process of formation that was unified in some respects and not in others. It
might become more of a nation in the future, as the interests of states were
better harmonized, but it could not be assumed to be wholly a nation already.
Moreover, the question was not one that required an unambiguous answer, for
those who thought it was a nation and those who did not could still work
together to prevent encroachments on liberty.

But Wilson rejected so ambiguous an answer to the question. For him an
American nation did exist and moreover had existed since the Declaration of
Independence or even before. The colonies, he asserted at the Federal Con-
vention, became independent "not *Individually* but *Unitedly*." He reported, and
took at face value, sentiments expressed—ironically, by Patrick Henry!—in the
Continental Congress of 1774–75 to the effect that Virginia, Massachusetts,
Pennsylvania are "no more." "We are now one nation of brethren. We must
bury all local interests & distinctions. This language continued for some time.
The tables at length began to turn. No sooner were the State Gov[ernmen]ts
formed than their jealousy & ambition began to display themselves."[58]

In Wilson's view it was the nation that created the states, not the other way
around.[59] The drafting and ratification of the Constitution did not create but
merely "perfected" an already existent Union. (Wilson's 1785 pamphlet *Considerations on the Bank of North America* argues that the people of the United
States, even under the Articles of Confederation, had granted the Continental
Congress the power to charter a national bank.) In the words of Samuel Beer,
for Wilson "the reallocation of power by the Constitution from state to federal government was simply a further exercise of the constituent sovereignty
which the American people had exercised in the past, as when they brought
the states themselves into existence."[60]

What was the source of Wilson's certainty that an American nation already
existed? At least part of the answer is biographical: Wilson, like Hamilton, immi-

grated to the colonies shortly before the Revolution and thus found it easier to attach himself to the cause of the nation than did most of those whose lifelong attachments were to particular colonies. But this is not an adequate explanation of Wilson's optimism about the nationalism of his compatriots. Hamilton, for example, was wholly national in his own loyalties but diagnosed with a cold and realistic eye the many factors that caused most Americans to give their allegiance to the states rather than the nation. What explains Wilson's confidence that his own nationalist sentiments were or could readily be shared by his fellow citizens?

Robert McCloskey, in his introduction to *The Works of James Wilson*, attributes to Wilson "a quality of mind that is curiously abstractive and romantic, a confidence in ideas and an impulse to push them to the limits of their implications without great regard for practicalities, a taste for large intellectual constructs and grand schemes."[61] Wilson was unable to distinguish between the possibility of an American nation and its present reality.

Samuel Beer offers another explanation which, without contradicting the character hypothesis, attributes somewhat more theoretical substance to Wilson's belief in a national, sovereign American people. Beer links Wilson's strong support of political participation with one of the premises of Thomas Reid, the Scottish common-sense philosopher who most influenced Wilson (and who is cited frequently in Wilson's *Lectures on Law* as well as quoted in his *Chisholm* opinion).[62] For Wilson, following Reid, an act of understanding was at the same time an act of will; reason and passion were not separate (as, Beer argues, they were in Madison's moral psychology).[63] This philosophical premise, applied to political participation, means that the very act of participation will create, not merely follow upon, the necessary degree of political attachment and understanding. In his 1789 speech against suffrage restrictions for elections to the Pennsylvania upper house, Wilson remarked:

> When a citizen elects to office ... he performs an act of the first political consequence. He should be employed, on every convenient occasion, in making researches after proper persons for filling the different departments of power; in discussing, with his neighbors and fellow citizens, the qualities that should be possessed by those who fill the several offices. ... A habit of conversing and reflecting on these subjects, and of governing his actions by the result of his deliberations, will form, in the mind of the citizen, a uniform, a strong, and a lively sensibility to the interests of his country.[64]

From this it would follow that a nation exists in the minds and hearts of ordinary citizens as soon as there exist opportunities for citizens to participate on national questions. This is consistent, too, with Wilson's assertion that an American nation came into existence during the crisis of 1774–75, for the political and military activities that took place during that period created for the first time a continent-wide forum for political participation and at the same time brought millions of new participants into political life.

In other words heightened participation can have the effect of telescoping political time. Recall Madison's gradual, emergent description of American nationhood; this was a process that could take generations, and Madison was not disposed to rush it. For Wilson, change in the political outlook of ordinary citizens could occur much more quickly if participation was encouraged and channeled in the right direction. Nor would this require the kind of showdown between national government and state governments that Hamilton anticipated; the process could be both rapid and harmonious.

Recall as well the importance Wilson placed upon political symbolism; this too may have encouraged him to believe a nation could develop quickly, because political symbols (unlike customs or law codes or economic practices) sometimes can change almost overnight. (The Revolution itself involved a breathtakingly rapid shift of political symbols.) Wilson may have hoped that through the right institutions and the right understanding of sovereignty, an American nation could come into existence in a relatively short time.

It would also follow that flawed understandings of sovereignty and perverted symbolism can have rapidly damaging effects as well. This explains why Wilson believed the *Chisholm* case—in which symbolism played a central part—so crucial: he may have regarded it as a crossroads in which the American people had a real choice between nationhood and parochial attachment to states. If so, then he must have regarded the aftermath of the case—the passage of the Eleventh Amendment to reverse the decision in the case—as a tragically missed opportunity to resolve an urgent question.

VI

It is on questions counterposing the sovereignty claims of a state to those of the nation—like the *Chisholm* case—that Wilson's conception of popular sovereignty is clearest and most directly practical in its implications. On other matters, however, the "panacea" of popular sovereignty is somewhat less helpful. One of these is the question of civil liberties.

One of the things Wilson was most well known for during the ratification contest was his argument to the effect that a bill of rights was unnecessary in the federal Constitution. In his State House Yard speech of October 6, 1787, Wilson claimed that a bill of rights would be superfluous because under the proposed constitution every power that was not positively granted to the national government was reserved to the people anyway: "It would have been superfluous and absurd to have stipulated with a federal body of our own creation, that we should enjoy those privileges, of which we are not divested either by the intention or the act, that has brought that body into existence."[65] In other words, a bill of rights makes no sense where the people themselves are sovereign, where the governing power is itself "of our own creation."

There is merit in this argument, and certainly bills of rights as traditionally understood—as special privileges and immunities from an otherwise comprehensive sovereign power—are inappropriate in a republican government. But what is missing here is any recognition that governments based upon the principle of popular sovereignty can threaten liberty in a different way than monarchies and aristocracies did.

It is not that Wilson was indifferent to civil liberties or willing to sacrifice them to the will of a passionate majority. Wilson was committed to civil liberties—not as completely as Madison was, but to a degree that was toward the liberal end of the spectrum of the age. Wilson probably was responsible for the Constitution's strict standard of proof in treason cases, having seen the abuse of the law of treason in Pennsylvania during the Revolution.[66] Like Madison he opposed religious discrimination of any kind.[67] He was thoroughly conversant with the history of English common-law liberties.[68] The Pennsylvania constitution he drafted included a provision that truth was a defense in criminal libel cases—the same moderately liberalizing reform which Hamilton would later argue for in New York.[69]

But one looks in vain in Wilson's writings for any recognition of the problem of reconciling civil liberties with the principle of popular sovereignty. What Madison had to say about freedom of the press and freedom of religion is interesting precisely because he recognized a tension between majority rule and civil liberties that must somehow be bridged. Wilson's remarks on civil liberties, on the other hand, are for the most part flat and dogmatic. He declared for liberty but would hardly be likely to persuade someone who disagreed. One would not suspect from reading Wilson that there were any important battles left to be fought over civil liberties.

Perhaps the reason is that here as elsewhere he was too ready to use the principle of popular sovereignty to harmonize all tensions. Just as he believed that the supremacy of the national government over the states could be achieved painlessly because the sovereign people create and supervise both, he seems not to have believed that majority rule would pose a serious threat to individual rights. (It is revealing that not once in the *Chisholm* opinion did he suggest that Georgia's refusal to pay its debts resulted from a selfish majority violating the rights of an individual.)

This is one thing Madison never lost sight of. He was as attached as Wilson was to the principle of popular sovereignty and so could appreciate the logic of Wilson's argument. Yet he did not let this prevent him from giving liberty some additional protections if he thought they would do some good. As he was changing his mind about a bill of rights, Madison in a letter to Jefferson referred to the claim that a bill of rights was unnecessary because the national government was limited to those powers enumerated in the Constitution. He said he accepted this argument to a certain degree, "though not in the extent argued by Mr. Wilson."[70] Madison seems to have recognized in Wilson a tendency to take a good idea too far.

VII

It is difficult to make a balanced critical appraisal of Wilson's accomplishments as statesman and theorist. This is partly because he has been studied so little by scholars, and because many standard histories of the period and most studies of Jefferson, Madison, and Hamilton (among others) pay little attention to Wilson. But the difficulty also stems from the man himself. The value of several of his particular accomplishments is clear—for example, his work at the Federal Convention, his role in the ratification debate, his revision of the Pennsylvania constitution, his encouragement of widespread political participation, his attempt to establish the authority of the Supreme Court. But the value of the overarching theory of popular sovereignty that guided him in those efforts is more questionable. One wonders whether in Wilson's case the whole is less than the sum of the parts.

Earlier I cited Gordon Wood's claim that the Federalist version of popular sovereignty was "disingenuous" in its democratic rhetoric and that it "obscured the real social antagonisms of American politics." The charge of disingenuity does not stick to Wilson; his democratic commitments were real. But one cannot deny that his thought tended to obscure "real social antagonisms"—not only antagonisms between status groups, which are Wood's principal concern, but also the antagonisms between national government and the states. Madison and Hamilton, whatever their other differences, were alike in the realism with which they described power relations and power struggles within a federal system. It is precisely this realism that was lacking in Wilson, who seems truly to have believed that the principle of popular sovereignty would eliminate such power struggles.

It has been pointed out that Wilson to a remarkable degree anticipated political developments that came much later: the transformation of the presidency into a democratic office; the popular election of senators that came with the Seventeenth Amendment; the one person–one vote requirement for electoral districts mandated by the Supreme Court in 1962.[71] But Wilson's ability—or his good fortune—to anticipate later political developments does not prove the truth or depth of his theory. He may have given theoretical expression to certain political and social tendencies without adequately understanding them—understanding, for instance, only their hopeful side while ignoring the dark side.

There were, after all, selfish and violent tendencies at work in American life—which touched Wilson's own life—that never found expression in his cheerful philosophy. During the war his opposition to price controls made his house a target of one of the fiercest outbreaks of mob violence of the Revolution.[72] His own addiction to get-rich-quick schemes is difficult to reconcile with his insistence that property is less important than "the cultivation and improvement of the human mind." My criticism here is not that Wilson failed in some cases to live up to his own principles (which is true of almost everyone). The problem is that there is no appreciation, even in his theory, for the kind of destructive passions that touched his own life.

I do not mean to argue against taking Wilson seriously, but only against taking him whole. His keenest insights are partial ones. This applies especially to the problem of reconciling the power of government and the liberty of citizens. Taken as a whole, Wilson's answer to this problem is inadequate. He seems to have believed that the principle of the sovereignty of the people removed all serious conflict between the power of government and the liberty of citizens. This is merely the obverse of the equally simple and straightforward belief that the power of government and the liberty of citizens are eternally antagonistic. Wilson in effect substituted one simple proposition for another.

But his conception of popular sovereignty did make an important contribution to the problem of reconciling power and liberty by directly confronting the traditional doctrine of sovereignty. Wilson clearly understood the symbolic dimensions of sovereignty and recognized the inappropriateness of the traditional doctrine of sovereignty in a republic. Wilson can perhaps be forgiven for mistakenly believing that removing one obstacle to the reconciliation of power and liberty would remove all obstacles.

The idea of "the sovereignty of the people," if it makes sense at all, does so only at a very high level of abstraction. On a day-to-day basis what we always observe, even in a democracy, is that a few govern the rest, subject to various limitations and challenges both formal and informal. Nor do we ever observe "the people" acting and thinking in unison—except perhaps in extreme cases where the whole society is threatened by a foreign enemy. In every ordinary case political life in a popular government is characterized by majorities and minorities on various issues, not by unity.

It is for this reason that some political theorists dismiss with contempt the whole idea of popular sovereignty.[73] But others approach it with a somewhat more nuanced skepticism. Edmund Morgan describes the idea that the people themselves rule as a "fiction," an exercise in make-believe: "Government requires make-believe. Make believe that the king is divine, make believe that he can do no wrong or make believe that the voice of the people is the voice of god. Make believe that the people *have* a voice or make believe that the representatives of the people *are* the people. Make believe that governors are the servants of the people." But in the same breath Morgan admits the value, even the indispensability, of such "fictions" because of the way they shape political reality without ever coinciding with it. In order to sustain our "willing suspension of disbelief" in our political fictions, we "often take pains to prevent their collapse by moving the facts to fit the fiction, by making our world conform more closely to what we want it to be."[74] The real merit of the idea of popular sovereignty is not its truth or falsity but its tendency to uphold the human value of liberty. I propose that Wilson's theory of popular sovereignty be likewise judged by its fruits—by what he was able to do with it.

Another consideration should be kept in mind. Not just the idea of "popular" sovereignty but every conception of sovereignty is extremely abstract. The idea that there must exist in every political order some final, supreme, unlimited power whose decisions are held to be legitimate by the community is already highly abstract; it is not a statement of fact but an axiom.[75]

Thus there is something unfair about judging Wilson's conception of popular sovereignty only by contrasting it with "the facts" of political life of his place and time—where one will observe all kinds of actions and events that do not fit the idea of a single, united, sovereign people. Wilson's understanding of sovereignty must also be judged against other theories and claims about sovereignty. It must be judged against, for instance, the claim that the governments of the states are sovereign, a claim no less abstract than Wilson's—and one which presupposes an idealized unity within a state that is just as questionable as Wilson's idealized national unity. If Wilson considered conceptions of sovereignty like the one advanced by Georgia to be pernicious to liberty or to national unity, he had no choice but to oppose them by means of a different conception of sovereignty. For sovereignty was a powerful idea at the time, and one must fight fire with fire; to work a variation on a famous Madisonian line, "Abstraction must be made to counteract abstraction."

Wilson did not succeed in defeating the abstraction against which he did battle—the doctrine of state sovereignty. But he did frame the terms in which the battle would eventually be fought. In his first inaugural address, Abraham Lincoln opposed the sovereignty claims of the secessionists with a very Wilsonian principle: "A majority, held in restraint by constitutional checks, and limitations, and always changing easily, with deliberate changes of popular opinion and sentiments, is the only true sovereign of a free people."[76]

Thomas Jefferson

1743–1826

5

Thomas Jefferson

LIBERTY, AND THE STATES

*The natural progress of things is for liberty to yield, and
government to gain ground.*
—Thomas Jefferson to Edward Carrington, May 27, 1788

*It is easy to foresee from the nature of things that the encroachments
of the state governments will tend to an excess of liberty which
will correct itself . . . while those of the general government will
tend to monarchy, which will fortify itself from day to day. . . .
I would rather be exposed to the inconveniencies attending too much
liberty than those attending too small a degree of it.*
—Thomas Jefferson to Archibald Stuart, December 23, 1791

*Confidence is everywhere the parent of despotism—free government
is founded in jealousy, and not in confidence.*
—Thomas Jefferson, Draft of the Kentucky Resolutions, 1798

T HUS FAR THIS WORK has examined three statesmen-theorists of the
Founding era who argued against any simple antagonism between the
power of government and the liberty of citizens; who believed that it
was possible under the right circumstances to make national government both
energetic and free. Madison's, Hamilton's, and Wilson's understanding of
national power and its proper limits differed in many ways. But all three would
have agreed with Madison's statement in his letter of October 17, 1788, that it
is inaccurate to assume "there is a tendency in all Governments to an augmentation of power at the expense of liberty." It is now time to turn to the
views of the man to whom the letter was written, and who held precisely the
view of power and liberty that Madison challenged.

There were—and continue to be—many different Thomas Jeffersons. Like the Bible, he can be cited in support of practically any side of any contest. His authority was invoked on both sides in the Civil War. In matters of political economy, he simultaneously furnishes arguments in favor of a more equal distribution of wealth and against the exercise of state power that would be necessary to bring this equality about. More recently the contradictory character of his utterances—as well as the gulf between principle and practice—in matters of slavery and race has been exhaustively researched and debated.[1]

The search for a single, unified Jefferson, for a portrait that will unite the public and private man in all his diversity and resolve all his tensions and contradictions, is forever destined to fail. The enormous range of Jefferson's own interests (political, religious, scientific, literary, architectural, agricultural), the length of his life, the form in which much of his thought was expressed— private letters where he tailored his response to a particular individual and public papers where he spoke for a movement or cause rather than as an individual—render any attempt to capture the whole man necessarily selective and one-sided. I do not attempt anything of the sort here.

Instead this chapter takes up only one aspect of Jefferson's thought: his opposition to an energetic national government and his willingness to endorse an extreme doctrine of state sovereignty in the belief that this would best preserve liberty against the encroachments of national power. This approach to Jefferson will necessarily be more critical than if the focus were religious liberty or political participation or the Declaration of Independence. The power and endurance of the Declaration were made possible because there Jefferson limited himself to a description of the characteristics of abusive government and the right to alter or abolish such a government; he did not claim in the Declaration that energetic government always tends toward abusive government. And yet that is what he believed. In his own more comprehensive political thought, there were close links between the struggle of liberty against despotism, over which the Revolution was fought, and the struggle over powerful national government in the 1790s. Jefferson's opposition to energetic national government and the remedies to which he was willing to resort were linked to his more general views of power and liberty.

At the core of Jefferson's political thought was suspicion of political power: his belief in an eternal struggle between the power of government and the liberty of citizens—an unequal struggle in which all the advantages lie on the side of power. The task of the statesman is not to create or expand power—power can always take care of itself—but to fortify liberty to make the contest more equal. All of Jefferson's actions and utterances as a public figure, even during those times when he cautiously favored giving additional powers to the national government, bore the stamp of this suspicion of power.[2]

In this respect Jefferson was faithful to the fear-of-power element in the English oppositional Whig tradition that so influenced American political thought of the Revolutionary era. Madison, Hamilton, and Wilson all accepted the premise that political power is dangerous if unchecked; but the overall tendency of their thought was to moderate this fear rather than reinforce it. Jefferson reinforced it and carried it to new lengths.

But Jefferson was no more a blind follower of tradition than the other three were. Instead he reinvented the Whig tradition in the course of adapting it to the wholly republican and partly federal conditions of the United States. David Mayer writes that Jefferson took the "Real Whig" jealousy of power and added a "federal aspect" (the subdivision of all power into distinct spheres and branches) and a "republican aspect" whereby all these distinct spheres and branches were "equally accountable to the 'rightful' majority will of the people."[3] Jefferson's opposition to energetic national government thus must be understood not as a simple application of a traditional dogma but in relation to Jefferson's own comprehensive synthesis of old and new ideas.

It is the problematic character of Jefferson's synthesis that concerns me here (and that most distinguishes this analysis of Jefferson from that of Mayer, who regards the synthesis as successful). It was a habit of Jefferson's to simplify radically what was at stake in any important political or constitutional question into two diametrically opposed principles: one side always represented liberty, the other power; one side aimed to preserve republicanism, while the other (whether they realized it or not) sowed the seeds of monarchy and privilege. Thus in Jefferson's synthesis energetic national government meant government in the interest of the few, while defense of liberty and popular sovereignty somehow turned naturally into endorsement of an extreme version of state sovereignty. For every important political contest is essentially between the principle of power and the principle of liberty; if the national government represents power, then state sovereignty becomes for practical purposes the embodiment of the principle of liberty. In Jefferson's Kentucky Resolutions the claim that "free government is founded in jealousy, and not in confidence" merges into his claim that the Constitution was created by a compact among sovereign states who retain the right, individually, to be final judge of the acts of the national government. It is Jefferson's identification of national-state authority contests with battles between "the few and the many" or between "monocrats and republicans" that deserves critical examination.

And this identification of state sovereignty with the principle of liberty was not merely a tactical move directed against the Alien and Sedition Acts. The constitutional theory upon which it is based was evident in Jefferson's thought even in the mid-1780s when he favored strengthening the powers of the national government. It lay in the background of his demand for the inclusion of a bill of rights and was central to his argument against the constitutionality of a national bank. It accounted for his claim in writing to Archibald Stuart on December 23, 1791, that even the "encroachments" of the states tend to reinforce liberty.[4]

Jefferson's tendency to reduce all political divisions to contests between power and liberty highlights both his virtues and his flaws as a political thinker. It exemplifies on the one hand his willingness to take the most comprehensive view of every political struggle, to look beyond its immediate and circumscribed details and consider it in the light of the entire range of human possibilities. This drive to generalize every contest onto a world-historical scale is what enabled Jefferson to write the Declaration of Independence the way he did—a document which, it should be noted, was produced in the course of a contest where Americans really did face a radical choice between two incompatible principles: either they remain part of the empire and attached to a king or separate and become republican.

On the other hand the tendency to generalize everything into a struggle between two opposed principles is not particularly appropriate to complex questions of separation of power or to the tangled workings of a federal system of government. It is unclear, to say the least, that in every question of how to allocate power between federal government and states or between executive, legislative, and judicial branches of government, one side represents republican principle and the other the urge to restore monarchy. Yet this was how Jefferson saw the world, and as a result he frequently used a sledgehammer for operations more suited to a scalpel.

This tendency to reduce everything into two opposed principles also allowed Jefferson to avoid choosing between the principle of majority rule and his own strong version of state sovereignty. Mayer writes that Jefferson "regarded the *lex majoris partis,* the law of the majority, as the natural law of every society of men."[5] This is true in one sense, but it depends upon a prior answer to the question of what constitutes a "society" or "people." It is by no means clear whether Jefferson would have allowed a national majority, on some matter of great importance, to override the will of a minority, if that minority constituted a majority within one state. The doctrine of state sovereignty set forth in the Kentucky Resolutions, taken at face value, would give precedence to a single state over a national majority. It is not clear whether Jefferson meant it that way; after all, he was confident that the majority of Americans opposed the kind of powerful national government the Kentucky Resolutions were intended to challenge. By radically simplifying the political alternatives at stake—strong national government equals antimajoritarian government equals unfree government—Jefferson was able to avoid ever having to choose between state and national versions of popular sovereignty. But the elements of his grand synthesis do not always occur naturally together, and Jefferson offered little guidance about what course to follow when these elements go their separate ways.

I

Before examining Jefferson's views on the specific question of national power, it helps to frame that question within the broader landscape of his political thought and political activity.

If the Declaration of Independence is the kind of political task best suited to Jefferson's cast of mind—a clear choice between two opposed principles— then the creation, maintenance, and interpretation of the federal Constitution posed a more difficult and much less straightforward problem for Jefferson's political thought. The Declaration dissolves a government; liberty and power were at war, and one had to take sides. The new federal Constitution on the other hand involved not the dissolution of old power but the creation of new power. Jefferson was not in principle opposed to creating new forms of power: the Declaration itself asserts the right of a people to do exactly this, and he himself supported a stronger national government of some kind in the 1780s. The picture of Jefferson sometimes drawn by his detractors—that he was a violent advocate of permanent revolution, an enemy of all law—is a complete misrepresentation, and it misses the real problem.[6] As a practical man Jefferson realized the need for effective government, at least some of the time and to some degree. But this practical need is necessarily in tension with the theoretical idea that power has all the advantages and always tends to increase at the expense of liberty. This tension came to the surface in Jefferson's views on national power during the mid-1780s.

Jefferson did make enormous efforts over a span of fifty years to reform the constitution and laws of Virginia. Among other things he pressed for religious liberty, a better separation of powers, genuine popular endorsement of the Virginia constitution, creation of structures for participatory local self-government, reform of the legal code, equality of representation among legislative districts, free public education, gradual abolition of slavery (at least early on—he retreated from this goal later), and distribution of fifty acres of public land free of charge to every white male citizen of the state.[7] With the exception of the bill for religious liberty, which was passed with Madison's help, most of Jefferson's efforts met with little success. But they were always imaginative and practical. Without question Jefferson understood the Virginia constitution and its problems from beginning to end.[8]

The federal Constitution, and national power more generally, posed problems of a different kind. Jefferson was out of the country during the period when the Constitution was created and ratified. Though he kept up on developments in America as much as possible, he never entered into the redesign of national government to the same degree that he was engaged with redesigning the government and laws of Virginia. Afterwards he accepted and participated in a national government very different from any he would have drawn up himself, and this must have influenced the way in which he understood and interpreted the Constitution.

Furthermore, the Virginia constitution did not involve any of the complications of federalism—of two separate systems of law and government exercising jurisdiction, and claiming a kind of supremacy, over the same body of citizens. In Virginia there were two basic entities: the government and the people; it was immediately clear who represented power and who liberty. In the federal context there are at least three entities: the national government, the state governments, and the people. In a power contest between the authority of the national government and the state governments, it is not immediately clear which side, if any, can claim to embody liberty against power.

Moreover, the Virginia constitution was directed toward a government which in its basic outlines was very old. The 1776 state constitution transformed Virginia from a royal colony to a republic; but however important the transformation, the fact remains that it was an alteration of an existing government which continued to enjoy the support and obedience of the populace throughout the transition. Thus when Jefferson turned his energy to reforming the constitution and laws of Virginia, an adequate degree of governmental power was already there. Jefferson did not need to propose the creation of new power or any significant expansion of existing power; power in Virginia could take care of itself, and he could turn his attention to limiting and redistributing that power in various ways.

The situation was very different on the national level. No national government of any kind had existed before the meeting of the First Continental Congress in 1774; the Articles of Confederation were drawn up hastily under wartime conditions, and they in turn were not reformed but set aside by the drafters of the federal Constitution. In short, everything related to national government involved not the reform and limitation of old power (as in Virginia) but the creation of new power. And this posed peculiar problems for a philosophy like Jefferson's which assumed that power can always take care of itself.

The difference between old power and new power leads in turn to a fundamental paradox related to Jefferson's understanding of popular sovereignty. For Jefferson innovation in the limitation of power was good—and this was the object of almost all of his proposed reforms of the constitution and laws of Virginia. It was when power needed to be limited that Jefferson appeared in his most radical light. Innovation in the creation or the exercise of power, in contrast, was almost always evil, a sign of corruption; here Jefferson urged that innovation in government be prevented with iron constitutional chains.

Jefferson's special hostility to new power, to innovations in the exercise of power, was deeply rooted in oppositional Whig tradition and its preoccupation with the tendency of government to fall away from its pure first principles. In *The Jeffersonian Persuasion* Lance Banning characterizes that tradition's perspective on political change:

> The classical-republican foundations of American constitutional thought taught that a constitution, once established, changed only for the worse. The accepted task for friends of liberty was neither counterrevolution nor reform. It was to guard against social and political degeneration, to force a strict adherence to the original principles of a government, to see that things became no worse. The revolutionary generation inhabited a mental universe that contained no familiar ways of thinking about progressive constitutional improvement, that encouraged men to think that constitutional change, like water, always flowed downhill.[9]

In Jefferson's own case the outlook Banning describes is reflected, among other places, in the wish Jefferson expressed to John Adams that the Articles of Confederation be preserved as a "religious relique," and in the Kentucky Resolutions where he said power must be bound down "by the chains of the Constitution."[10]

Now at this point Jefferson's political thought must appear rather puzzling.

This after all is the man who made it a fundamental principle that every generation is free from the power of previous generations, that no generation has a right to make a perpetual law or a perpetual constitution. Jefferson did have a plan for "progressive constitutional improvement"—a constitutional convention every nineteen years. How is it possible to reconcile the Jefferson who was especially suspicious of innovations in government—of new power—with the Jefferson who left each generation free to rewrite all its constitutions and laws?

The answer is that Jefferson's radical right of the people to innovate and his conservative opposition to innovations in government are two sides of the same idea, and both are founded on the fundamental opposition between government on one side and people on the other. Only if power and liberty represent two antagonistic essences that can never blend do Jefferson's complete endorsement of alterations made by the people and his complete condemnation of alterations initiated by the government make sense.

The equal priority of Jefferson's hostility to innovations in power and his endorsement of the people's right to begin anew is evident from the particular form in which Jefferson would have institutionalized this general principle. It is not enough, he wrote on September 6, 1789, to Madison, that each generation merely enjoy the right to repeal or change any constitution or law; they must be forced to begin again.

> It may be said that the succeeding generation exercising in fact the power of repeal, this leaves them as free as if the constitution or law had been expressly limited to 19. years only. In the first place, this objection admits the right, in proposing an equivalent. But the power of repeal is not an equivalent. It might be indeed if every form of government were so perfectly contrived that the will of the majority could always be obtained fairly and without impediment. But this is true of no form. The people cannot assemble themselves; their representation is unequal and vicious. Various checks are opposed to every legislative proposition. Factions get possession of the public councils. Bribery corrupts them. Personal interests lead them astray from the general interests of their constituents; and other impediments arise so as to prove to every practical man that a law of limited duration is much more manageable than one which needs a repeal.[11]

Notice here that fear of government power is integrally related to the right of each generation to begin anew. All change that occurs at the initiative of government is corruption. The possibility that government might initiate some alterations that would advance liberty and be accepted as such after the fact by the people themselves—which is Hamilton's perspective—is excluded from the beginning in Jefferson's way of posing the problem. Likewise excluded is the possibility of in-between cases, where a change occurs partly through the initiative of someone in power and partly as an expression of a genuine but unclear popular demand. For Jefferson it is all-or-nothing: either a change comes entirely from the people and reflects their natural right to be free of the authority of the past, or it comes from government and is corruption.[12]

This might be one of the reasons he had such reservations about the Constitution and the political movement behind it. Whatever its particular merits and flaws as a design for a more effective national government, it was clearly not generated by the kind of direct, spontaneous popular demand that Jefferson would have preferred. (There was no clear and direct opposition to the Constitution either—the people were in between and pulled both directions. But for Jefferson this was not a clear enough endorsement.) Jefferson doubtless also realized that in 1787 to speak of a single American people—in the directly political sense of the word—involved an exercise of power on the part of a political elite and required a leap of faith, an act of "confidence," on the part of the people. Thus the same principle of jealousy that made him suspicious of power would have led him to resist the attempt to transform the United States into a single nation—unless this attempt came spontaneously and unequivocally from the people themselves, which it did not. Jefferson was willing in the end to accept the Constitution, but only on terms designed to halt the exertion of power that had brought the document into existence and to ensure that there would be no future innovations without a clear and direct popular mandate.

II

How did Jefferson conceive of the relation between the national government, the state governments, and the people? How is his understanding of federalism linked to his more fundamental view of the antagonism between power and liberty?

To this question there might appear to be a simple, brief, and authoritative answer. In his first inaugural address (1801), Jefferson described as one of the "essential principles of our Government . . . the support of the State governments in all their rights, as the most competent administrations for our domestic concerns and the surest bulwarks against antirepublican tendencies; the preservation of the General Government in its whole constitutional vigor, as the sheet anchor of our peace at home and safety abroad."[13] Here, as in the Declaration of Independence, Jefferson succeeded in putting into clear and elegant language a widely shared general principle; here too, as with the Declaration, the power of the formulation depended on Jefferson's suppressing specifics upon which men would not agree. All of the truly divisive questions were left open. Where exactly is the line drawn between the "rights of states" and the "constitutional vigor" of the national government? Who decides where this line is drawn? Was Jefferson here renouncing the strong version of state sovereignty he put forth in the Kentucky Resolutions—or restating it at a more comfortable level of generality?

To approach these very difficult questions, it helps to go back in time to the mid-1780s and reconstruct Jefferson's understanding of national union before the whole problem was transformed by the work of the Federal Convention. While Jefferson was serving in the Continental Congress in 1783-84, he drafted a "Report for a Plan of Government for the Western Territory" which among other things assumed a power in the national government to exclude slavery from the Northwest Territory. From 1784 to 1789 he served as minister to France, spending much of his time and energy attempting to negotiate commercial treaties and assuring European creditors that the United States would eventually honor its financial obligations.[14] Both this year in the Continental Congress and his diplomatic service acquainted him with the defects of the Confederation. A snapshot of his political views in the mid-1780s would have classified him among the nationalists: like Madison he was especially concerned with the lack of adequate power in Congress over trade and supported the proposal to "take the commerce of the states out of the hands of the states and to place it under the superintendence of Congress, so far as the imperfect provisions of our constitution will admit, and until the states shall by new compact make them more perfect." In the same letter he proposed that the interests of the states "ought to be made joint in every possible instance in order to cultivate the idea of our being one nation, and to multiply the instances in which the people shall look up to Congress as their head."[15] Here Jefferson sounds as nationalist as Alexander Hamilton or James Wilson.

But the picture is a misleading one.[16] Jefferson did favor vesting the Continental Congress with additional powers over commerce. But his reform suggestions were subject to peculiar kinds of inhibitions, and the idea of America being a single nation "in every possible instance" was merely a hasty and oversimplified statement on Jefferson's part which he corrected in other writings around the same time. His real view of the matter is expressed in several places including two letters to Madison and the "Answers and Observations for Démeunier's Article." In writing to Madison on February 8, 1786, Jefferson, after praising the Virginia assembly for its resolution in favor of giving the national government the power to regulate commerce, immediately placed limits on the nationalizing tendency of such a move: "The politics of Europe render it indispensably necessary that with respect to everything external we be one nation only, firmly hooped together. Interiour government is what each state should keep to itself." By implication, at least, the separate states were indeed nations unto themselves with respect to everything not "external." Jefferson made this point in even stronger form in writing to Madison on December 16, 1786 (and it is possible that Jefferson was already quietly resisting a disturbing nationalizing tendency he had noticed in Madison's letters). Jefferson acknowledged the failure of the Commercial Convention (at Annapolis in 1786) and mentioned the proposed "full meeting in May" (1787) of a convention for "a broader reformation." He then characterized the proper task of such a convention: "To make us one nation as to foreign concerns, and keep us distinct in Domestic ones, gives the outline of the proper division of powers between the general and particular governments."[17] At no point during this period of Jefferson's supposed nationalism did he propose trusting the national government with any powers comparable to those later vested in the national government by the Constitution.

The first thing to notice is the very limited and specific character of the additional powers Jefferson wanted to place in the national government. In his "Answers and Observations for Démeunier's Article" (1786), he called the Confederation "a wonderfully perfect instrument, considering the circumstances under which it was formed," and then went on to propose three specific alterations: (1) "To establish a general rule for the admission of new states into the Union"; (2) to change the way the quotas of money contributed by the states were apportioned (from reading Jefferson's description one would think that the Confederation was already adequately funded, and the only problem was to make the degree of sacrifice more equal); and (3) to give Congress a power to regulate the commerce of the states (which he also urged in letters to Madison, Monroe, and others). Jefferson himself testified to the contrast between his reform proposals and the transformation of power effected by the Federal Convention when on November 13, 1787, he listed for John Adams his objections to the proposed Constitution and added, "Indeed I think all the good of this new constitution might have been couched in three or four new articles to be added to the good, old, and venerable fabrick, which should have been preserved even as a religious relique."[18]

The limited and specific character of Jefferson's reform proposals circa 1786 is not by itself particularly surprising. Very few people, perhaps no one, could have then foreseen the extent and direction of the work of the future Federal Convention. It is certainly no failing on Jefferson's part that he did not anticipate the work of the convention, or that he was taken by surprise when he learned of it.

What is revealing, however, is the difficulty Jefferson had reconciling with his political principles even the limited reforms he himself had recommended. Equally revealing are his speculations about how the reforms might be brought about and his background assumptions about the single or plural character of American nationhood.

However limited in scope the reforms he had proposed, they would in fact represent a significant increase in the power of the national government. As a practical man, trying to formulate a united commercial policy and preserve respect for the nation abroad, Jefferson recognized the need for these additional powers. From the perspective of his political principles, however, any increase of power in government was suspect. Jefferson's method of resolving this tension was to so widen the frame of reference that what in the American context would appear to be strong government shows itself still to be weak government compared to Europe. In his "Answers and Observations for Démeunier's Article," having listed the additional powers needed and even having suggested that Congress in a last resort should coerce recalcitrant states (with a naval force, "as being more easy, less dangerous to liberty, & less likely to produce much bloodshed"),[19] Jefferson immediately turned around and praised the weakness of American governments in contrast to European governments whose energy was based on armed force. It is as though, having just caught himself taking the side of power, he could only relieve his political conscience by finding some larger context within which what he had just recommended (including the coercion) would still appear to be erring on the side of liberty. He had enormous difficulty making a principled justification for an expansion of power; instead he reaffirmed his principled hostility to power as though he had never sided with power at all. It seems the left hand should not know what the right is doing.

Also revealing is the way in which Jefferson imagined the necessary augmentation of power in the Confederacy might occur. He suggested two very different roads. The first could be described as a stealth campaign: the change would be accomplished through the backdoor of the treaty power vested in the Continental Congress; the treaty power should be used to acquire a more general power to regulate the commerce of the states. In writing on June 17, 1785, to Monroe, he stated: "Congress, by the Confederation have no original and inherent power over the commerce of the states. But by the 9th article they are authorized to enter into treaties of commerce. The moment these treaties are concluded the jurisdiction of Congress over the commerce of the states springs into existence, and that of the particular states is superseded so far as the articles of the treaty may have taken up the subject."[20] (He floated the same idea in his "Answers and Observations for Démeunier's Article.") What is peculiar here is that Jefferson seems to have believed that a significant shift of power from states to Confederation could be accomplished immediately and painlessly, without any need for an extended public debate on the matter or any popular ratification of the increased power.

The other path he suggested is quite different, nearly the opposite of a stealth campaign. On February 1, 1785, Jefferson wrote to Richard Price:

> Since the peace it was observed that some nations of Europe, counting on the weakness of Congress and the little probability of a union in measure among the States, were proposing to grasp at unequal advantages in our commerce. The people are become sensible of this, and you may be assured that this evil will be immediately redressed, and redressed radically. I doubt still whether in this moment they will enlarge those powers in Congress which are necessary to keep the peace among the States. I think it possible that this may be suffered to lie till some two States commit hostilities on each other, but in that moment the hand of the union will be lifted up and interposed, and the people will themselves demand a general concession to Congress of means to prevent similar mischeifs.[21]

Here, instead of a stealth campaign lacking any popular involvement, Jefferson went to the opposite extreme and suggested that a crisis brought about by aggressive states would lead the people themselves spontaneously to demand greater powers in Congress. This outcome would be relatively easy to reconcile with Jefferson's own principle of jealousy of power, because it could be understood as liberty—the spontaneous act of the people—rising up against the arrogant and destructive power of states. (This is, by the way, one of the very few passages in which Jefferson placed the national government on the liberty side of the power-liberty dualism and the states on the power side.

Everywhere else in his writings, and especially during the 1790s, the national government represents power and state sovereignty represents liberty.) In this case the innovation was not dangerous because it would have proceeded clearly and spontaneously from the side of the people.

It is not clear which of the two paths—the stealth campaign or popular demand in a crisis—Jefferson preferred or considered more likely; he proposed both around the same period of time. However different the two scenarios are from one another, they have at least one thing in common: neither depends upon any modification of the public's jealousy of power—in the first case because the public's involvement is minimal, and in the second case because it can be understood as turning that very principle of jealousy against the overweening power of states. In neither case is there any need for a deliberate public campaign, of the kind later carried on by the Federalists in the ratification debate, to persuade the public that its traditional hostility to power is excessive. There is a curiously passive and reactive character to Jefferson's crisis scenario: rather than allowing political elites to mount a deliberate political campaign to augment the powers of Congress before a crisis occurs—a campaign that would itself be an exercise of power arousing Jefferson's suspicions—he would rather wait until there was an unmistakable popular demand for the change. Either make the change, simply and quickly, without confusing the public with new political principles (the stealth approach) or wait until it demands them itself. Here we see the complications that arose when Jefferson attempted to make an augmentation of power consistent with principles that cast suspicion on any augmentation of power.

III

Jefferson's objections to the Constitution when he first saw it are well known: writing on December 20, 1787, to Madison, Jefferson listed as his chief objections the lack of a bill of rights and the absence of any bar to continual reelection of the chief executive. These objections are important enough, and they display Jefferson's characteristic fear that without provisions to the contrary, power will augment itself at the expense of liberty.

But these two objections taken in isolation provide only a very partial view of Jefferson's reservations about the proposed Constitution. They refer merely to provisions in the document itself, which he ultimately came to accept—after the addition of a bill of rights—and even treated as a sacred text. What worried him more than anything in the document itself, and foreshadowed more about his politics in the 1790s, was his suspicion about the political movement behind the Constitution. His suspicions were not directed against Madison himself, to whom he communicated his fears. In the same letter to Madison in which he listed his objections to the proposed Constitution, Jefferson warned against overreaction to "the late rebellion in Massachusetts."

In the close of the letter, in what could be read as its central point, Jefferson wrote: "I own I am not a friend to a very energetic government. It is always oppressive. The late rebellion in Massachusetts has given more alarm than I think it should have done. Calculate that one rebellion in 13 states in the course of 11 years, is but one for each state in a century & a half. No country should be so long without one."[22] This remark is one of a series of similar observations Jefferson had made within the year in letters (all written from France) to various correspondents, urging Americans to avoid overreacting to popular disorders (like Shays' Rebellion), to refrain from excessive counterforce, and not to let such disorders shake their faith in popular government. These remarks go to the core of Jefferson's political thought and thus deserve to be quoted at length.

Writing to Edward Carrington on January 16, 1787, at a time when panic over Shays' Rebellion was near its peak in America, Jefferson wrote:

> The tumults in America, I expected would have produced in Europe an unfavorable opinion of our political state. But it has not. On the contrary, the small effect of these tumults seems to have given more confidence in the firmness of our governments. The interposition of the people themselves on the side of government has had a great effect on the opinion here. I am persuaded myself that the good sense of the people will always be found to be the best army. They may be led astray for a moment, but will soon correct themselves. The people are the only censors of their governors: and even their errors will tend to keep these to the true principles of their institution. To punish these errors too severely would be to suppress the only safeguard of the public liberty. The way to prevent these irregular interpositions of the people is to give them full information of their affairs thro' the channel of the public papers, & to contrive that those papers should penetrate the whole mass of the people. The basis of our government being the opinion of the people, the very first object should be to keep that right; and were it left to me to decide whether we should have a government without newspapers or newspapers without a govern-

ment, I should not hesitate a moment to prefer the latter. . . . Cherish therefore the spirit of our people, and keep alive their attention. Do not be too severe upon their errors, but reclaim them by enlightening them. If once they become inattentive to the public affairs, you & I, & Congress & Assemblies, judges & governors shall all become wolves.[23]

On January 30, 1787, Jefferson wrote Madison "to learn your sentiments on the late troubles in the Eastern states." He admitted that the acts of the rebels were "absolutely unjustifiable; but I hope they will provoke no severities from their governments." He worried that

those characters wherein fear predominates over hope . . . may conclude too hastily that nature has formed man insusceptible of any other government but that of force, a conclusion not founded in truth, nor experience. Societies exist under three forms sufficiently distinguishable. 1. Without government, as among our Indians. 2. Under governments wherein the will of every one has a just influence, as is the case in England in a slight degree, and in our states, in a great one. 3. Under governments of force: as is the case in all other monarchies and in most of the other republics. To have an idea of the curse of existence under these last, they must be seen. It is a government of wolves over sheep. It is a problem, not clear in my mind, that the 1st condition is not the best. But I believe it to be inconsistent with any great degree of population. The second state has a great deal of good in it. The mass of mankind under that enjoys a precious degree of liberty & happiness. It has it's evils too: the principal of which is the turbulence to which it is subject. But weigh this against the oppressions of monarchy, and it becomes nothing. *Malo periculosam libertatem quam quietam servitutem.* Even this evil is productive of good. It prevents the degeneracy of government, and nourishes a general attention to the public affairs. I hold it that a little rebellion now and then is a good thing, & as necessary in the political world as storms in the physical. Unsuccessful rebellions indeed generally establish the encroachments on the rights of the people which have produced them. An observation of this truth should render honest republican governors so mild in their punishment of rebellions, as not to discourage them too much. It is a medicine necessary for the sound health of government.[24]

He made a similar point, more briefly, in a February 22, 1787, letter to Abigail Adams: "The spirit of resistance to government is so valuable on certain occasions, that I wish it to be always kept alive. It will often be exercised when wrong, but better so than not to be exercised at all."[25]

To William S. Smith on November 13, 1787, he suggested for the first time that the Constitution itself might have been designed with the intention of giving the chief executive the power to react repressively to popular uprisings. His critical reaction to continual reeligibility of the executive led him to the rebellion and liberty theme: "Our Convention has been too much impressed by the insurrection of Massachusetts: and in the spur of the moment they are setting up a kite to keep the hen-yard in order. I hope in God this article will be rectified before the new constitution is accepted."[26]

All of these observations from earlier letters form the background for understanding Jefferson's remark to Madison on December 20, 1787, that "I own that I am not a friend to a very energetic government. It is always oppressive." It is clear that what most troubled Jefferson was not the Constitution itself—despite his criticism of specific provisions—but the fear that the political movement to form a more energetic government was motivated, at least in part, by a loss of faith in popular government: a failure of republican spirit. He interpreted the political situation as one in which, regardless of the specific details of the Constitution itself, the fundamental question was whether Americans would retain their faith in popular government or forsake it.

Furthermore, energy in government for Jefferson meant repressive energy—force, bayonets. He made this point explicit in his "Answers and Observations for Démeunier's Article on the United States in the *Encyclopédie Methodique*" (1786): "It has been said too that our governments both federal and particular want energy; that it is difficult to restrain both individuals & states from committing wrong. This is true, & it is an inconvenience. On the other hand that energy which absolute governments derive from an armed force, which is the effect of the bayonet constantly held at the breast of every citizen, and which resembles very much the stillness of the grave, must be admitted also to have it's inconveniences. We weigh the two together, and like best to submit to the former."[27]

The passages quoted above raise a wide range of important themes and problems related to power and liberty.

1. Nowhere in this series of letters did Jefferson actually encourage popular uprisings like Shays' Rebellion, which he called unjustifiable. (Several years

later he would likewise condemn the Whiskey Rebellion, while opposing excessively oppressive countermeasures.) Jefferson was not an advocate of violent
rebellion for its own sake. He was pleased that in Massachusetts the mass of
citizenry sided with the law and implied that the rebels were ignorant about
the true causes of their distress. His central purpose was to prevent a remedy
that was worse than the disease: disorder is bad, but repression is worse. In calling such occasional uprisings necessary, he was adopting the detached perspective of a scientist: given human nature on the one hand and the nature of
government on the other, such events will occur with a frequency directly pro-
portional to the repressive force of government. Conclusion: if you do not like
uprisings, make the yoke of government as light as possible.

2. Energy in government is repressive energy. There seems to be little place
in Jefferson's political thought for a concept of energy in government that is
not repressive in character. In fact, governments, even in Jefferson's time, did
many things besides repress disorder with force: building roads and canals,
chartering banks (Jefferson had no objection to state banks), coining money,
educating citizens, to name a few. All of these things display energy; none of
them can be adequately characterized as a "bayonet at the breast." And yet Jefferson, even though he supported all of these governmental activities considered individually, nevertheless spoke in general terms as though the entire
function of government is repressive.

3. In any attempt to balance liberty and power, one should always err on
the side of liberty. In practice this means tolerating a degree of popular disorder despite its inconveniences. One cannot have the best of both; either you
will have a government too weak or a government too strong: "We weigh the
two together, and like best to submit to the former." A perfect balance between
power and liberty is impossible: because all the advantages lie on the side of
power, any perfect balance will soon tip toward an excess of power. Therefore
the proper policy is deliberately to aim for an excess of liberty, trusting that
this excess will compensate for the natural advantages of power. "The people
are the only censors of their governors; and even their errors will tend to keep
these to the true principles of their institution."

4. Insofar as popular disorder in a republic requires a remedy, that remedy is predominantly of a nongovernmental character: better information, better public education, a people willing to fly to the support of the law. The best
line of policy for government is negative: do not repress with excessive force;
leave the newspapers free. The solution, in short, is not better government but
a better people.

We can gain some perspective on Jefferson's recommendation here by comparing it with George Washington's response to reports of Shays' Rebellion. Washington's reaction was one of concern but not panic, and it shows a fundamentally different view of the responsibilities of government than that of Jefferson. On October 31, 1786, Washington wrote Henry Lee: "Know precisely what the insurgents aim at. If they have *real* grievances, redress them if possible; or acknowledge the justice of them, and your inability to do it in the present moment. If they have not, employ the force of government against them at once."[28] For Washington, the appropriate degree of force to be used in suppressing a popular rebellion was to be determined not, as with Jefferson, according to some sweeping view of the entire range of human political orders from Indian communities to absolute monarchies but according to the rather more specific question of whether the grievances that spurred the rebellion were real or imaginary. In suggesting that the grievances might be real, Washington at the same time indicated that the problem might be not a government too strong but a government too weak. Redressing real grievances requires a government capable of redressing them, which the government of Massachusetts, under the financial confusion of the 1780s, clearly was not. (And obviously Washington hoped that a stronger national government might be part of the solution.) This stress on government's responsibilities was wholly absent in Jefferson. And Washington's observations allow for the possibility—which Jefferson's do not—that government could be strong in some respects and weak in others. Massachusetts might be strong enough to repress the rebellion and yet too weak to solve the financial problems that caused it in the first place.

5. For Jefferson the question of how a popular uprising should be handled in a republican political order could not be answered in narrowly pragmatic terms but instead must take into consideration the entire range of human political possibilities—from American Indian communities to absolute monarchies, as he wrote to Madison on January 30, 1787. Every alteration in the relation between government and people signifies a shift toward one or the other of the two poles, anarchy and absolutism. A decision made in a republic to repress a popular uprising forcibly, even if the uprising was unjust and the governors honest, is nevertheless a move—however modest—in the direction of absolutism. There exists no purely republican context for political action; the sparks of monarchy and absolutism are always there, ready to flare up in a crisis.

This range of human political possibilities is itself less a function of institutional design (which could hardly be arranged according to a simple bipolar continuum) than of human psychology: it is a matter of spirit, a question of whether hope or fear predominates. That is why the motives behind the proposed Constitution matter more than the provisions themselves.

This tendency to see all political contests in terms of a bipolar political psychology illustrates at the same time the strengths and the limitations of Jefferson's political philosophy. At its best it provided Jefferson with an especially keen eye for the fragility of republican commitments in others and insulated him against panic at the first sign of trouble. Even at a great distance from events, Jefferson's political instincts led him to distrust apocalyptic reports of Shays' Rebellion; and in retrospect he was right. He also had good reason to distrust the republican commitments of those who opposed or remained indifferent to the move to strengthen national government until Shays' Rebellion occurred and then became enthusiasts for national government. Sometimes important political choices do involve a choice between fear and hope, between siding with power and siding with liberty; and when this is the case Jefferson's maxim to err on the side of liberty will always remain appropriate advice.

But Jefferson's penchant for reducing everything to a clash of two opposed principles is not especially useful in understanding the structural problems connected with the Articles of Confederation. For example, in his "Answers and Observations for Démeunier's Article," Jefferson attempted to explain why Rhode Island had been such an obstructive force within the Confederation. His answer? The state had too many merchants and thus lacked the proper republican spirit.[29] Jefferson failed to mention that many other states—including Virginia, despite its lower proportion of merchants—at one time or another were just as obstructive within the Confederation as Rhode Island, and that the Articles of Confederation themselves, by requiring unanimity for any significant change, encouraged obstructive tactics by a single state. The problem here had far more to do with state sovereignty than with republican spirit, and it is precisely this kind of structural problem that was least amenable to Jefferson's mode of analysis.

Jefferson's political thought was most at home when political contests could be reduced to a clash of two opposed principles. The question of whether and how to suppress Shays' Rebellion, for example, immediately involved only the government and people of Massachusetts. In contrast, the debate over the Constitution and over the legitimate powers of the national government during the 1790s was not merely about government on one side and people on the other. It involved an authority contest between two different levels of government and raised the difficult question of whether "the people" meant the people of the United States, the people of each individual state, or some hybrid of the two. Jefferson's elemental antagonism between power and liberty thus had to play itself out in this more complex and ambiguous political landscape.

IV

It is not at all surprising that Jefferson and Hamilton should have become political opponents during the 1790s. They differed on so many things—on their visions of America's economic future,[30] on the proper balance between power and liberty, on the power of the executive, on public finance and debt,[31] to name a few—that it is somewhat surprising that they did not become enemies sooner. Madison broke with Hamilton before the conflict between Jefferson and Hamilton had heated up. When it did flare up, its violence was increased to some degree by factors purely personal, and I make no effort here to explain that side of it, important as it might be.

But although the conflict itself is not difficult to explain, the particular form that Jefferson's opposition took requires some discussion. First, Jefferson became convinced not only that Hamilton's policies were unwise or unjust, not only that their effects posed a threat to liberty and republican government, but that Hamilton was in fact a monarchist who deliberately aimed to subvert the Constitution and restore a hereditary political order. Second, Jefferson early on came to the conclusion that the proper remedy to the danger from national government was to defend and promote state sovereignty—even to the point of excess, as he suggested to Archibald Stuart on December 23, 1791. For if the national government represents power, then within the terms of the dualism the states represent liberty. To push state sovereignty further than is strictly proper is, in effect, to err on the side of liberty. There ceased to be any distinction in Jefferson's mind between the people's resistance to powerful government and the resistance of states to the power of the national government. The same dualism that made Hamilton into Caesar made the state governments into freedom fighters.

Lance Banning's *The Jeffersonian Persuasion* provides a good starting point for understanding Jefferson's suspicions of Hamilton, which were shared in some form by many others. Banning begins the study with a quote from Jefferson's "Anas," written in 1818 and looking back to the political battles of the 1790s. The party struggles of the 1790s, Jefferson claimed, "were contests of principle between the advocates of republican and those of kingly government." Banning adds: "Countless times, not just in public, but in letters to each other and even in notations to themselves, Republicans insisted that what they opposed was nothing less than a conspiracy against liberty." What were the grounds, Banning asks, for the conviction of Jefferson and many others that Alexander Hamilton and the Federalist party actually sought to subvert the Republic? "For there was, in the new nation, no influential group of men who really plotted to reverse the Revolution." *The Jeffersonian Persuasion* is an attempt to reconstruct the world of eighteenth-century oppositional thought from within which Federalist policies could appear to be conspiracies against liberty. Banning also describes some of the challenges faced by the Republicans after 1800, when, he argues, "the party's triumphs and its failures were the products, in large part, of its attempt to govern in accordance with an ideology that taught that power was a monster and governing was wrong."[32]

The Whig opposition of Walpole's day feared the subversion of the English constitution through an excessively powerful executive: "Identifying liberty with Parliament and power with the court, opposition tracts portrayed the constitution as a battlefield where liberty was constantly besieged by the executive." An imbalance in the constitution was at the same time a symptom of a moral corruption beginning in the centers of power and spreading outward: "Depravity of morals is a product and a symptom of a change within the government." And the main instrument of power and corruption was the public debt. Borrowing led to extravagance and higher taxes, which led to poverty and dependence, immorality and corruption, a process which "could have no other consequence than absolute destruction of the nation's freedom."[33]

Turning to the American context, Banning describes how the policies of Alexander Hamilton as treasury secretary played directly into all of the inherited fears and suspicions about power and executive influence. Although Hamilton's program in fact was "aimed against the old American evil of localism" and was conceived by a man "who sought nothing less than to be the classical legislator of a great American state," he appeared to Jefferson and many others to be deliberately corrupting men with his scheme of public finance.[34] His commercial and manufacturing policies would have the effect of enriching a favored few at the expense of the independent farmer, the necessary social base of a republican political order. Anyone who would deliberately pursue such perverse policies, it necessarily followed within this framework of thought, must be aiming to subvert the Republic itself and to restore a hereditary political order.

Banning is describing a broad political ideology, not Jefferson's alone. But it is easy enough to show that his characterization applies to Jefferson. As early as 1792 Jefferson spoke of the "Monarchical federalists" who supported the new Constitution "merely as a stepping stone to monarchy." In a letter to Washington later the same year, Jefferson wrote of "that corps under the command of the Secretary of the Treasury for the purpose of subverting step by step the principles of the constitution" as though it were a simple matter of fact.[35] Clearly from Jefferson's perspective the step from Hamilton's fiscal policies to a conspiracy to restore monarchy was a short and obvious one. And Jefferson had come to this conclusion about Hamilton before the nation became passionately divided over the French Revolution; that event and the foreign policy quarrels it engendered may have reinforced Jefferson's conviction that Hamilton was a monarchist, but the idea was already there.

The value as well as the limitations of Banning's *Jeffersonian Persuasion* arises from its being a study of the ideology of a party rather than the thought of an individual. On the one hand it is absolutely necessary in understanding Jefferson to consider him in relation to the party he led and the ideology he helped formulate. It is essential to know, for example, that Jefferson was not alone in his extravagant suspicions of Hamilton and the Federalists; if these suspicions reveal something about the cast of Jefferson's mind, they also demonstrate that this cast of mind was shared in some degree by many others. Jefferson's peculiar gift, here as with the Declaration of Independence, was to generalize and systematize what was on the minds of many others.[36]

On the other hand a study of a party ideology is limited by its focus on the points of agreement shared by thinkers and statesmen in other respects very different from one another. The same measures can be supported or opposed for quite different reasons; there may be shared perception of a danger but very different remedies. *The Jeffersonian Persuasion* has little to say about how and why Jefferson's response to the perceived danger of Federalist policy took the form of a very strong version of states' rights and state sovereignty. Banning notes that Hamilton himself designed the policies to counteract the "evil of localism," but he does not discuss the place of localism in the Jeffersonian persuasion at length. In his chapter on "The Principles of Ninety-Eight,"[37] Banning analyzes Madison's Virginia Resolutions, not Jefferson's Kentucky Resolutions which assert the right of each state, individually, to be the final judge of the acts of the federal government and which describe the Constitution itself as created by a compact among the states. Because the ideas expressed in the Kentucky Resolutions were not orthodox even within the party Jefferson led, and because they have no obvious counterpart in the oppositional Whig tradition with which Banning links Republican political thought, it is perhaps appropriate that they are not emphasized in his study. But any study of Jefferson's thought must account for the place of states' rights, both in his diagnosis of the evils of Hamilton's (and Federalist) policy and in his manner of opposing those policies.

V

Jefferson's opposition to a national bank was based in part on his rejection of the "corrupt" fiscal power it could be used to support and the executive influence it would entail, and in that respect it was a continuation of the Whig objections. But there are some other specifically Jeffersonian elements to his "Opinion on the Constitutionality of a National Bank." If, as I have argued, two analytically separable issues—the power of government in relation to the liberty of citizens and the power of the national government in relation to the authority of states—are systematically conflated in Jefferson's political thought, at least after 1787, then this tendency should be visible in Jefferson's argument against the Bank.

It was the Bank controversy that sealed Madison's break with Hamilton and inaugurated Madison's and Jefferson's close political cooperation of the 1790s. An examination of Jefferson's argument against the Bank will help clarify the similarities and differences between Madison and Jefferson.

It is helpful first to summarize Madison's objection to the Bank, with which Jefferson's argument overlaps in part but from which it diverges in several important respects. Madison's objections preceded Jefferson's, and at the time (1791) Madison appeared to be far more troubled about the Bank than Jefferson was. Madison's argument was in a nutshell this: although the Constitution could have been written and ratified giving the national government power to charter banks, it was not. Such a power was considered and rejected, and the people ratified it with the clear understanding that such a power was excluded. To override the clear understanding of the people—an understanding national in scope, not limited to any one state—was a clear threat to liberty. Madison also criticized a method of construing the Constitution whereby every means to a end specified in the text becomes in turn an end; this new end entails new means, which again become ends, so that the Constitution becomes infinitely expansive, contrary to the people's clear understanding that the power of the national government was limited.

Some of the arguments Jefferson put forth in his "Opinion on the Constitutionality of a National Bank" echo Madison's argument: Jefferson like Madison claimed that the power in question was rejected "by the Convention which formed the Constitution." Jefferson's claim that "to take a single step beyond the boundaries thus specially drawn around the powers of Congress, is to take possession of a boundless field of power, no longer susceptible of any definition," is a simplified version of Madison's objection to an infinitely expansive method of textual construction.[38]

But blended with these objections is a peculiar version of states' rights theory which has no counterpart in Madison's argument against the Bank:

> Can it be thought that the Constitution intended that for a shade or two of *convenience*, more or less, Congress should be authorised to break down the most ancient and fundamental laws of the several States; such as those against Mortmain, the laws of Alienage, the rules of descent, the acts of distribution, the laws of escheat and forfeiture, the laws of monopoly? Nothing but a necessity invincible by any other means, can justify such a prostitution of laws, which constitute the pillars of our whole system of jurisprudence. Will Congress be too straight-laced to carry the constitution into honest effect, unless they may pass over the foundation-laws of the State governments for the slightest convenience of theirs?[39]

The implication here is that there is some clear and natural distinction between the sphere of legislation of the states and that of the national government—so natural that any national law that has any significant effect on the operation of a state law, if that state law is legitimate in its own sphere, is presumptively unconstitutional. This presumption of a clear and natural difference between national and state spheres of activity is absent from Madison's constitutional theory, which recognized that interference occurred as a matter of course and that the boundary between the spheres was to some degree artificial—but had to be respected all the same. Madison also made clear, in *Federalist* No. 39 and elsewhere, that the decision about where to draw the line between national and state power had to be made at the national level; here too he differed fundamentally from Jefferson.

Jefferson's presumption of a clear and natural difference between national and state spheres of activity also turns up in his remarks about commerce: "If [chartering a national bank] was an exercise of the power of regulating commerce, it would be void, as extending as much to the internal commerce of every State, as to its external. For the power given to Congress by the Constitution does not extend to the internal regulation of the commerce of a State, (that is to say of the commerce between citizen and citizen,) which remain exclusively with its own legislature; but to its external commerce only, that is to say, its commerce with another State, or with foreign nations, or with the Indian tribes."[40] The especially important phrase here is "as much." Jefferson did not deny that the operations of the Bank would extend to interstate and foreign commerce. But it could not do so without also having an effect on commerce within a state. Merely to demonstrate that a national law has an effect on commerce within a state (as the Bank clearly would) is enough to demonstrate its unconstitutionality, for there is no legitimate sphere of overlap and interference between state and national power; wherever interference occurs, the state power takes precedence, and the national power is void.

Jefferson's remarks about the "ancient and fundamental laws of the several States" that would be altered by the operation of the Bank reveal something else about his thinking. However much Jefferson valued the Anglo-Saxon legal heritage, it was nevertheless a basic principle with him that the people of every generation have the right to repeal any law or constitution and begin again from scratch. That is the central point of Jefferson's insistence to Madison on September 6, 1789, that "the earth belongs to the living" and that "no society can make a perpetual constitution, or even a perpetual law."[41] Jefferson never wavered from this principle. What then is the meaning of his invoking here certain "ancient and fundamental laws of the several States" as though they were unchangeable? The answer is that they are changeable—by the people of the state. They are not changeable by the national government of the United States (except perhaps in cases of "invincible necessity"). Whether this was because Jefferson believed that the national people have no right to interfere in the business of the people of a state, or merely that the Bank bill did not truly reflect the will of the (national) people, is an open question. As in so many other cases, including the Kentucky Resolutions, Jefferson was able to frame the alternatives in a way that made it unnecessary for him to choose between national and state majorities: power and privilege lay entirely on one side, liberty and states' rights on the other.

VI

Jefferson wrote his draft of the Kentucky Resolutions during a crisis, when political passions ran extremely high and it was not unreasonable to believe that the fate of the republican experiment hung in the balance. The ratification contest and the controversy over the national bank had been primarily contests between national power and state sovereignty; neither of these fit readily into the Jeffersonian dualism of democracy versus oligarchy. But much of the Federalist political propaganda of the late 1790s played completely into Jefferson's view of what the contest was about. One is struck by the extent to which a fear of Jacobinism overshadowed the earlier Federalist concern for preserving the integrity of national power against the sovereignty claims of the states.[42]

But if the conflicts of the late 1790s had indeed begun to resemble contests over democracy versus oligarchy, then Jefferson's response is all the more puzzling. For his solution to a perceived threat to popular government was to insist on an extreme version of state sovereignty whereby each state, individually, reserved the right to judge and nullify the acts of the national government. The logic by which Jefferson linked problem and remedy is, to say the least, unclear. Some of Jefferson's most sympathetic biographers have found it difficult to swallow the Kentucky Resolutions. Merrill Peterson can only defend them as extreme tactics for extreme circumstances: "In the final analysis it is impossible to say precisely what Jefferson's theory was in the Resolutions of '98. They were not conceived in the oracular realm of constitutional law but in a desperate struggle for political survival. . . . [Jefferson] pursued 'a political resistance for political effect,' without much regard for nuances and ambiguities of doctrine."[43]

There is no question that the tone of the Kentucky Resolutions is desperate. It is quite possible that Jefferson's response to the crisis was deliberately extreme; perhaps he consciously decided to err on the side of liberty. But it still must be asked how state sovereignty came to represent liberty in the first place. The threat posed to civil liberties by the Alien and Sedition Acts are side issues in the Kentucky Resolutions; the central issue is the total amount of power assumed by the national government at the expense of state authority. The Kentucky Resolutions were a response to a crisis, but they built upon elements already present in Jefferson's thought even during the mid-1780s when he supported stronger national government. They also may be linked to certain aspects of Jefferson's argument for a bill of rights during the ratification contest and to his "Opinion on the Constitutionality of a National Bank."

The Kentucky Resolutions use the language of international law, of treaties and their enforcement, to characterize the Union and the Constitution. The government of the United States is a product of a "compact" between the states: "As in all other cases of compact among powers having no common judge, each party has an equal right to judge for itself, as well of infractions as of the mode and measure of redress." Although it is true that this right would only be invoked when the national government has "assumed [powers] which have not been delegated" under the Constitution, it is also the case that the state, not the national government, is the "final judge of the extent of the powers delegated to itself."[44] Therefore, although the doctrine would only be invoked when the powers assumed by the national government threatened liberty, the state is the judge of what threatens liberty. Because the government of a state is likely to regard any significant interference with its powers as a threat to liberty, the effect of Jefferson's formulation is to make the national government's threat to liberty look much more expansive than it would be if liberty were defined independently of state sovereignty.

The treaty language of the Kentucky Resolutions echoes what Jefferson said about the Union in the mid-1780s, when he favored adding some powers to national government. In his "Answers and Observations for Démeunier's Article," he described the United States not as a nation but as a confederation of nations united by a "compact" which was essentially a treaty: "It has been often said that the decisions of Congress are impotent because the Confederation provides no compulsory power. But when two or more nations enter into compact, it is not usual for them to say what shall be done to the party who infringes it. Decency forbids this, and it is unnecessary as indecent, because the right of compulsion naturally results to the party injured by the breach. When any one state in the American Union refuses obedience to the Confederation by which they have bound themselves, the rest have a natural right to compel them to obedience."[45] The problem here is obviously different from that to which the Kentucky Resolutions were addressed. But the underlying constitutional theory is the same. The authority of the national government is derived not from any single American people (as it is for James Wilson, and in a qualified way for Madison) but from the natural right of all nations to enter into treaties and enforce and break those treaties at their own risk. It would follow, of course, that the recalcitrant state would have just as much natural right to resist the compulsion as the other states have to impose it.

If then the national government is a creation of the states, not of a single American people, where then are "the people"? The assumption of power by the national government cannot threaten popular government unless there is a people to threaten.

Jefferson's answer seems to be that for purposes of the Union, the collectivity of the states is the American people. For purposes of union, the "consent of the governed" is indistinguishable from the consent of the states. The general government, he claimed in the Kentucky Resolutions, has assumed a power "to bind the States . . . by laws made, not with their consent, but by others against their consent: that this would be to surrender the form of government we have chosen, and live under one deriving its powers from its own will, and not from our authority."[46] The consent of the people and the consent of the states have here become one and the same. There is no way of distinguishing them even in principle—no possible theoretical ground from which one could question whether the American people have really consented to this extreme version of state sovereignty. Sovereign states are the people.

This same conflation of liberty and the authority of states is implicit throughout the Kentucky Resolutions. Jefferson saw no essential difference between proclaiming that "free government is founded in jealousy, and not in confidence" and insisting that each state has the right to nullify acts of the national government. Jealousy of power is here jealousy directed toward the national government. The same degree of jealousy is never directed against the power and sovereignty claims of the states. State governments may threaten liberty internally, through the power they exercise over their own citizens in "domestic" concerns. But externally, considered as members of the federation, their power does not threaten liberty but only advances it.

Jefferson made exactly the same conflation of "people" and "states" a decade earlier during the ratification debate. In listing his objections to the proposed Constitution for Madison on December 20, 1787, Jefferson, while arguing for the necessity of a bill of rights, included a curious line of argument that is incomprehensible except under the assumption that "the people" and "the states" are one and the same. Jefferson referred to James Wilson's argument to the effect that a bill of rights was unnecessary because under the Constitution the people of the United States reserve to themselves every power not granted to the government; whereas the constitutions of the states required bills of rights because the state governments proceeded under the opposite assumption, assuming all powers not specifically reserved to the people. (Presumably Jefferson had seen a copy of Wilson's October 6, 1787, State House Yard speech or heard a summary of the argument.)[47] To this line of argument Jefferson replied: "To say, as Mr. Wilson does that a bill of rights was not necessary because all is reserved in the case of the general government which is not given, while in the particular ones all is given which is not reserved, might do for the audience to whom it was addressed, but is surely a gratis dictum, opposed by strong inferences from the body of the instrument, as well as from the omission of the clause of our present confederation which had declared that in express terms."[48]

One of Jefferson's objections to Wilson's argument is easy enough to understand: to Jefferson "strong inferences from the body of the instrument" suggested the possibility of expanding the power of the national government. It would be helpful to know what specific inferences Jefferson had in mind (he did not elaborate), but he demonstrated here a healthy skepticism toward Wilson's notion that the general principle "all not given is reserved" would of itself prevent abuses of power.

The strange part of the passage comes at the end, where Jefferson spoke of "the omission of the clause of our present confederation" which had "declared in express terms" the principle that "all is reserved which is not given." Wilson had meant a declaration that all power that is not given to the national government is reserved to the people of the United States. There is no clause to this effect in the Articles of Confederation; the very concept of a single American people is foreign to the document. The "clause of our present confederation" about which Jefferson spoke can only be its Article II: "Each state retains its sovereignty, freedom, and independence, and every power, jurisdiction, and right, which is not by this confederation expressly delegated to the United States, in Congress assembled."

In short, Jefferson saw no essential difference between the people of the United States reserving all powers not granted to the national government and the states reserving to themselves such powers. Nothing could have been further from Wilson's meaning; Wilson saw a strong opposition between the sovereignty of the people and a state's own assertion of sovereignty. It does not matter whether Jefferson misunderstood Wilson's point or understood it and disagreed with it. In either case Jefferson's own view is clear: the "people of the United States" and the community of sovereign states were for Jefferson equivalent terms. It would naturally follow, then, that in any contest between national government and the authority of states, the former represents power and the latter liberty.

For Jefferson—in contrast to Madison—there seems to have been no legitimate instance in which the national government could exercise authority over a state in a way that advanced liberty. Madison's original draft of a bill of rights would have used national authority to prohibit a state from restricting freedom of speech, press, or religion. Despite his attachment to religious liberty, Jefferson would never have supported a bill of rights that added new powers to the national government.

VII

Why did Jefferson's defense of liberty against power take the form of an unequivocal endorsement of state sovereignty? This man so closely identified with national questions, who put the nation's fundamental principles into words, who spent nearly a decade representing the American nation to the world (first as ambassador to France and then as secretary of state), who created and led the first national political party: why would he speak this way about the states, as though no American nation existed at all?

One possible explanation is that he believed states were the best "fence" to liberty (to employ a Lockean term). Jefferson's first concern, the argument would go, was liberty, not state sovereignty. But a national government that does not respect the reserved powers of states will not respect the private and public liberties of the people either. Thus liberty and state sovereignty, though not identical, would in practice stand or fall together.

This is in essence Madison's view of the threat posed by the national government in the 1790s, and to some degree it also characterizes Jefferson's view. But Jefferson took state sovereignty much further than can be explained by a reliance on it to be a "fence" to liberty. The metaphor of a fence to liberty implies that liberty lies beyond the fence. In the Kentucky Resolutions there ceases to be any distinction between the fence and what it is supposed to protect.

Let us consider another possible explanation for the strong link Jefferson believed to exist between liberty and state sovereignty. Jefferson's strong endorsement of states' rights and state sovereignty can be readily, but misleadingly, assimilated to one of his most attractive and enduring ideas: his proposal to encourage political participation by giving as much responsibility as possible to local communities. Writing to P. S. DuPont de Nemours in 1816, Jefferson argued for a participatory structure of local government and claimed that "action by the citizens in person, in affairs within their reach and competence, and in all others by representatives, chosen immediately, and removable by themselves, constitutes the essence of a republic."[49] In his 1816 reply to Samuel Kercheval, who had asked his advice on reforming the Virginia constitution, Jefferson advised: "Divide the counties into wards of such size as that every citizen can attend, when called on, and act in person. Ascribe to them the government of their wards in all things relating to themselves exclusively. . . . [This] will relieve the county administration of nearly all its business, will have it better done, and by making every citizen an acting member of the government, and in the offices nearest and most interesting to him, will attach him

by his strongest feelings to the independence of his country, and its republican constitution."[50]

There is a superficial resemblance between ascribing to each local community, in relation to the government of the state, "all things relating to themselves exclusively" and reserving to each state all "domestic" business, leaving
the national government only that "foreign" and "external" business to which
the states individually were incompetent. But there is a fundamental difference: at no point did he suggest that each local community was the final judge
of the acts of the state government, or that local communities were themselves
the judge of where their own competence and rightful sphere of authority
began and ended, or that local communities could nullify state laws that they
considered unjust. Under Jefferson's ideal Virginia constitution, local governments would have a measure of power and citizens a sphere of participation;
but they are not sovereign. Yet in relation to the national government, Jefferson's states were the ultimate judges of where their authority began and ended;
they did not merely exercise those powers for which they were "competent"
but were themselves the judge of their own competence. Jefferson, in short,
treated states in relation to national government very differently than he
treated local governments in relation to states. It is possible that Jefferson himself may have thought that he was applying the same principles in both cases,
but in fact he was not.

There is one final misleading, or at least insufficient, explanation for Jefferson's attachment to state sovereignty that should be considered. The claim
has sometimes been made that Jefferson was first and last a Virginian and that
his true attachments were to his own state, not the wider United States. He did
after all refer to Virginia as "my country." One might hypothesize that his
strong attachment to states' rights, especially during periods when Virginia was
outvoted in Congress, reflected a powerful, even automatic and instinctive
attachment to Virginia's outlook and needs. Stanley Elkins and Eric McKitrick
in *The Age of Federalism* speak of a "Virginia principle" which disposed men
of talent and experience—above all Jefferson and Madison—to "see everything
in what can only be called, perhaps helplessly, a Virginia way."[51] It would follow that Jefferson's support of state sovereignty and his conflation of state sovereignty with liberty itself ultimately reflected a powerful attachment to
Virginia and an instinctive opposition to anything that threatened its economic
interests and political influence.

This explanation is not easily dismissed and must be at least partly true.

But at the same time there is much evidence that challenges the picture of Jefferson as a provincial Virginian. His criticism of Virginia's constitution and laws was vigorous—not what one would expect from a man whose attachment to its way of life was instinctive and unquestioning.

In certain respects Jefferson was a greater American nationalist than anyone else, even something of a fanatic about it. He wanted the fame of America's heroes broadcast around the world: not just Washington of Virginia but Franklin of Pennsylvania.[52] His peculiar insistence on demonstrating that American animals were just as large as those of the Old World certainly demonstrates a kind of American nationalism.[53] He was interested in and proud of the scientific accomplishments of men from every state.[54] As a diplomat in Europe he was troubled by the reports of anarchy and degeneracy in the United States generally, not just in Virginia. When Virginia passed the Statute on Religious Freedom that Jefferson had drafted, he was of course proud for Virginia; but at the same time he was proud for the entire United States.[55]

Politically as well, at least in certain respects, he was a kind of universal citizen of the United States. A narrowly provincial Virginian could not have written the Declaration of Independence and thereby codified a set of principles shared by the whole United States. During his period of opposition in the 1790s, even as he was giving voice to extreme versions of states' rights dogma, he was creating the first truly national political party and keeping in contact with like-minded men from around the nation. One of the best formulations of his principles from the late 1790s comes in a letter to Elbridge Gerry of Massachusetts.[56] And although he supported a theory of states' rights that could easily justify secession, he at the same time was genuinely anguished at the prospect.[57]

Thus in certain respects Jefferson had a very strong sense of a single American people linked by shared political principles, a common scientific community, geographical similarity, and many other things. But the American people in this sense was tied together entirely through voluntary—i.e., nongovernmental—bonds. If the American people (or "nation") was defined politically, Jefferson would immediately have to face the question of where citizens' ultimate loyalties should lie, with the state or the nation. But if the American people was defined in nonpolitical terms, there would never be a need to choose between the United States and one's own state. Insofar as there was a single American "people," for Jefferson it was not a people defined by participation in shared political institutions (as it was for James Wilson) but in other ways. David Mayer speaks of Jefferson's attraction to the concept of a "natural society": "the idea that there was a natural order of social life, separate and distinct from civil government." Certainly Jefferson's insistence on complete religious liberty was designed to protect from the coercion of government the kind of "natural" and wholly voluntary society constituted by religious belief and also by the community of science. But one can also ask whether Jefferson saw the American federation itself (both before and after the Constitution) as such a "natural society": as a voluntary or nearly voluntary community of sovereign states. The idea has roots in Jefferson's political thought from the earliest period of his public career. Mayer points out that Jefferson's *Summary View of the Rights of British America* (1774) was the only important pamphlet of the Revolution that took the historical view "that the settlers had quit their allegiance upon emigrating to America and had then voluntarily agreed to again become subjects of the king"; Americans were never subjects of the king but from the beginning "a separate, sovereign people."[58] The similarities are striking between this and Jefferson's compact theory of the Union as expressed in the Kentucky Resolutions.

In his less idealistic moments, even Jefferson knew that the Union cannot be entirely consensual. Rhode Island, he wrote in 1786, could be coerced if it acted in ways that disrupted the workings of the whole. (It is hard to imagine Jefferson allowing Virginia to be coerced.) But the Union can at least approach this ideal of pure consensus, insofar as there is a clear, obvious, and natural distinction between national and state business of the kind upon which his argument against a national bank depended. The distinction is so clear that no authoritative judge is required: the people (or the peoples, separately by state) can make the judgment themselves. In a few, very precisely defined set of cases, the federation would need coercive powers (and even here the sovereign state retains a natural right to resist). In all other cases states are left politically entirely to themselves—which does not mean that they close in upon themselves in provincial isolation, but rather that their citizens interact with citizens from other states in purely voluntary ways. That would seem to be Jefferson's ideal, and perhaps the single best explanation for his conflation of state sovereignty with liberty itself. Sovereign states are thus not merely fences to liberty but models of liberty in their mutual relations. (The irony is that the United States, understood in this fashion, would be more free than the states internally, for none of the states would concede a purely consensual bond to their cities and counties. The political authority of the United States becomes in a sense the victim of the higher standards to which Jefferson held it.)

VIII

It is impossible to discuss the question of Jefferson's attachment to state sovereignty without at least a brief mention of slavery. Were Jefferson's attachment to states' rights and the connection he saw between states' rights and liberty itself grounded on a fear of national interference with this peculiar institution which Jefferson himself condemned but did little to change?

Jefferson's thoughts on slavery and on the related problem of race are too complicated to attempt to discuss here. The idea of a permanent antagonism between the power of government and the liberty of citizens explains a great deal of what Jefferson did and said, but it cannot account for his inhibitions about acting against slavery or his thoughts on race. Even less are his thoughts on slavery and race somehow a key to explaining his understanding of power and liberty—as though his whole philosophy of liberty, including the Declaration, were a rationalization of white supremacy. If the Declaration was such a rationalization, it was an especially counterproductive one.

The essentials of Jefferson's doctrine of state sovereignty were already in place in the 1780s, the high point of his willingness to speak and act publicly against slavery, including his willingness to employ congressional power to restrict slavery from the Northwest Territory. So on chronological grounds the hypothesis that he took up a strong version of state sovereignty in order to defend slavery against national interference fails. Insofar as there was a connection in Jefferson's thought between state sovereignty and defensiveness about slavery, it ran in the other direction. Once having convinced himself by the 1790s, on other grounds, that the national government was the most dangerous power, and that state sovereignty represented the principle of liberty in relation to that power, the possibility of national power employed against state authority on behalf of liberty was excluded almost by definition. This is, I believe, the best explanation of the elderly Jefferson's response to the Missouri Compromise in 1820.[59] Jefferson, for better or worse, thought in terms of dualisms, and any practical steps by the national government directed against slavery (even steps similar to those Jefferson himself had supported in the 1780s) would have run afoul of the dualism whereby any increase of national power at the expense of the states meant a net loss of liberty. In Jefferson's world, where the power of government was always arrayed against the liberty of citizens, there was simply no conceptual room for the paradoxes of slavery.

IX

Jefferson's legacy is extraordinarily diverse. In *The Jefferson Image in the American Mind,* Merrill Peterson shows how, almost from the moment of his death, rival versions of the "true" Jefferson split off and did battle with one another over slavery, states' rights, equality, and many other things. *The Jefferson Image* was published in 1960; the contest of rival legacies has continued unabated since then, with some new themes and new emphases.[60]

Given this diversity, it is somewhat arbitrary what aspect of Jefferson one chooses to emphasize when one turns to present-day American life. But certainly the side of Jefferson I have developed here, his distrust of centralized power and attachment to state sovereignty, is, for political reasons, of greater relevance today than it has been for a long time. One erstwhile federal responsibility after another is being devolved to states and local communities, partly for budgetary reasons, partly out of ideological opposition to "big government" as such. The Supreme Court decision in *Jay Printz v. United States* (1997) has resurrected the doctrine of "dual sovereignty" in order to deny the federal government the authority to require state and local officials to carry out federal laws and regulations. In his majority opinion Justice Scalia cited Alexander Hamilton for support in ways that stand his ideas on their head and leave his corpse spinning in the grave. But Jefferson could have been cited without great distortion.

It is true there is much in Jefferson that runs counter to the current political climate. His support for roughly equal distribution of property and his reservations about capitalism do not easily fit. His opposition to governmental promotion of religion does not fit the current conservative agenda either. But this only proves that Jefferson was more consistently suspicious of government power than are many present-day conservatives. On those matters to which modern conservatives turn their somewhat selective suspicion of government power, they can find authentic support in Jefferson. There is distortion in appropriating him this way, but no more than is inevitable in the political use of a figure who lived two centuries ago. Rival versions of Jefferson's legacy are subject to the same limitations.

Now to the conservative appropriation of Jefferson there is a radical counterargument that must be taken seriously. In *The Radical Politics of Thomas Jefferson,* Richard K. Matthews argues that Jefferson's central idea was that "the earth belongs to the living," which makes Jefferson, in Matthews's words, "America's first and foremost advocate of permanent revolution." Matthews is especially interested in the potentially strong Jeffersonian case for redistribution of property. For property laws are merely instrumental to happiness and can be altered as circumstances change; while the right of each generation to free itself of the burdens of the past (which would include past distributions of property) is as fundamental as the right of every individual to life, liberty, and the pursuit of happiness.[61] Matthews concedes that Jefferson's agrarian vision has become unattainable and that some other aspects of his thought, such as his views of blacks and women, have to be revised for modern-day radical politics. But the necessary revisions are in keeping with Jefferson's own progressive view of human nature and human society. By implication, at least, the more conservative aspects of Jefferson's thought drop out as social conditions change; what remains is a radical participatory democracy capable of continually remaking the world.

There is no question that Matthews has effectively drawn out one important aspect of Jefferson's thought, and he is correct to stress Jefferson's willingness to revise property laws in an egalitarian direction. The problem with Matthews's radical reading is that it does not take into account Jefferson's suspicion of energetic government—a suspicion which was at least as central to his thought as the principle that "the earth belongs to the living." Indeed, as I have argued, in Jefferson's thought the right of each generation to rewrite laws and constitutions was inseparable from his fear of political power and its encroachments over time, which make such new beginnings necessary.

This does not by itself preclude a Jeffersonian redistributive politics. What it does preclude, or at least makes very difficult, is any redistribution that would require substantial exercise of political power. And it is difficult to imagine any modern-day redistribution, even fairly modest ones, that would not depend upon a far more energetic government than Jefferson would tolerate. None of the redistributionist measures Jefferson himself supported, such as abolition of entail and primogeniture and the allocation of fifty acres of public land free of charge to every adult white male, require the kind of energetic government that a substantial redistribution of wealth would. By exaggerating the actual redistributive effects of such measures, Jefferson could have it both ways: support a fairly equal distribution of wealth and oppose energetic (especially national) government. Conversely, he was able to convince himself that were it not for energetic government like that practiced by Hamilton, a rough equality of wealth could have been maintained. It is at the very least an open question which way Jefferson would have gone if forced to choose between his commitment to equality and his hostility to energetic government.

This is not to say that a progressive or radical modern-day appropriation of Jefferson is illegitimate. Every modern-day appropriation of Jefferson will be partial, because the diverse pieces of his political vision no longer fit together as they once did (and the fit was questionable even in his own time). As partial appropriations of Jefferson go, the one called for by Matthews is as well grounded as any. My point is only that progressives and radicals who hope to make an exclusive claim to Jefferson's legacy and to delegitimize the conservative appropriation are bound to be disappointed. Jeffersonian faith in the people and Jeffersonian hostility to energetic national government may be found on both ends of the contemporary political spectrum.

Suspicion and distrust of governmental power are central to the enduring political appeal of Jefferson's writings, in both its right-wing and left-wing variants. Populist community organizers suspicious of a distant, inegalitarian, capitalist federal government can quote Jefferson in their contests with conservatives suspicious of a distant, leveling, collectivist federal government.

The Whig hostility to power, which Jefferson shared, is sometimes described as antimodern in orientation. J. G. A. Pocock describes the American Revolution in a way that would probably apply to Jefferson, as founded in a "dread of modernity."[62] Drew McCoy's *The Elusive Republic* describes the way in which Jefferson's political economy and his policy toward the West were designed to delay as much as possible the evolution from a virtuous and healthy agricultural economy to a corrupt and dependent manufacturing economy. Lance Banning describes the Jeffersonians' ever-present fear of "conspiracies against liberty," rooted in the concerns and fears of eighteenth-century English oppositional Whig thought. In all of these respects Jefferson and the political movement he led can be accurately portrayed as antimodern, as hostile to the creation of a modern state and to modern large-scale capitalist economies.

But this is only half the picture. If in certain respects Jefferson is antimodern, it is equally true that there are few things more modern than this Jeffersonian hostility to the power of the modern state. We continually create and institutionalize expansive state powers and at the same time fear or rage against our own creation in a way that is very Jeffersonian. However rooted in Whig tradition Jefferson's concerns were, he was able to elevate them to a level of generality that continues to speak to our time.

What makes Jefferson remarkable is that almost everything he said continues to speak to us: not only his elegant formulation of the principles of popular government but also his hasty judgments, oversimplifications, and stark dualisms. In his strengths as well as his weaknesses Jefferson remains the single best "expression of the American mind."

6

Conclusion

But every difference of opinion is not a difference of principle.
We have called by different names brethren of the same principle.
We are all Republicans, we are all Federalists.
—Thomas Jefferson, First Inaugural Address, 1801

WHAT NEW LIGHT DOES the problem examined in this work—the relation between the liberty of citizens and the degree of power vested in national government—shed on our understanding of the founding of the Republic and the controversies of its first few decades? This has been a study of four individuals, but between them they cover a very wide spectrum of political and theoretical alternatives.

Once more we can draw upon Jefferson to pose the terms of the problem. Was the battle over the degree of power to be vested in the national government a contest between adherents of fundamentally different principles of government? Was it on the contrary merely a "difference of opinion" among men and women who shared the same principles but disagreed about what policies and institutional arrangements would best realize those shared principles in practice?[1]

As is so often the case, Jefferson can be cited in support of either side of the argument. His first inaugural address suggests that Jefferson himself in calmer moments accepted the partisan divisions of the 1790s as differences over how to put into practice shared principles. Everyone, after all, claimed to be republicans; everyone claimed to accept the fundamentals of the Constitution with its separation of powers and partition of authority between national and state governments, however much they disagreed over where to draw that line. If Jefferson's words are taken this way, however, they would be first and foremost as a self-criticism, for Jefferson had as strong a tendency as anyone to magnify differences of opinion into differences of principle.

Cecelia Kenyon's classic essay on the Antifederalists, "Men of Little Faith,"

puts forth a version of the "difference of opinion" thesis, at least with respect
to the ratification contest. Kenyon characterizes the Antifederalists as men who
shared with the supporters of the Constitution the same fundamental commitment to republican government and to written constitutions with separated powers, but who, because of a "profound distrust of man's capacity to
use power wisely and well," could not bring themselves to support a national
constitution founded upon those shared principles.[2] Kenyon's essay is specifically directed toward the contest over the ratification of the Constitution, so
its applicability to the battles of the 1790s is not immediately clear. (She mentions Jefferson only to point out that he had far more faith in the people than
the Antifederalists did.)

But one could construct a similar description of the divisions of the 1790s:
the Jeffersonians, so the argument would go, believed in the need for an effective national government but balked at the means necessary to make it real,
while the Federalists believed in reserving some authority to the states and in
the principle of freedom of the press but panicked too quickly at real or imagined excesses in the exercise of states' rights and civil liberties.

On the other side of the argument, however, must be placed Jefferson's
own unshakable belief that Hamilton and his followers were secret monar-
chists who fully intended to subvert the Republic and the Constitution. When
Jefferson spoke in his inaugural address of "brethren of the same principle,"
he did not have Hamilton or those fully committed to Hamilton's policies in
mind. Even if the charge of monarchism and antirepublican subversion is set
aside—as it should be—the fact remains that something about the way Hamilton sought to expand the power of the national government aroused enormous fears in Jefferson and in many others. Jefferson himself believed that the
principle at stake in the contest of the 1790s was the same principle for which
he and others had fought the Revolution. Even if one disagrees with Jefferson
on this (reminding oneself that Hamilton, too, wrote and fought against the
king and Parliament of England), Jefferson's conviction that he and Hamilton
adhered to fundamentally different political principles cannot be lightly dismissed. Even if it is false, the fact that someone of Jefferson's stature believed
it requires some kind of explanation.

And there have been and continue to be scholars who see not merely differences over the practical applications of shared principles but basic contests
of principle in the battle over the ratification of the Constitution, the Bank of
the United States, and the other major controversies between Federalists and
Republicans in the 1790s. Historians differ on what these fundamental differ-

ences of principle are: some see liberalism versus republicanism; some see democracy versus oligarchy; some consider the contest over political and economic visions of the nation's future the most important—for instance, Jefferson's agrarian ideal versus Hamilton's commercial and industrial vision.[3]

It is not my purpose here either to resolve this means-ends dispute or to take a clear side. Instead I want to use it to call attention to the peculiarity of the problem to which this work is addressed: the problem of the degree of power vested in government (and specifically in national government). There is something about power itself and the practical problems connected with it that defies the means-ends categorization: power is always both means and end, and by its very nature it can be only imperfectly defined and controlled. The men of the age did divide over democracy and political economy and many other issues. But they also divided over the nature of power itself and its practical dynamics in ways that cannot be simply reduced to a matter of who holds power or what it is used to do. Power is a strange thing. No one of the time understood it very well, nor has anyone else.

The central question of this work has been whether, and in what respects, increasing the power of government diminishes the liberty of those subject to its authority. Madison's, Hamilton's, Wilson's, and Jefferson's answers to this question have been examined. Now it is appropriate to step back and ask: what kind of problem is this? For it is in certain respects a very peculiar problem.

I

The problem of how much power to vest in national government is a peculiar one, first of all, because it could be interpreted either as a quite specific, circumscribed, subordinate problem or as the central problem of the republican experiment. It all depends on how the question is approached and what background assumptions are made about the character of power.

Considered as a narrow and specific problem, it would look something like this. All sides in the dispute over the degree of power to vest in national government admitted the necessity of a national power capable of providing for the common defense, regulating commerce between the states, paying the nation's debts to citizens and foreigners, and many other things. All sides admitted that power is necessary and yet conceded that it is dangerous and thus accepted a wide range of checks and limitations: separation of powers, frequent elections, specific constitutional prohibitions on government action. Hamilton and Wilson praised "energy" in government and criticized those who would place undue restrictions on public power, but both men fully supported an array of checks and restraints that would look like a straitjacket to a European statesman of the age. The differences seem to be ones of degree and emphasis: men who agreed on the extremes to be avoided drew the line in different places; they agreed about what the dangers were but disagreed about which of these dangers was most pressing under the circumstances.

Before the ratification of the Constitution, the question of how much power to vest in national government involved disagreements over constitutional design, which are not the same as disagreements over fundamental political principles. After the ratification of the Constitution, the problem became even more circumscribed: how to interpret certain ambiguous passages ("necessary and proper") in a document accepted as authoritative by all sides. Whether the national government should have the power to charter banks and other corporations is certainly an important enough issue for purposes of ordinary politics, but it hardly seems to involve issues as great as those over which the Revolution was fought. Whether the national government should have power to restrict the press through the Sedition Act raised more obvious issues of principle. But the principle at stake is confused by the fact that many of those—including Jefferson—who opposed it did so not because of the type of restrictions it placed on the press (Jefferson favored similar kinds of restrictions at the state level) but because of the national power it assumed. Aside from the issues of national authority involved, the types of restrictions Jefferson and Hamilton would have placed upon press liberty were broadly similar.[4]

In these and many other respects differences over the degree of power to be vested in national government can be portrayed as a second- or third-order problem, a family quarrel among "brethren of the same principle." The heat of the political blaze of the 1790s, the argument would go, owed more to partisan enthusiasm, to the youthful insecurities of a new nation, and to the economic and sectional interests at stake than to any fundamental principle of republican government.

It is true that the quarrels over national power involved differences of degree. But what gave these differences of degree such enormous significance was the elusive and dynamic character of political power itself: no one could be sure that it would keep to the degree assigned to it. The arguments concerned not merely differences over how much power ought to be assigned to each branch and level of government; they were also arguments over whether that assignment was stable or unstable and the probable direction of change.

Madison, for example, opposed the national government's having a power to charter a bank not because of the power immediately at stake but because he feared that the constitutional justification Hamilton sought for this power would set in motion an indefinitely expansive effect: each means in turn would become an end, thus allowing new and more expansive means. Jefferson's suspicion of a powerful national government was based on a more extreme and more general version of the same fear: in all times and all places the tendency of power is to expand and break its bounds, and for this reason it must be held in place by "iron chains." But one does not have to hold a Jeffersonian view of power to recognize its unstable and elusive character. Hamilton feared instability and change in the opposite direction: the degree of power assigned to the national government by the Constitution would diminish over time and be rendered merely nominal, unless it was given additional supports as soon as possible. Hamilton and Jefferson had wholly opposed views of the probable direction of change, but they both believed political power is very difficult to define and control.

These differing views of how power is likely to shift and in what direction are linked to different theoretical views of the character of power itself and its relation to popular consent. These theories are never spelled out explicitly and at length; it is unreasonable to expect the equivalent of Hobbes's *Leviathan*. But the rudiments of theories are present. For example, Madison was convinced that what matters above all is not the amount of power vested in national government (within a fairly broad range) but whether there exists a clear understanding—a "sense of the people"—about how much and what kind of power national government shall have. If such an understanding is there and is honored, then even a fairly energetic national government is safe. If there is no clear understanding, or—even worse—if there is one, but it is violated, then there is nothing to prevent power from expanding without limit. There is an implicit theory here about what causes power to remain stable or become unstable. It differs from Jefferson's conviction that the tendency is everywhere for government to gain, and liberty to yield, ground and from Hamilton's conviction that the national government "must swallow up the State powers, otherwise it will be swallowed up by them." Both Jefferson's and Hamilton's views of the matter are likewise based upon implicit theories of power that could in principle be reconstructed.

The problem of power is on one hand the central problem of republican government and for that reason extremely wide-ranging in character; it is on the other hand an extremely fine-grained problem in which important distinctions (such as the difference between Madison's and Jefferson's reasons for opposing Hamilton's policies) can be easily overlooked or misunderstood.

It is a broad problem because if it cannot be resolved, republican government is unsustainable. The Revolution came about, in the first instance, because in the colonists' view the king and Parliament had exercised a power that knew no boundaries, that overleaped even those limits accepted under the English constitution. The introductory chapter of this work argues that the Declaration of Independence is directed not so much to powerful government as to abusive government; the practical relation between the amount of power vested in government and the tendency toward abuse of power is left unspecified. But energetic government can be prevented from becoming an abusive government only if political power, elusive as it is, can be defined and controlled with at least rough accuracy. And men and women can differ enormously over how to accomplish this even if they share the same republican principles.

Consider once again Kenyon's description of the Antifederalists as "men of little faith": they shared the same principles of government as the supporters of the Constitution but would not apply those principles on the national scale because of a "profound mistrust" of power. This characterization presupposes that their fear of power was taken to a pathological degree. If on the contrary their view of power—which has much in common with Jefferson's view of power—is accepted, then the whole problem is transformed. If one accepts the premise that every power that can be abused will be abused, if this is one's diagnosis of what led to the Revolution in the first place, and one considers it an obvious truth that even the other side is capable of comprehending, then the tables are turned: it then becomes the Antifederalists who kept the faith and the supporters of the Constitution who turned their back on it. This demonstrates how much depends upon one's underlying view of the dynamics of power.

Because the Revolution was fought to protect liberty from the encroachments of power, deciding how much power to vest in government is an extremely broad problem. But it is at the same time a very specific, fine-grained, detail-dependent problem. It is not one in which there are only two sides; it is not like the act of declaring whether one supports or opposes independence and republican government. In arguments over how much power to vest in a republican form of government, fierce political battles may be fought over differences so subtle they can be easily overlooked or misrepresented by historians and even by the participants themselves. This is one of the reasons Madison's apparent reversal on national power has always been so difficult to explain (or so easy to explain on false grounds). We too easily assume that Jefferson and Hamilton represented the two genuine possibilities of the age and that everything in between is slippery inconsistency. We find it hard to believe that there can be a position on national power in between Jefferson and Hamilton, equally distant from both, possessing a theoretical integrity of its own. Yet this was precisely Madison's case.

The implications of this extend beyond our interpretation of Madison. Every inch of the territory between Jefferson and Hamilton, which we thought we knew so well, deserves to be newly explored from the perspective of the problems raised in this work. Our received view of the possibilities of the age makes it difficult to believe that someone could be as democratic as Jefferson and as nationalist as Hamilton—at least in a form that possesses any consistency. But James Wilson was nothing if not consistent. His case demonstrates that the possibilities of the age were not arranged along a single axis; that commitment to democracy and support for energetic national government were separable dimensions even then.

II

This peculiar problem of power was not addressed in a vacuum. It is not as though the quantity of power to vest in national government was the only significant division of the age. The statesmen of the age also differed in their visions of the American economic future, in their views of the appropriate degree of democracy, in their attachment to their own state and sectional interests, and many other things. They differed, in short, not only over how much national power there should be but also over who should hold it and what it should be used to accomplish.

These are separable problems, both in logic and in practice. For this reason understanding a theorist-statesman's view of national power provides no magic key unlocking all the disputes of the age; it cannot and should not be used to explain everything. But the reverse is also the case: positions on national power cannot be explained as simple reflections of quarrels over democracy, substantive policy goals, or partisan maneuvering. The peculiar problem of national power was always connected to, but never reducible to, the other problems and divisions of the age.

Given a particular statesman's position on the question of how much power to place in national government, one cannot immediately know how much faith in democracy that statesman had or what he would have used the power of government to accomplish. Two theories of republican government— one founded in suspicion of power (Jefferson), the other valuing energetic government and asking for a generous measure of trust (Wilson)—can be democratic to an equal degree. The converse is also true: two theorists of republican government (Hamilton and Wilson) may be equally committed to energetic government and yet differ significantly in their degree of faith in the political capacity of the people at large.

The same holds for commitment to substantive policy goals. In the sphere of political economy, Jefferson's and Madison's views were broadly similar: both supported policies designed to preserve the predominantly agrarian character of the nation and believed (excessively) in the efficacy of commercial sanctions in relations among nations. But on matters of national power, constitutional interpretation, and state sovereignty, their views diverged widely even during their periods of closest political cooperation.

What is distinctive about Jefferson is precisely that he conflated all three of these problems that I have argued must be understood separately: how much power, who holds it, and what policies it will be used to advance. From Jefferson's perspective a powerful national government was necessarily also one that ignored the voice of the people and favored speculators and industrialists at the expense of virtuous farmers. Energetic government equals government in the interest of the rich and powerful, equals oppressive government, equals antirepublican government. Though it is impossible to answer such a question here, it is worth asking: to what degree are scholars of the period still under the sway of Jefferson's description of what the contests of the 1790s were about?

One of the purposes of this work has been to disaggregate the elements of this Jeffersonian synthesis; to show that at least in the late 1780s and early 1790s, the range of political possibilities was much more diverse and fluid than we usually recognize. But Jefferson's radical simplification of the political divisions of the age—in which every political division is described as a contest between those who have faith in the people and those who side with power and privilege—would not have had such enormous and enduring influence unless it contained an element of truth. Sometimes this is indeed what is at stake in the contest. If one considers what Federalism had become by the late 1790s, as panic over the French Revolution and the fever of possible war with France or England took its toll, one finds its spokesmen falling all too often into exactly the antidemocratic mold cut out for them by Jeffersonian ideology. Opposition to the power of national government and to the policies of those in control of the government was attributed to an inflamed, democratic, Jacobin mob.

To a certain degree Hamilton himself fell into this trap. Although he was never a democrat, Hamilton's contributions to *The Federalist* and his public reports as treasury secretary display a degree of faith in the deliberative capacity of the people at large that gives way to a behind-the-barricades tone by the late 1790s—though the early faith in the public reappeared when he argued the *Croswell* case in 1803.

A scholar who believes that the divisions of the age were essentially between "democrats" and "oligarchs" (in other words, one who accepts Jefferson's own categories) might claim that what the Federalists had become by 1800 was already marked out in 1787. The move to strengthen the national government in the first place, the argument would go, was motivated above all by a fear of the democratic mob; panic over the French Revolution is merely the old fear of Shays' Rebellion raised to a higher level.

There are at least two problems with this way of reading 1800 back into 1787. First, it ignores the wide range of problems the advocates of the Constitution sought to address that had nothing directly to do with fear of a democratic mob; problems, for example, caused by claims of state sovereignty that could not be solved even if "the better sorts of people" were in control of state governments.

Second, it does not take into account the way in which the range of political possibilities can be narrowed over time, sometimes as a result of unforeseeable events, sometimes by deliberate efforts to eliminate the possibility of any middle ground. There was a richness to the political spectrum in 1791 that was gone by 1798 (if not sooner). In 1791 Hamilton would willingly have made common cause with men more democratic than himself in his battle against overly powerful states; his enemy was not democracy but state sovereignty. The question is at least worth asking whether a democratic nationalism of the kind that came into its own in the mid-nineteenth century could have developed earlier if the events of the 1790s had not intervened. James Wilson pointed in that direction, but he lacked Jefferson's capacity for political and moral leadership.

It should also be stressed that all four of the men examined here were theorists as well as statesmen. One of the tasks of a statesman is to navigate a course among the available political choices. But one of the tasks of a theorist is to call into question the very way in which those choices are framed in the first place and to propose other ways of constructing the range of choices even if realizing these new options are not possible immediately. Madison, Hamilton, and Wilson, all in different ways, attempted to frame in a new way the possibilities of reconciling the power of government and the liberty of citizens. Jefferson, in contrast, reaffirmed the received wisdom on power and liberty. But in doing so he did not blindly defer to tradition or merely follow tracks clearly laid out; he reinvented the tradition itself in a republican form and introduced elements that had no counterpart in the English original. Jefferson did not take the range of political choices as a brute fact; he himself helped create the range—much more effectively, in fact, than did any of the other three.

III

This work has occasionally referred to the crisis leading up to the Civil War. The link is an obvious one to make, because division over the rightful power of national government was one of the two great unresolved problems that produced the Civil War—slavery was the other. One of the principal themes running through the analysis of Madison, Hamilton, Wilson, and Jefferson has been the conflict between nation and states. I have criticized scholarly attempts to present the nation-state conflict of the 1780s and 1790s as derivative of some other more fundamental conflict, such as democracy versus oligarchy. I have stressed Hamilton's fear of a sovereignty contest between national government and states in which the advantages would lie with the states, Wilson's attempt to substitute the idea of popular sovereignty for the perverse doctrine of state sovereignty, and Jefferson's extreme version of state sovereignty in the Kentucky Resolutions. No matter how often one reminds oneself of the danger of reading history backwards, it is impossible to prevent knowledge of the Civil War from influencing analysis of earlier nation-state conflicts. In reading Jefferson's Kentucky Resolutions of 1798, it is impossible to forget the use made of his writings by the nullificationists of the 1830s and by the secessionists in the Civil War.

But there are also differences between the earlier and later contests over national power, and these are as important as the similarities. The most obvious difference is the role played by slavery in the crisis leading up to the Civil War; slavery was not the issue that drove the contests over national power in 1787 or 1798. Slavery did indeed lurk like "a serpent under the table" at the Federal Convention, and it was never far from the minds of Jefferson and many others. It could easily have become the central issue in contests over national power—at enormous political cost—but was deliberately neutralized at the convention by mutual agreement of northern and southern delegates.

A second difference is that the national government was new and untried in 1787 and relatively so even in 1800, whereas it was no longer new in 1861. This gives a very different cast to the type of despotism feared by the southern secessionists as compared to the Antifederalists or the Jeffersonians of the 1790s. The Antifederalist and Jeffersonian fear of national power was closely connected with the novelty both of the republican experiment itself and of the national government. It was not completely unreasonable to suspect that some men might secretly renounce their republican principles and return to the monarchism in which they had been brought up; it was not unreasonable to fear that a wholly new set of national institutions could be bent to the interests of designing men. It was precisely the vagueness of the threat posed by national power that most characterized the fears of the Antifederalists, Jefferson, and even Madison: once power has overstepped its boundaries, there is no way of predicting what it will do. (Thus Madison's fear that if the national government began chartering corporations in violation of a clear understanding that it had no such power, then it might also "take up the care of religion into their own hands.") It was this same powerful but vague fear that Hamilton believed would be remedied by the ordinary actions of the national government itself.

By the time of the Civil War, in contrast, the power of the national government was no longer a novelty; there was a tradition and decades of precedent to give its operations a stable and predictable character. The men who led the secession of the southern states were not driven by vague fears but by something quite specific: the national government under Republican control would restrict the expansion of slavery and abolish it in the long run. To them this was despotism; they did not need to speculate about what else the national government might do.

The problem of sovereignty provides one of the clearest links between the conflicts of the 1780s and 1790s and the crisis leading up to the Civil War. It was in the name of state sovereignty that Georgia refused to be sued for debt and refused even to appear before the Supreme Court; it was in the name of popular sovereignty that James Wilson rejected Georgia's claim. Sixty-eight years later it was in the name of state sovereignty that the southern states—including Georgia—seceded from the Union; it was in the name of popular sovereignty that Lincoln opposed them. In this case the continuities are impossible to overlook.

Nevertheless there are subtle differences even here. The discourse on sovereignty of the 1780s and 1790s has an experimental and tentative character. Not everyone was locked into dogmatic either/or propositions on sovereignty. Madison, for example, was relatively unconcerned about strict consistency on matters of sovereignty. At least some of those who employed the concept of state sovereignty may have used it primarily to express their opposition to a system whereby all political power was concentrated in the national government—without necessarily intending to make the states into final and absolute authorities. The importance of Wilson's conception of popular sovereignty, whereby "the people" freely decide how much authority each level and branch of government shall have, is that it provides a theoretical language whereby one can oppose complete consolidation without running to the other extreme and placing excessive power in the states.

The extreme version of state sovereignty expressed in Jefferson's Kentucky Resolutions is sometimes explained (and defended) as a tactic employed in a particular crisis rather than the invocation of a principle. The preceding chapter casts doubt on this interpretation by showing that similar notions of state sovereignty may be found even in Jefferson's writings of the mid-1780s when he favored adding powers to the national government. But if the tactical interpretation of the Kentucky Resolutions is accepted (and Jefferson's use was at least partly tactical), then it is further evidence of the fluid and undogmatic ways in which the concept of sovereignty could be employed in the early years of the Republic. (Whatever his intentions, however, Jefferson contributed greatly to the dogmatic version of state sovereignty later employed by the nullificationists and secessionists.)

The final and perhaps most important difference between the national-state contests of the early Republic and those that led up to the Civil War involves the principle of majority rule. Those who defended state sovereignty and state power during the ratification contest and during the battle over Hamilton's policies were persuaded that the majority of the American people were on their side. (Whether they were correct in believing this is impossible to determine and does not change the point.) Madison regarded the Virginia Resolutions as a way of using the machinery of the states to express a position supported by a majority of Americans. Jefferson's Kentucky Resolutions are quite different; taken at face value they would allow a single state to resist the authority of a clear national majority. But in practice Jefferson, like Madison, believed that the majority was on his side. So he did not have to choose explicitly between his commitment to majority rule and the strong version of state sovereignty set forth in the resolutions. There is at least some doubt about which way Jefferson would have gone if forced to make such a choice.

For the southern nullifiers and secessionists, all doubt on this point was removed: state sovereignty took precedence over a national majority, which was just another form of despotic power over their own state and their own peculiar way of life. And for the antimajoritarian theorists—John C. Calhoun, for instance—majority tyranny did not mean the same thing that it meant for Madison. Madison feared a passionate and impulsive majority but believed that if prevented from having its way too quickly, the majority would tend over time toward moderation and justice. The nullifiers and secessionists, in contrast, were certain that the majority of the American people were against them and their way of life; and it made no difference whether this majority was transient or enduring.

They found much better support in Jefferson than in Madison. But even Jefferson could be cited in support only after much of what he stood for had been jettisoned.[5] Jefferson's condemnation of slavery had to be rejected. His strong commitment to democracy and majority rule had to be downplayed, not only with regard to issues pitting national government against the states but also on issues internal to states, because this would have threatened the control of the large plantation owners. His principle that "the earth belongs to the living" had to give way to a defense of custom and inviolable property rights. All that remained was Jefferson's doctrine of state sovereignty and a doctrine of revolution stripped of the faith in natural rights that had given it life.

Jefferson, like the Bible, was quoted on both sides of the Civil War. There is no way of answering the question of what side he really belonged to. It is more important to realize that Jefferson put together a sweeping synthesis of elements that do not always occur together. The elements of the Jeffersonian synthesis came apart as soon as he died, if not sooner.[6] One can if one likes criticize Jefferson for the use made of some of these elements after his death. But we can probably learn more from a critique of Jefferson's faith that all of these elements—majority rule, state sovereignty, natural rights, opposition to energetic government—belong naturally together in the first place. The present work has examined Jefferson, and the age as a whole, in that spirit.

IV

What form does this peculiar problem—deciding how much power to vest in national government—take in our own time? And what can we learn from the efforts of Madison, Hamilton, Wilson, and Jefferson to address that problem more than two hundred years ago?

Can it be said that we face a moment of critical decision about the scope and purpose of national power? It is always easy to claim that the decisions one's own generation must make are somehow especially critical ones. There have been many moments of critical decision with regard to national power since the passing of the Founding generation, the Civil War standing at the top of the list and the New Deal era close behind. It would be presumptuous to claim that the critical decisions we face are somehow more critical than those faced by our grandmothers or our great-grandfathers.

But the form the problem of national power takes today and the type of decisions that must be made are distinctly different than ever before. Through much of United States history, the problem was one of deciding whether to expand national power, and how to do so in a way consistent with liberty. This has been particularly the case throughout most of the twentieth century: from the beginning of the century until the late 1970s, the range of activities touched by one branch or another of the national government was always on the increase.

Today—at least within the domestic sphere—we are no longer discussing whether to expand national power and how to go about it. We are discussing whether to shrink it and how to do so. Even those who oppose this reduction in the scope of national government are, in this political climate, forced to talk about where and where not to cut government.

This is a political contest in which all of us—scholars included—are partisans to some degree. The temptation in such a struggle is to reach for any available weapon. And the authority of the Founders has always been an especially effective political weapon. It always gives an argument an additional rhetorical charge to claim that on some current political or constitutional question Madison, or Jefferson, or Hamilton—or perhaps even all three!—would take your side entirely. (Perhaps Wilson, too, will someday enjoy this ambiguous honor.)

This is an abuse of the Founders' authority. We cannot with any certainty predict what side they would have taken on a question that arises under political, social, and economic circumstances they could not possibly have foreseen. Jefferson, for example, opposed both powerful government and powerful private corporations. There is no way of determining with certainty which side he would take in a question pitting the power of the former against that of the latter. One can make a Jeffersonian argument either way, and that is legitimate;

but one cannot lay claim to Jefferson himself. And the same goes for all the other statesmen of the Founding era, with respect to all the other developments they did not foresee or intend.

But abuse of the Founders' authority is possible in the first place only because there are some undeniable kinships between our power-liberty problems and theirs. They would certainly recognize something of themselves in our current arguments over the power of national government even if they prudently refrained from taking sides. It is fair at least to imagine them posing questions to us based on their own experience with problems of liberty and power. I will close with reflections of my own inspired by the passionate arguments of men long dead. I employ quotation marks around their names to relieve them of responsibility for what follows.

V

One of the arguments advanced by the advocates of smaller government is that the current size and scope of government has had the effect of stifling the liberty and energy of citizens to a dangerous degree. Occasionally this argument is made with the help of Alexis de Tocqueville's prediction that the American love of equality combined with centralization of power would lead to a kind of soft despotism. The only way to prevent this suffocation of liberty, it would follow, is to reduce the power of national government significantly; the energy and initiative of a free citizenry will rise up to fill the space vacated by government.

The question that must be asked here is: does every reduction of the size and scope of government increase the quantity of freedom? Or will some reductions increase liberty and others diminish it? We could think of this as a choice between a "Jeffersonian" and a "Madisonian" perspective on power and liberty. If there is an inherent antagonism between the power of government and the liberty of those subject to its authority, then it almost does not matter where one begins the process of reducing government. All reductions lead to greater liberty; "more liberty" and "less government" are equivalent expressions.

On the other hand, if there is no inherent antagonism between the power of government and the liberty of those subject to its authority, then it makes a very great difference where one reduces the power of government and how one proceeds to do so. In this case if one hopes to increase liberty by cutting back on government, one would have to proceed in an issue-specific manner:

one would have to first identify particular types of government activities that restrict freedom too much or whose purposes could be accomplished in a less restrictive manner and then decide what to cut and where. In this case liberty is defined independently, rather than as the simple inverse of government power. And one would have to admit the possibility that at least some of the time, preserving and advancing liberty require more government in some specific respect. The degree of power vested in government and the range of liberty—public and private—enjoyed by citizens become two different matters whose interrelation in practice is complicated and not readily predictable.

There are methods of reducing the power of government that presuppose a "Jeffersonian," inherently inverse relation between power and liberty. One such method can be described as cutting off the blood supply. By drastically reducing the revenues available to government, one can force cutbacks to occur even though one cannot know what will be cut. One can in this way significantly reduce the power of a regulatory agency without actually repealing the regulations it is charged with enforcing; one simply reduces the funds needed to enforce the law, knowing that as a result there will be less government—somewhere. Another way of forcing a general reduction of power would be to impose "constitutional shackles" (to use a Hamiltonian epithet)—such as the proposal that all tax increases require a two-thirds majority (while tax cuts would still require only a simple majority). One cannot know for certain what would be cut as a result of such a rule, but one can predict with certainty that it would lead to less government on the whole. And it would follow—by the logic of the inverse relation between power and liberty—that every such reduction expands liberty.

Only on the "Jeffersonian" presupposition that all power inhering in government is that much less liberty enjoyed by the people can one be confident that such across-the-board reductions of national power will expand the range of liberty enjoyed by citizens. If in contrast power and liberty are defined independently and issue-specifically, a general deficit-forced cutback of government would be at least as likely to hinder liberty as to advance it—especially if what is and what is not cut are determined by the degree of political power enjoyed by those whose interests are at stake.

Not every cutback in the activities and responsibilities of the federal government, however, has followed this "cut off the blood supply" logic. Some of the most significant cutbacks have been issue-specific in character, the most prominent example being the elimination of Aid for Families with Dependent Children as a federal entitlement. Many of those responsible for the elimination of the federal entitlement believe that the federal welfare system caused families to remain trapped in poverty by creating a culture of dependency. This shift of ultimate responsibility for poverty to the states was accompanied by a number of rules intended to force people off welfare and into work. The end result, according to proponents of the change, will be to improve the lives of people in poverty: make them more energetic, more responsible, more free.

The argument that the federal commitment to welfare should be eliminated does not logically entail that all federal responsibilities should be cut back. One can believe that the federal welfare system makes Americans less free without claiming that the federal government is too powerful in every respect. However, many of those who supported the elimination of welfare as a federal entitlement did indeed subscribe to both propositions. And this leads to what I believe is the central question that must be asked of those who supported the recent changes in the welfare system. Given that one of the aims of the policy is to lead people out of dependency and into freedom: is that a result which one hopes and expects will occur but which might also fail? Or is it regarded as a result which is, by definition, already accomplished in the cutback itself?

In the first case one would have to monitor the policy carefully to see whether in fact it is producing the intended effects—improved job prospects, greater personal responsibility, independence—and be willing to alter it if those effects turn out to be very different from what was expected. In the second case there is no need either to monitor the policy or to change it because the cutback of government responsibility is of itself supposed to make people more free: they immediately become more free when government ceases to support them, and what they do with their lives afterward is their own problem.

And here the fundamental distinction between the two ways of conceiving power and liberty returns in full force. Are the power of government and the liberty of citizens simple inverses of each other? If so, then it would follow that people in poverty become more free as a direct result of the elimination of government aid. If on the other hand the power of government and the liberty of citizens are not simple inverses of each other—if instead they are separately defined and practically connected in ways not easily predictable—then greater personal freedom and responsibility are merely possible results of the radical changes in our nation's approach to poverty; it could come out otherwise.

The cutbacks of federal power have not been unopposed. But the opposition has for the most part a rather confused and untheoretical character. The general tendency among the opposition has been to accept the principle that national government should be cut but oppose its being taken too far. Thus fundamental conflicts are resolved, temporarily, by splitting the difference. The opponents of significant reductions in federal responsibilities have as yet no principled answer to the question of what should and what should not be cut—much less a publicly convincing argument against making significant cuts at all. The policies to which they object are driven by a principled opposition to big government on the grounds that it stifles freedom; this requires a principled response which also speaks of freedom.

The closest approximation to a principled response is a historical justification of an expansive role for government. Opponents of massive cutbacks of federal power point out that through most of American history, it has been the national government that has tended to protect and expand civil and political liberties while state and local governments have often been the most restrictive of liberty. It was the national government that ended slavery and segregation and that has defended the rights of religious dissenters from intolerant local communities.

All of this is true enough, and too easily forgotten by enthusiasts for "devolution." The historical record serves as a reminder that national power and liberty sometimes do expand together. The argument challenges the other side to explain why they believe the current cutbacks of federal power will not simply lead back to the same kind of intolerance and inequality federal power sought to remedy in the first place.

But a historical argument by itself is insufficient. The fact that at several key moments in the past an expansive national government went hand in hand with an expansion of liberty does not prove that the same remedy is appropriate in the present and future. The effects of policies always change over time. A particular expansion of national power could be liberty-enhancing at one point and yet set in motion a series of effects that diminish liberty later. For example, one of the arguments in favor of transferring certain responsibilities to state and local governments is that when too many important decisions are made at the national level, political participation by ordinary citizens tends to evaporate. This "Jeffersonian" line of argument resonates with people at both ends of the political spectrum. Whether the expansion of federal power is in fact the cause of the political alienation complained of and whether devolution of responsibilities is an appropriate remedy are open questions. But to those who believe centralization of power is the cause, it is no answer at all merely to point to the good things the federal government has accomplished in the twentieth century.

Instead the whole question of national power has to be considered anew, giving due attention to the historical record but without assuming that the same solutions are appropriate now as were appropriate thirty or sixty years ago. One of the most inspiring characteristics of Madison was his willingness to consult history while rejecting many of its conventionally accepted lessons (like the assumption that republics were unsuited to large territories). In this as in other respects, we ought to approach contemporary problems of power and liberty in a "Madisonian" spirit.

Notes

Abbreviations

LWJM   *Letters and Other Writings of James Madison.* 4 vols. Philadelphia, 1865.

PAH   Harold C. Syrett et al., eds. *The Papers of Alexander Hamilton.* 27 vols. New York, 1961–87.

PJM   William T. Hutchinson et al., eds. *The Papers of James Madison.* Chicago and Charlottesville, Va., 1962—.

PTJ   Julian P. Boyd et al., eds. *The Papers of Thomas Jefferson.* Princeton, N.J., 1950—.

TJW   Merrill Peterson, ed. *Thomas Jefferson: Writings.* New York, 1984.

WJW   Robert G. McCloskey, ed. *The Works of James Wilson.* 2 vols. Cambridge, Mass., 1967.

1. Introduction

1. *TJW,* 917.

2. *PJM* 11:299.

3. A good example is Morgan, *American Slavery, American Freedom.*

4. These passages are cited and discussed in chaps. 3 and 5.

5. The entire correspondence between Madison and Jefferson is collected in Smith, *Republic of Letters.*

6. For example: on June 2, according to Madison's own notes, "Mr. [Madison] & Mr. Wilson observed" (jointly) that it was bad policy to make the chief executive removable by request of state legislatures (Farrand, *Records* 1:86); on June 6 Madison seconded Wilson's motion to give the judiciary a share in the revision of laws (ibid., 1:138); on June 7 Madison and Wilson led the opposition to Dickinson's motion that "members of the 2nd branch ought to be chosen by the individual Legislatures" (ibid., 1:150–54). On June 19 Hamilton "assented to the doctrine of Mr. Wilson" that the states separated from Britain "not *Individually* but *Unitedly*" (ibid., 1:324); on June 21 Madison, Wilson, and Hamilton led the opposition to the proposal that members of the lower house be appointed by the state legislatures.

7. Bailyn, *Faces of Revolution*, 230. See also Rakove, *Original Meanings*, 143.

8. The claim that Jefferson was influenced above all by Scottish moral philosophy is advanced in Wills, *Inventing America*.

9. On this point I agree with Zuckert, who argues that the "Lockean political philosophy" and "Whig political science" were "modes of political analysis proceeding at different levels and addressing different questions" rather than mutually exclusive competing traditions (*Natural Rights and the New Republicanism*, xix).

10. For the political philosophy of the Declaration, see Zuckert, *Natural Rights Republic*.

11. Jefferson to Henry Lee, May 8, 1825, *TJW*, 1501.

12. Jefferson to Edward Carrington, May 27, 1788, *PTJ* 13:208.

13. "What makes [rights] insecure is not stated. . . . Perhaps the Declaration remains silent on the nature and severity of the threat to rights because that topic escaped the 'harmonizing sentiments of the day'" (Zuckert, *Natural Rights Republic*, 28).

14. The ambiguities of the Declaration in this regard are discussed in Pocock, "States, Republics, and Empires," 59–60.

15. Bailyn, *Ideological Origins;* Wood, *Creation of the American Republic;* Banning, *Jeffersonian Persuasion*.

16. Trenchard and Gordon, *Cato's Letters*, 803–4.

17. *PTJ* 13:208.

18. For example, Diamond's essay "*The Federalist*, 1787–1788." However, in "*The Federalist*'s View of Federalism," Diamond distinguishes between Madison and Hamilton.

19. Mason, "*The Federalist*—A Split Personality."

20. Epstein, *Political Theory of* The Federalist; Millican, *One United People*.

21. Recent exceptions to this common assumption include Banning's *Sacred Fire of Liberty* and Rakove's *Original Meanings*, which are discussed in the following chapter. Madison's consistency is also a central theme of McCoy, *Last of the Fathers*.

22. Elkins and McKitrick, *Age of Federalism*, 230–41.

23. Ibid., 79.

24. On this theme, see McCoy, *Elusive Republic*.

25. Jefferson to Madison, Sept. 6, 1789, *TJW*, 959–64.

26. Hobbes, *Leviathan*, chap. 21.

27. See, for example, Banning, "Some Second Thoughts on Virtue"; Zuckert, *Natural Rights Republic*, 202–10.

2. James Madison on Power and Liberty

1. Farrand, *Records* 1:464.

2. Bailyn describes the dissident Whig tradition which the American colonists had incorporated into their political worldview: "Most commonly the discussion of power centered on its essential characteristic of aggressiveness: its endlessly propulsive ten-

dency to expand itself beyond legitimate boundaries. . . . [Power] inhered naturally in government and was the possession and interest of those who controlled government, just as liberty, always weak, always defensive . . . inhered naturally in the people and was their peculiar possession and interest" (*Ideological Origins*, 56–59). See also Wood, *Creation of the American Republic*, 3–45.

3. Madison to Jefferson, March 19, 1787, *PJM* 9:318.

4. Farrand, *Records* 1:318–19, 2:440, 589. For Madison's continued concern after the Federal Convention about the lack of a negative, see Madison to Jefferson, Oct. 24, 1787, *PJM* 10:205–20.

5. See Madison to Nicholas P. Trist, Dec. 1831, *LWJM* 4:204–11, where Madison attacked the "preposterous and anarchical" doctrine of nullification and distinguished it from the Virginia Resolutions of 1798. For the elderly Madison's battles with the doctrine of nullification, see McCoy, *Last of the Fathers*, 119–70.

6. Madison insisted on his own consistency over time in his December 1831 letter to Nicholas P. Trist, *LWJM* 4:204–11.

7. Banning, *Sacred Fire of Liberty*, 2–3. See also Riemer, who asks: "How, many wonder, could Madison, the powerful and prophetic nationalist of 1787, become by the late 1790s the narrow, pedantic advocate of states' rights?" (*James Madison*, 5). Riemer follows with a capsule description of various explanations offered over the years for Madison's political shifts.

8. Gay, *James Madison*, 172. For another late nineteenth-century view, see Hunt, *Life of James Madison*, 211.

9. See, for example, Burns, *James Madison*.

10. "In policy he remained an advocate of the use of federal power for the public good, up to the limit of its discernible existence. But the spectacle of chronic abuse of that power propelled him into a lifelong argument against some of the most important principles he had helped to plant in the Constitution" (Brant, *James Madison*, 332; see also 12–13, 132–39). Brant's claim that Madison reversed his constitutional principles is challenged by Banning, *Sacred Fire of Liberty*, 1–14, 158.

11. Hamilton himself believed a "very material change" in Madison's political principles had occurred (Hamilton to Edward Carrington, May 26, 1792, *PAH* 11:426–45).

12. Brant, *James Madison*, makes much of Madison's supposed reversal on the issue of implied powers. See also Elkins and McKitrick, *Age of Federalism*, 230–41.

13. Banning, *Sacred Fire of Liberty*, 120, 164, 22.

14. Rakove, *Original Meanings*, 287.

15. Madison to Jefferson, Oct. 17, 1788, *PJM* 11:299.

16. Ibid., 14:191.

17. Banning writes: "The 'liberty' [Madison] wished to save . . . was not just liberty defined as the inherent rights of individuals, but also liberty defined as popular control" (*Sacred Fire of Liberty*, 9–10; see also 185).

18. See Ketcham, *James Madison*, 72–73, and Banning, *Sacred Fire of Liberty*, 85–86.

It is significant that much later, as president during the War of 1812, Madison "never hinted at measures abridging freedom of speech or press, even in the face of rampant obstruction of his government's policies and countless cases of outright treason in the 'eastern states' of New England" (McCoy, *Last of the Fathers*, 12).

19. For contrasting views of Madison's proposed negative on state laws, see Hobson, "The Negative on State Laws"; Zuckert, "Federalism and the Founding"; and Banning, *Sacred Fire of Liberty*, 113–21.

20. *PJM* 11:299.

21. On the differences between Madison and the Antifederalists with respect to the purpose of a bill of rights, see Goldwin, *From Parchment to Power*, 75–95.

22. *PJM* 12:208.

23. Goldwin, *From Parchment to Power*, says almost nothing about Madison's proposal to use the Bill of Rights to limit the states. Banning discusses it briefly in *Sacred Fire of Liberty*, 288–89.

24. Hobson, "The Negative on State Laws," 234.

25. On Madison's anticipation of the Fourteenth Amendment, see Rakove, *Original Meanings*, 337–38, and Banning, *Sacred Fire of Liberty*, 288.

26. *PJM* 14:427.

27. "To a Resident of Spotsylvania County," Jan. 27, 1789, ibid., 11:428–29.

28. Madison to Jefferson, Oct. 17, 1788, ibid., 297.

29. Ibid., 295–300.

30. Speech in Congress, June 8, 1789, ibid., 12:204–5, 198.

31. The importance Madison placed on educating public opinion through a bill of rights is also noted in Rakove, *Original Meanings*, 335, and Goldwin, *From Parchment to Power*, 71–73.

32. Madison to Washington, April 16, 1787, *PJM* 9:382–87.

33. Banning, *Sacred Fire of Liberty*, 139.

34. Goldwin quotes, and argues against, scholars who maintain that Madison's support for a bill of rights "was forced by the pressure of public opinion" (*From Parchment to Power*, 96–102).

35. Ibid.

36. Farrand, *Records* 2:615. That Madison's resolution would have included banks is evidenced by the remarks of Rufus King and James Wilson in the ensuing discussion.

37. Hamilton to Edward Carrington, May 26, 1792, *PAH* 11:432.

38. McCoy, *Last of the Fathers*, 80–81.

39. Whether Madison's opposition to the Bank is consistent with his earlier support for a national negative on all state laws depends upon how the proposed negative is understood. Hobson, "The Negative on State Laws," presents the negative as evidence of a strong nationalism from which Madison later retreated. Zuckert describes it as principally preventive in purpose: to arm "the general government with a negative power to help secure rights and the steady dispensation of justice within

the States, rather than with positive power to provide those things directly itself"
("Federalism and the Founding," 196). Chartering a bank would constitute a positive
rather than negative federal power.

40. Banning, *Sacred Fire of Liberty*, 22.

41. For discussion of this phrase from *Federalist* No. 45, see Rakove, *Original
Meanings*, 177, and Banning, *Sacred Fire of Liberty*, 229–30.

42. *PJM* 13:374.

43. Ibid., 375–76.

44. Ibid., 378.

45. Ibid., 377–78.

46. Ibid., 374.

47. Rakove points out that Madison's motion at the convention to grant Congress
a power of incorporation "obviously presumed that such authority did not yet exist
elsewhere in the Constitution" (*Original Meanings*, 355).

48. *PJM* 13:380–81.

49. Ibid., 375.

50. For analysis of Madison on the understanding of the ratifiers as key to constitutional interpretation, see Rakove, *Original Meanings*, 339–65, and McCoy, *Last of
the Fathers*, 73–83.

51. *PJM* 16:295–96.

52. Madison to Nicholas P. Trist, Dec. 1831, *LWJM* 4:204–11. For discussion, see
McCoy, *Last of the Fathers*, 80–81.

53. "Address and Reasons of Dissent of the Minority of the Convention of Pennsylvania," in Storing, *Antifederalist*, 213.

54. Farrand, *Records* 1:324.

55. John C. Calhoun dissected *Federalist* No. 39 with scorn and concluded that
Madison was both confused and disingenuous (*A Discourse on the Constitution and
Government of the United States*, 108–16).

56. *PJM* 14:139.

57. For Madison's and Jefferson's disagreements over the wording of the protest
resolutions, see McCoy, *Last of the Fathers*, 145–46.

58. *TJW* 449.

59. *PJM* 17:189.

60. See, for instance, Hamilton's *Federalist* No. 28.

61. There is an enormous literature on *Federalist* No. 10. The best starting point
is Adair, "That Politics May Be Reduced to a Science." For a thorough examination of
the literature on *Federalist* No. 10, see Gibson, "Impartial Representation and the
Extended Republic."

62. Here I agree with Banning, who writes that "taken by itself, [*Federalist* No. 10]
leads almost inevitably to serious distortion of his views. . . . Madison had *never* considered majority excess the only problem for republics" (*Sacred Fire of Liberty*, 208–10).

63. Ibid., 218.

64. *PJM* 9:350.

65. Epstein, *Political Theory of* The Federalist, 100–101.

66. Gibson, "Impartial Representation and the Extended Republic," 284, 288.

67. Riemer, *James Madison*, 11–20.

3. Alexander Hamilton as Libertarian and Nationalist

1. For Hamilton's financial wizardry, see McDonald, *Alexander Hamilton*, esp. 118–210. For the theory underpinning Hamilton's foreign policy, see Stourzh, *Alexander Hamilton and the Idea of Republican Government*, 126–205. For Hamilton's administrative theory, see Flaumenhaft, *Effective Republic*.

2. A widely used American politics textbook describes Hamilton, along with Gouverneur Morris, as "an extreme antidemocrat, primarily concerned with protecting property holders" (Edwards et al., *Government in America*, 35).

3. Flaumenhaft, *Effective Republic*, argues that Hamilton wanted citizens to turn away from popular, public liberty in favor of private, "negative" liberty. For a contrasting view, see Epstein, who argues that both Hamilton and Madison doubted "the feasibility and even the desirability of quieting men's political impulses" (*Political Theory of* The Federalist, 6).

4. Miller claims that in his June 18 speech at the Federal Convention, Hamilton renounced any idea of "protecting the individual against the exercise of arbitrary power" and in doing so turned his back on the republicanism of his youth (*Alexander Hamilton*, 161).

5. Madison's notes for June 26, in Farrand, *Records* 1:424. Madison recorded Hamilton as saying in the same speech that he did not "think favorably of Republican Government." This remark, however, has no counterpart in Yates's notes for the same speech. Yates would certainly have been on the lookout for any evidence of antirepublicanism in Hamilton.

6. Speech in New York Ratifying Convention, June 30, 1788, *PAH* 5:16–17.

7. *PJM* 14:427.

8. Ibid., 191.

9. I like Rossiter's characterization: Hamilton "was conservative and radical, traditionalist and revolutionary, reactionary and visionary, Tory and Whig all thrown into one. . . . He may well be the most unclassifiable man of pronounced views in all the history of American thought and politics" (*Alexander Hamilton and the Constitution*, 182).

10. McDonald, *Alexander Hamilton*, emphasizes the radical side of Hamilton in contrast to the social and economic conservatism of Madison and Jefferson.

11. Roche, "The Founding Fathers," 800. Kohn in *Eagle and Sword* portrays Hamilton as an outright militarist who was more than happy to rule by force alone if he could get away with it.

12. Hamilton to Timothy Pickering, Nov. 4, 1803, Farrand, *Records* 3:397–98.

13. Hamilton's republicanism is described and defended at length in Stourzh, *Alexander Hamilton and the Idea of Republican Government.*

14. A fairly typical example of the monarchism charge is found in an 1810 letter from John Eppes to Madison, where Eppes claimed that Hamilton's plan of a constitution "contains proof clear as holy writ that the idol of the Federal party was not a Monarchist in Theory merely, but the open zealous and unreserved advocate for the adoption of the monarchical system in this Country" (Farrand, *Records* 3:418).

15. Wood, *Creation of the American Republic,* 471–518.

16. Farrand, *Records* 1:284, 289.

17. The quote is from Yates's notes on Hamilton's June 18 speech (Farrand, *Records* 1:298–99).

18. *PAH* 2:651.

19. Speech, June 24, 1788, ibid., 5:68.

20. Speech at New York Ratifying Convention, June 25, 1788, ibid., 5:81.

21. For the conception of a power-liberty balance in Whig political thought, see Bailyn, *Ideological Origins,* 76–77, and Wood, *Creation of the American Republic,* 18–28.

22. Speech at Federal Convention, Sept. 8, 1787, Farrand, *Records* 2:553–54.

23. *PJM* 14:191.

24. New York Assembly, "Remarks on an Act for Regulating Elections," Jan. 24, 1787, *PAH* 4:23.

25. New York Assembly, "Remarks on an Act for Regulating Elections," Jan. 30, 1787, ibid., 4:31–32.

26. New York Assembly, "Remarks on an Act concerning Murder," Feb. 8, 1787, ibid., 4:39.

27. For detailed description of the law cases, see Goebel, *Law Practice* 1:197–543. For "Phocion," see *PAH* 3:483–97, 530–58.

28. For the proposal to give slaves freedom in exchange for fighting, see Hamilton to John Jay, March 14, 1779, *PAH* 2:17–19.

29. For Jefferson's inconsistencies in matters of press freedom, see Levy, *Jefferson and Civil Liberties.* Smith, *Freedom's Fetters,* characterizes Hamilton's outlook on press freedom (and that of the Federalists generally) as purely partisan in character: he (and they) supported it for their friends and opposed it for their enemies.

30. The *Croswell* case, including Hamilton's briefs and reports of his oral argument, is discussed in detail in Goebel, *Law Practice* 1:775–848.

31. Ibid., 1:809, 825.

32. Ibid., 829.

33. "Report of 1800," *PJM* 17:343–46, 337.

34. Madison, speech in Congress, Nov. 27, 1794, cited in Smith, *Freedom's Fetters,* 432.

35. Levy, *Legacy of Suppression,* shows that Madison's sweeping defense of press liberty was exceptional in the extreme. For the most part, "progressive" opinion went

only so far as to oppose prior restraint and allow truth as a defense. In this respect Hamilton's efforts at liberalization, while not unique, place him toward the liberal end of the spectrum of the age.

36. Federal Convention, June 18, Farrand, *Records* 1:287.

37. Madison's words as recorded by Nicholas Trist, Sept. 27, 1834, ibid., 3:533–34.

38. Remark at Federal Convention, June 29, 1787, ibid., 1:466.

39. "The State governments possess inherent advantages, which will ever give them an influence and ascendancy over the national government; and will forever preclude the possibility of federal encroachments. That their liberties indeed can be subverted by the federal head, is repugnant to every rule of political calculation" (speech in New York Ratifying Convention, June 20, 1788, *PAH* 5:26).

40. The phrases come from *Federalist* No. 28, where Hamilton argued that any action by the national government posing a serious threat to liberty could be easily put down by the combined actions of the states. He made a similar claim in his June 21 speech at the New York Ratifying Convention (ibid., 38).

41. Hamilton, *Federalist* No. 23.

42. Examples of Hamilton's use of the concept of popular sovereignty include *Federalist* No. 78 (on judicial review) and *Federalist* No. 84 (why a bill of rights is unnecessary).

43. June 18 speech, Farrand, *Records* 1:290.

44. "Opinion on the Constitutionality of a Bank," *PAH* 8:98.

45. Ibid., 111.

46. Powell, "The Original Understanding of Original Intent," 71.

47. Lofgren, "The Original Understanding of Original Intent?" 122.

48. *PAH* 8:99–100.

49. "The Vindication No. I," ibid., 11:462–63.

50. McDonald claims that at the time the Constitution was framed it was still widely believed that the total amount of wealth remains constant (*Novus Ordo Seclorum*, 99). So Hamilton's economic argument in his "Report on Manufactures" was more innovative than it appears to twentieth-century readers.

51. *PAH* 8:98, 105, 131.

52. Ibid., 103.

53. Hamilton to Gouverneur Morris, Feb. 29, 1802, ibid., 25:544.

54. McDonald stresses the importance of appearances in Hamilton's political economy. Establishing public credit "involved the creation of illusions. . . . The marketplace dealt in beliefs as well as facts" (*Alexander Hamilton,* 164).

55. "Report Relative to a Provision for the Support of Public Credit" (1790), *PAH* 6:97.

56. Ibid., 2:242.

57. Hamilton to James Duane, Sept. 3, 1780, ibid., 417.

58. Speech at New York Ratifying Convention, June 27, 1788, ibid., 5:95.

59. "Sir, there is something in an argument, that has been urged, which, if it proves any thing, concludes against all union and all government; it goes to prove, that no powers should be entrusted to any body of men, because they may be abused" (speech in New York Ratifying Convention, June 21, 1788, ibid., 57).

60. Elkins and McKitrick describe the considerations that guided Washington in the formation of his cabinet. Because the legitimacy of the national government itself was still fragile, his appointees had to be not merely men of merit but also "First Characters" who would bring the weight of their own reputations to the support of the new government (*Age of Federalism*, 52–55). Hamilton probably had similar considerations in mind for the Senate proposed in his June 18 speech.

4. James Wilson and the Idea of Popular Sovereignty

1. For example, Bailyn, *Ideological Origins;* Wood, *Creation of the American Republic;* Morgan, *Inventing the People;* Beer, *To Make a Nation.*

2. Remark at Federal Convention, May 31, 1787, Farrand, *Records* 1:49.

3. Speech at Pennsylvania Ratifying Convention, Nov. 26, 1787, *WJW* 2:771.

4. Jefferson to Madison, Dec. 20, 1787, *TJW* 917.

5. See Wilson's pamphlet *Considerations on the Bank of North America* (1785) in *WJW* 2:824–47.

6. For the way in which Wilson saw juries and common law as expressions of popular sovereignty, see Stimson, "A Jury of the Country."

7. Wilson, speech in Pennsylvania Ratifying Convention, Dec. 4, 1787, in Jensen, *Documentary History* 2:477.

8. McCloskey, in his Introduction to *The Works of James Wilson,* observes that "posterity's neglect of Wilson is nothing short of astonishing when it is measured against his claims to be remembered" (*WJW* 1:2). For an excellent biography of Wilson, see Smith, *James Wilson.*

9. For the pamphlet, see *WJW* 2:720–46. For Wilson's argument in the pamphlet, see Dennison, "The Revolution Principle."

10. For Wilson's importance at the Federal Convention, see Farrand, *Framing of the Constitution,* 197–98. For Wilson and the creation of the presidency, see DiClerico, "James Wilson's Presidency," and McCarthy, "James Wilson and the Creation of the Presidency."

11. See Madison to Washington, April 16, 1787, *PJM* 9:385.

12. For a comparative study of Wilson, Madison, and Gouverneur Morris on property and suffrage, see Nedelsky, *Private Property and the Limits of American Constitutionalism.*

13. Alexander Graydon, quoted in Smith, *James Wilson,* 303.

14. Wilson's views on natural law are the focus of much of the older scholarly literature on Wilson's thought; see Hall, *Political and Legal Philosophy of James Wilson,*

35–67. For a more modern and secular characterization of Wilson's conception of natural law, see Velasquez, "Rethinking America's Modernity."

15. Hall, *Political and Legal Philosophy of James Wilson*, contains an excellent bibliography of both recent and older scholarly articles on Wilson.

16. Morgan, *Inventing the People*, 55–77.

17. Bailyn, *Ideological Origins*, 198.

18. Cited ibid., 201–2.

19. *Considerations on the Nature and Extent of the Legislative Authority of the British Parliament*, in *WJW* 2:720–46.

20. For a description of the "useful ambiguities" that guided the workings of colonial government before Parliament attempted to assert its unambiguous sovereignty, see Morgan, *Inventing the People*, 122–48. See also Greene, *Peripheries and Center*, which argues that the empire would have been unworkable before 1763 if the principle of full parliamentary sovereignty had been enforced in practice.

21. Storing, *Anti-Federalist*, 211. See also Virginia's *The Impartial Examiner*, ibid., 281.

22. Farrand, *Records* 1:287.

23. Wood, *Creation of the American Republic*, 383.

24. Ibid., 562. For a critique of Wood's interpretation of the "disingenuous" Federalist version of popular sovereignty, at least as applied to James Wilson, see Dennison, "The Revolutionary Principle," 183–91.

25. Morgan, *Inventing the People*, 53.

26. Ibid., 245.

27. Ibid., 255.

28. *WJW* 2:770.

29. Farrand, *Records* 1:253 (June 16).

30. Wood, *Creation of the American Republic*, 562.

31. Farrand, *Records*, 1:48.

32. Ibid., 49.

33. Ibid., 69.

34. Ibid., 132–33.

35. For example, the Pennsylvania Minority writes: "The representation ought to be fair, equal, and sufficiently numerous, to possess the same interests, feelings, opinions, and views, which the people themselves would possess, were they all assembled" (Storing, *Anti-Federalist*, 214).

36. Farrand, *Records* 1:361.

37. Ibid., 605.

38. See, for example, ibid., 179–80 (June 9), 482–84 (June 30).

39. Ibid., 483.

40. Ibid., 405–6.

41. Ibid., 322, 356 (June 19 and 26).

42. Onuf, *Origins of the Federal Republic,* 201. See also Onuf, "State Sovereignty and the Making of the Constitution."

43. *WJW* 1:292–93.

44. See, for example, Farrand, *Records* 1:65–68 (June 1), 96–100 (June 4).

45. *WJW* 1:414–15. Beer comments on this passage in *To Make a Nation,* 372.

46. *WJW* 2:785.

47. For Wilson's advocacy of widespread political participation, see Conrad, "Metaphor and Imagination," and Nedelsky, *Private Property and the Limits of American Constitutionalism.*

48. *WJW* 2:786.

49. Ibid., 1:72–73.

50. Seed, in his survey of Wilson's political thought, occasionally falls into speaking of Wilson's "divided sovereignty" (*James Wilson,* 76).

51. *Chisholm v. Georgia,* in Friedman and Israel, *Justices* 1:98–101.

52. *WJW* 1:103–12.

53. Friedman and Israel, *Justices* 1:103.

54. My stress on the importance of symbolism in Wilson's thought converges in certain respects with the discussion of Wilson's metaphors in Conrad, "Imagination and Metaphor."

55. "Wilson took very seriously this ubiquitous metaphor 'the People' as an established reality in American politics" (ibid., 54).

56. Storing, *Anti-Federalist,* 213, 297, 115.

57. See the discussion of these passages in the following chapter.

58. Farrand, *Records* 1:324, 166.

59. Rakove lends support to Wilson's contention that the Union came first and created the states (*Original Meanings,* 163–64). Abraham Lincoln in his July 4, 1861, message to Congress in special session made the same argument: "The Union is older than any of the States; and, in fact, it created them as States" (Lincoln, *Speeches and Writings,* 256).

60. Beer, *To Make a Nation,* 324.

61. *WJW* 1:9.

62. For Reid's influence on Wilson's political thought, see Conrad, "Metaphor and Imagination"; Stimson, "A Jury of the Country"; Hall, *Political and Legal Philosophy,* 68–89.

63. Beer, *To Make a Nation,* 367.

64. *WJW* 2:788.

65. Wilson, "Speech in the State House Yard," Philadelphia, Oct. 6, 1787, in Jensen, *Documentary History* 2:167–68.

66. Smith, *James Wilson,* 119–23, 246.

67. See, for example, *WJW* 1:71.

68. Ibid., 334–68.

69. For Wilson's views on liberty of the press, see Levy, *Legacy of Suppression*, 201–3.

70. Madison to Jefferson, Oct. 17, 1788, *PJM* 11:297.

71. See, for example, McCloskey's Introduction to *WJW* 1:1–48.

72. Smith, *James Wilson*, 129–39.

73. Crick, *In Defense of Politics*. See also Crick, "Sovereignty," in the *International Encyclopedia of the Social Sciences*.

74. Morgan, *Inventing the People*, 13–14.

75. Hinsley writes: "Men do not wield or submit to sovereignty. They wield or submit to authority or power. Authority and power are facts as old and ubiquitous as society itself; but they have not everywhere and at all times enjoyed the support or suffered the restraints which sovereignty, a theory or assumption about political power, seeks to construct for them. Although we talk of it loosely as something concrete which may be lost or acquired, eroded or increased, sovereignty is not a fact. It is a concept which men in certain circumstances have applied—a quality they have attributed or a claim they have counterposed—to the political power which they or other men were exercising" (*Sovereignty*, 1).

76. Lincoln, *Speeches and Writings*, 220.

5. Thomas Jefferson, Liberty, and the States

1. For recent scholarship on Jefferson, see Onuf, "The Scholars' Jefferson." For recent examinations of Jefferson on slavery and race, see the essays by Lucia Stanton, Paul Finkelman, and Scot A. French and Edward L. Ayers in Onuf, *Jeffersonian Legacies*.

2. Mayer's recent book-length study *The Constitutional Thought of Thomas Jefferson* puts Jefferson's "principle of jealousy" at the center of his political thought.

3. Ibid., xi.

4. *TJW*, 983.

5. Mayer, *Constitutional Thought*, 103.

6. O'Brien's *The Long Affair* is the most recent installment; the basic image goes back to Federalist campaign tracts of the 1790s.

7. These are covered (among other places) in *Notes on the State of Virginia*, in Jefferson's draft constitution for Virginia (1776), and in his Bill for Establishing Religious Freedom, Bill for Proportioning Crimes and Punishments, and Bill for the More General Diffusion of Knowledge. All may be found in *TJW*.

8. For Jefferson's efforts to reform Virginia's constitution and laws, see Peterson, *Thomas Jefferson and the New Nation*, 97–165. For the political theory underlying Jefferson's reform proposals, see Zuckert, *Natural Rights Republic*, 202–43.

9. Banning, *Jeffersonian Persuasion*, 113.

10. *TJW*, 914, 455.

11. Ibid., 963.

12. Sloan, *Principle and Interest*, argues that debt was the central concern of Jef-

ferson's Sept. 6, 1789, letter to Madison and of Jefferson's entire public and private career. Jefferson's principle that one generation should not have to pay the debts of another, Sloan argues, is the most original and characteristically Jeffersonian variation on the otherwise commonplace eighteenth-century idea that one generation has no right to bind another.

13. *TJW*, 494.

14. Peterson, *Thomas Jefferson and the New Nation*, 241–389.

15. Jefferson to Monroe, June 17, 1785, *TJW*, 804, 806. See also Jefferson to Madison, Feb. 8, 1786, and his "Answers and Observations for Démeunier's Article," ibid., 848, 575–77.

16. Peterson claims that Jefferson's experience in Europe "made him a nationalist" (*Thomas Jefferson and the New Nation*, 314). But Peterson's portrayal of Jefferson in this period is very selective, overemphasizing his "nationalist" expressions and ignoring the letters and documents in which he spoke of the American states as separate nations.

17. Smith, *Republic of Letters*, 1:410, 458.

18. *TJW*, 575–79, 914.

19. Ibid., 579.

20. Ibid., 805–6.

21. Ibid., 798–99.

22. Ibid., 917–18.

23. Ibid., 880–81.

24. Ibid., 881–82.

25. Ibid., 889–90.

26. Ibid., 911.

27. Ibid., 579.

28. Allen, *George Washington*, 337.

29. *TJW*, 577.

30. For comparison of Jefferson's political economy with that of Hamilton, see McCoy, *Elusive Republic*, 136–65.

31. See Sloan, *Principle and Interest*, 125–201.

32. Banning, *Jeffersonian Persuasion*, 13, 14, 273. The original passage from the "Anas" may be found in *TJW*, 663.

33. Banning, *Jeffersonian Persuasion*, 63, 46, 67.

34. Ibid., 140.

35. Jefferson to Washington, May 23, Sept. 9, 1792, *TJW*, 988, 995.

36. Sloan's *Principle and Interest* describes how in Jefferson's case the critique of debt taken over from Whig ideology was powerfully strengthened by Jefferson's own lifelong personal struggle with inherited debts.

37. Banning, *Jeffersonian Persuasion*, 246–70.

38. *TJW*, 416–21.

39. Ibid., 420. Sloan points out that in this passage Jefferson was, among other things, attempting to protect "the reforms of the law of property and inheritance that had been one of his principal accomplishments in Virginia" against the "giant engine" represented by the Bank (*Principle and Interest*, 172–73).

40. *TJW*, 417.

41. Ibid., 959–64.

42. Typical of this brand of late 1790s Federalism was Timothy Pickering, whom McKitrick and Elkins describe as "a doctrinaire Federalist persuaded that jacobinism lurked in every corner and must be hunted down without stint or mercy" (*Age of Federalism*, 625).

43. Peterson, *Thomas Jefferson and the New Nation*, 615.

44. *TJW*, 449, 453.

45. Ibid., 578.

46. Ibid., 455.

47. The words of Wilson to which Jefferson was most likely responding are: "When the people established the powers of legislation under their separate governments, they invested their representatives with every right and authority which they did not in explicit terms reserve. . . . But in delegating federal powers, another criterion was necessarily introduced, and the congressional authority is to be collected, not from tacit implication, but from the positive grant expressed in the instrument of union. Hence it is evident, that in the former case everything which is not reserved is given, but in the latter the reverse of the proposition prevails, and everything which is not given, is reserved. This distinction being recognized, will furnish an answer to those who think the omission of a bill of rights, a defect in the proposed constitution: for it would have been superfluous and absurd to have stipulated with a federal body of our own creation, that we should enjoy those privileges, of which we are not divested either by the intention or the act, that has brought the body into existence" (Jensen, *Documentary History* 2:167–68).

48. *TJW*, 916.

49. Ibid., 1387; discussed in Mayer, *Constitutional Thought*, 132–33.

50. *TJW*, 1399.

51. Elkins and McKitrick, *Age of Federalism*, 26. Jefferson is likewise portrayed as first and foremost a typically debt-ridden Virginia planter in Sloan, *Principle and Interest*.

52. See, for example, Jefferson to St. John de Crèvecoeur, Jan. 15, 1787, where Franklin's inventions are characterized as "our inventions," in contrast to the English who try to steal the credit (*TJW*, 877–78).

53. See *Notes on the State of Virginia*, Query VI, ibid., 165–82.

54. See, for example, Jefferson to David Rittenhouse (a scientist from Philadelphia), July 19, 1778, ibid., 762–64.

55. See Jefferson to George Wythe, Aug. 13, 1786, ibid., 857–60. In denying the

charge of "our" anarchy and in speaking of "a people . . . who are in perfect tranquillity" and so able to pass such a statute, Jefferson spoke in a way that could apply either to Virginia or to the whole United States.

56. Jefferson to Elbridge Gerry, Jan. 26, 1799, ibid., 1055–62.

57. See Jefferson's June 4, 1798, letter to John Taylor of Caroline, who had openly broached the idea of secession (ibid., 1048–51). In his response Jefferson sounds almost like Lincoln in his criticism of the "resort to a scission of the Union" on a "temporary superiority of the one party" and the precedent this sets for secessions within secessions. But Jefferson did not question the right, either natural or constitutional, of a state to secede; he merely argued that it was not yet necessary when other means of resistance still remained.

58. Mayer, *Constitutional Thought,* 70, 39, 37.

59. Jefferson to John Holmes, April 22, 1820, to Albert Gallatin, Dec. 26, 1820, *TJW,* 1433–35, 1447–50. The Gallatin letter is especially revealing of Jefferson's inability to get past the power-liberty divisions of the 1790s: "The Federalists compleatly put down, and despairing of ever rising again under the old division of whig and tory, devised a new one, of slave-holding, & non-slave-holding states . . . calculated to give them ascendancy by debauching their old opponents to a coalition with them." Onuf, "Thomas Jefferson, Missouri, and the 'Empire for Liberty,'" shows how Jefferson's response to the Missouri Compromise was rooted in his long-standing concern for equality among states and sections.

60. For current scholarly controversies over Jefferson, see Onuf, "The Scholars' Jefferson." For a snapshot of current popular interest in Jefferson, see Ellis, *American Sphinx,* 3–23.

61. Matthews, *Radical Politics,* 125, 19–52.

62. Pocock, "Virtue and Commerce in the Eighteenth Century," cited and discussed in Zuckert, *Natural Rights Republic,* 204.

6. Conclusion

1. *TJW,* 493.

2. Kenyon, "Men of Little Faith," 38.

3. See McCoy, *Elusive Republic;* Sloan, *Principle and Interest.*

4. This is not to deny that Jefferson and Hamilton thought about press liberty in quite different ways. The same type of restriction can be given quite different theoretical justifications. Jefferson's attempt to distinguish legitimate press liberty from "demoralising licentiousness" is discussed in Mayer, *Constitutional Thought,* 166–84.

5. For the selective use of Jefferson by the nullifiers, see Peterson, *Jefferson Image,* 36–66.

6. See ibid.

Bibliography

Adair, Douglass. "That Politics May Be Reduced to a Science: David Hume, James Madison, and the Tenth *Federalist*." In Douglass Adair. *Fame and the Founding Fathers*. New York, 1974.

Allen, William B., ed. *George Washington: A Collection*. Indianapolis, 1988.

Bailyn, Bernard. *Faces of Revolution: Personalities and Themes in the Struggle for American Independence*. New York, 1990.

——. *The Ideological Origins of the American Revolution*. Cambridge, Mass., 1967.

Banning, Lance. *The Jeffersonian Persuasion: Evolution of a Party Ideology*. Ithaca, N.Y., 1978.

——. *The Sacred Fire of Liberty: James Madison and the Founding of the Federal Republic*. Ithaca, N.Y., 1995.

——. "Some Second Thoughts on Virtue and the Course of Revolutionary Thinking." In Terence Ball and J. G. A. Pocock, eds. *Conceptual Change and the Constitution*, 194–212. Lawrence, Kans., 1988.

Beer, Samuel. *To Make a Nation: The Rediscovery of American Federalism*. Cambridge, Mass., 1993.

Boyd, Julian P., et al., eds. *The Papers of Thomas Jefferson*. Princeton, N.J., 1950—.

Brant, Irving. *James Madison: Father of the Constitution, 1787–1800*. Indianapolis, 1950.

Burns, Edward McNall. *James Madison: Philosopher of the Constitution*. New York, 1938.

Burns, James MacGregor. *The Deadlock of Democracy: Four Party Politics in America*. Englewood Cliffs, N.J., 1963.

Calhoun, John C. *A Discourse on the Constitution and Government of the United States*. In Ross M. Lence, ed. *Union and Liberty: The Political Philosophy of John C. Calhoun*. Indianapolis, 1992.

Conrad, Stephen A. "Metaphor and Imagination in James Wilson's Theory of Federal Union." *Law and Social Inquiry* 13 (1988): 1–70.

Crick, Bernard. *In Defense of Politics*. Chicago, 1962.

——. "Sovereignty." In the *International Encyclopedia of the Social Sciences* 15:77–82. Macmillan, 1968.

Dahl, Robert A. *A Preface to Democratic Theory*. Chicago, 1956.

Dennison, George. "The 'Revolutionary Principle': Ideology and Constitutionalism in the Thought of James Wilson." *Review of Politics* 39:2 (1977): 157–91.

Diamond, Martin. "*The Federalist*, 1787–88." In Leo Strauss and Joseph Cropsey, eds. *The History of Political Philosophy*, 659–79. 3d ed. Chicago, 1987.

———. "*The Federalist's* View of Federalism." In William A. Schambra, ed. *As Far as Republican Principles Will Admit: Essays by Martin Diamond*, 108–43. Washington, D.C., 1992.

DiClerico, Robert E. "James Wilson's Presidency." *Presidential Studies Quarterly* 17:2 (1987): 301–17.

Edwards, George C., III, et al. *Government in America*. 7th ed. New York, 1996.

Elkins, Stanley, and Eric McKitrick. *The Age of Federalism: The Early American Republic, 1788–1800*. Oxford, 1993.

Ellis, Joseph J. *American Sphinx: The Character of Thomas Jefferson*. New York, 1997.

Epstein, David F. *The Political Theory of* The Federalist. Chicago, 1984.

Farrand, Max. *The Framing of the Constitution of the United States*. New Haven, 1913.

———. *The Records of the Federal Convention of 1787*. 4 vols. New Haven, 1937.

Flaumenhaft, Harvey. *The Effective Republic: Administration and Constitution in the Thought of Alexander Hamilton*. Durham, N.C., 1992.

Friedman, Leon, and Fred L. Israel, eds., *The Justices of the United States Supreme Court, 1789–1969: Their Lives and Major Opinions*. Vol. 1. New York, 1969.

Gay, Sidney Howard. *James Madison*. Boston, 1890.

Gibson, Alan. "Impartial Representation and the Extended Republic: Towards a Comprehensive and Balanced Reading of the Tenth *Federalist* Paper." *History of Political Thought* 12:2 (1991): 263–304.

Goebel, Julius, Jr., ed. *The Law Practice of Alexander Hamilton*. 2 vols. New York, 1964.

Goldwin, Robert A. *From Parchment to Power: How James Madison Used the Bill of Rights to Save the Constitution*. Washington, D.C., 1997.

Greene, Jack P. *Peripheries and Center: Constitutional Development in the Extended Polities of the British Empire and the United States, 1607–1788*. New York, 1990.

Hall, Mark David. *The Political and Legal Philosophy of James Wilson, 1742–1798*. Columbia, Mo., 1997.

Hamilton, Alexander, James Madison, and John Jay. *The Federalist Papers*. Ed. Clinton Rossiter. New York, 1961.

Hinsley, F. H. *Sovereignty*. New York, 1966.

Hobbes, Thomas. *The Leviathan*. London, 1651.

Hobson, Charles. "The Negative on State Laws: James Madison, the Constitution, and the Crisis of Republican Government." *William and Mary Quarterly*, 3d ser., 36:2 (1979): 215–35.

Hunt, Gaillard. *The Life of James Madison*. New York, 1902.

Hutchinson, William T., et al., eds. *The Papers of James Madison*. Chicago and Charlottesville, Va., 1962—.

Jensen, Merrill, ed. *The Documentary History of the Ratification of the Constitution.* Vol. 2. Madison, Wis., 1976.

Kenyon, Cecelia. "Men of Little Faith: The Anti-Federalists on the Nature of Representative Government." *William and Mary Quarterly,* 3d ser., 12:1 (1955): 3–43.

Ketcham, Ralph. *James Madison: A Biography.* New York, 1971.

Kohn, Richard. *Eagle and Sword: The Federalists and the Creation of the Military Establishment in America, 1783–1802.* New York, 1975.

Levy, Leonard. *Jefferson and Civil Liberties: The Darker Side.* Cambridge, Mass., 1963.

——. *Legacy of Suppression: Freedom of Speech and Press in Early American History.* Cambridge, Mass., 1964.

Lincoln, Abraham. *Speeches and Writings, 1859–1865.* Ed. Don E. Fehrenbacher. New York, 1989.

Lofgren, Charles A. "The Original Understanding of Original Intent?" In Jack N. Rakove, ed. *Interpreting the Constitution: the Debate over Original Intent,* 117–50. Boston, 1990.

Madison, James. *Letters and Other Writings of James Madison.* Vol. 4. Philadelphia, 1865.

Mason, Alpheus T. "*The Federalist*—A Split Personality." *American Historical Review* 57:3 (1952): 593–643.

Matthews, Richard K. *The Radical Politics of Thomas Jefferson: A Revisionist View.* Lawrence, Kans., 1984.

Mayer, David N. *The Constitutional Thought of Thomas Jefferson.* Charlottesville, Va., 1994.

McCarthy, Daniel J. "James Wilson and the Creation of the Presidency." *Presidential Studies Quarterly* 17:4 (1987): 689–96.

McCloskey, Robert G., ed. *The Works of James Wilson.* 2 vols. Cambridge, Mass., 1967.

McCoy, Drew R. *The Elusive Republic: Political Economy in Jeffersonian America.* Chapel Hill, N.C., 1980.

——. *The Last of the Fathers: James Madison and the Republican Legacy.* Cambridge, 1989.

McDonald, Forrest. *Alexander Hamilton: A Biography.* New York, 1979.

——. *Novus Ordo Seclorum: The Intellectual Origins of the Constitution.* Lawrence, Kans., 1985.

Miller, John C. *Alexander Hamilton: Portrait in Paradox.* New York, 1959.

Millican, Edward. *One United People: The* Federalist *Papers and the National Idea.* Lexington, Ky., 1990.

Morgan, Edmund S. *American Slavery, American Freedom: The Ordeal of Colonial Virginia.* New York, 1975.

——. *Inventing the People: The Rise of Popular Sovereignty in England and America.* New York, 1988.

Nedelsky, Jennifer. *Private Property and the Limits of American Constitutionalism: The Madisonian Framework and Its Legacy.* Chicago, 1990.

O'Brien, Conor Cruise. *The Long Affair: Thomas Jefferson and the French Revolution, 1785–1800.* Chicago, 1996.

Onuf, Peter S. *The Origins of the Federal Republic: Jurisdictional Controversies in the United States, 1775–1787.* Philadelphia, 1983.

——. "The Scholars' Jefferson." *William and Mary Quarterly,* 3d ser., 50:4 (1993): 671–99.

——. "State Sovereignty and the Making of the Constitution." In Terence Ball and J. G. A. Pocock, eds. *Conceptual Change and the Constitution,* 78–98. Lawrence, Kans., 1988.

——. "Thomas Jefferson, Missouri, and the 'Empire for Liberty.'" In James P. Ronda, ed. *Thomas Jefferson and the Changing West: From Conquest to Conservation,* 110–53. Albuquerque, N.Mex., 1997.

——, ed. *Jeffersonian Legacies.* Charlottesville, Va., 1993.

Peterson, Merrill. *The Jefferson Image in the American Mind.* New York, 1960.

——. *Thomas Jefferson and the New Nation.* New York, 1970.

——, ed. *Thomas Jefferson: Writings.* New York, 1984.

Pocock, J. G. A. "States, Republics, and Empires." In Terence Ball and J. G. A. Pocock, eds. *Conceptual Change and the Constitution,* 55–77. Lawrence, Kans., 1988.

Powell, H. Jefferson. "The Original Understanding of Original Intent." In Jack N. Rakove, ed. *Interpreting the Constitution: The Debate over Original Intent,* 53–115. Boston, 1990.

Rakove, Jack N. *Original Meanings: Politics and Ideas in the Making of the Constitution.* New York, 1996.

Riemer, Neal. *James Madison: Creating the American Constitution.* Washington, D.C., 1986.

Roche, John. "The Founding Fathers: A Reform Caucus in Action." *American Political Science Review* 55:4 (1961): 799–816.

Rossiter, Clinton. *Alexander Hamilton and the Constitution.* New York, 1964.

Seed, Geoffrey. *James Wilson.* Millwood, N.Y., 1978.

Sloan, Herbert E. *Principle and Interest: Thomas Jefferson and the Problem of Debt.* New York, 1995.

Smith, James Morton. *Freedom's Fetters: The Alien and Sedition Laws and American Civil Liberties.* Ithaca, N.Y., 1956.

——. *The Republic of Letters: The Correspondence between Thomas Jefferson and James Madison, 1776–1826.* 3 vols. New York, 1995.

Smith, Page. *James Wilson, Founding Father.* Chapel Hill, N.C., 1956.

Stimson, Shannon. "'A Jury of the Country': Common Sense Philosophy and the Jurisprudence of James Wilson." In Richard B. Sher and Jeffrey R. Smitten, eds. *Scotland and America in the Age of the Enlightenment,* 193–208. Princeton, N.J., 1990.

Storing, Herbert J., ed. *The Anti-Federalist.* Abridged by Murray Dry. Chicago, 1985.

Stourzh, Gerald. *Alexander Hamilton and the Idea of Republican Government.* Stanford, Calif., 1970.

Syrett, Harold C., et al., eds. *The Papers of Alexander Hamilton.* 27 vols. New York, 1961–87.

Trenchard, John, and Thomas Gordon. *Cato's Letters: or, Essays on Liberty, Civil and Religious, and Other Important Subjects.* 2 vols. Indianapolis, 1995.

Velasquez, Eduardo A. "Rethinking America's Modernity: Natural Law, Natural Rights, and the Character of James Wilson's Liberal Republicanism." *Polity* 29:2 (1996): 193–220.

Wills, Garry. *Inventing America: Jefferson's Declaration of Independence.* Garden City, N.Y., 1978.

Wood, Gordon S. *The Creation of the American Republic.* Chapel Hill, N.C., 1969.

Zuckert, Michael P. "Federalism and the Founding: Toward a Reinterpretation of the Constitutional Convention." *Review of Politics* 48:2 (1986): 166–210.

——. *Natural Rights and the New Republicanism.* Princeton, N.J., 1994.

——. *The Natural Rights Republic: Studies in the Foundation of the American Political Tradition.* Notre Dame, Ind., 1996.

Index